MAKING EMPLOYMENT RIGHTS EFFECTIVE

There has been an enormous expansion of individual employment rights in Britain but their practical impact in terms of delivering fairer workplaces can be questioned. Taking as its starting point the widespread acknowledgement of problems with the major enforcement mechanism, the Employment Tribunals, this collection brings together experts from law, sociology and employment relations to explore a range of alternative regulatory and non-regulatory approaches to enforcement and to securing compliance and to consider factors affecting variation in the extent to which legal rights have meaning and impact at the workplace. Thus this book addresses issues key to contemporary policy and academic debate.

Chapters discuss the growth in employment rights and their enforcement mechanisms (Gillian Morris), problems with the employment tribunal system and the current and potential role of alternative dispute resolution (Linda Dickens); reflect on the long experience of enforcement of equality rights (Bob Hepple) and agency enforcement of health and safety legislation under the 'better regulation' agenda (Steve Tombs and David Whyte); evaluate the potential of various 'reflexive law' mechanisms, including corporate governance (Simon Deakin, Colm McLaughlin and Dominic Chai), and of procurement (Christopher McCrudden) as strategies for delivering fairness at the workplace. The mediation of statutory rights, influencing how they shape workplace practice are illuminated further in chapters on trade unions and individual legal rights (Trevor Colling), the management of employment rights (John Purcell) and regulation and small firms (Paul Edwards).

Making Employment Rights Effective

Issues of Enforcement and Compliance

Edited by
Linda Dickens

·HART·
PUBLISHING
OXFORD AND PORTLAND, OREGON
2012

Published in the United Kingdom by Hart Publishing Ltd
16C Worcester Place, Oxford, OX1 2JW
Telephone: +44 (0)1865 517530
Fax: +44 (0)1865 510710
E-mail: mail@hartpub.co.uk
Website: http://www.hartpub.co.uk

Published in North America (US and Canada) by
Hart Publishing
c/o International Specialized Book Services
920 NE 58th Avenue, Suite 300
Portland, OR 97213-3786
USA
Tel: +1 503 287 3093 or toll-free: (1) 800 944 6190
Fax: +1 503 280 8832
E-mail: orders@isbs.com
Website: http://www.isbs.com

British Library Cataloguing in Publication Data
Data Available

ISBN: 978-1-84946-256-3

Typeset by Compuscript Ltd, Shannon
Printed and bound in Great Britain by
MPG Books Ltd

Preface

The completion of this book owes much to the support given to me by colleagues in the Industrial Relations Research Unit and the Industrial Relations and Organisational Behaviour Group of Warwick Business School, University of Warwick. I am grateful for their unselfish collegiality during 2011—a difficult time both institutionally and for me personally. Throughout the project valuable administrative and secretarial assistance was provided with cheerful enthusiasm by Natalie Johnson. Above all I wish to record my thanks to Michael Terry who performed many and diverse roles essential to my work on this publication and more generally.

Linda Dickens

Contents

List of Contributors

Dominic Heesang Chai is Assistant Professor of Strategy and International Management at Seoul National University.

Trevor Colling is Associate Professor in the Industrial Relations and Organisational Behaviour Group, Warwick Business School, and a member of the Industrial Relations Research Unit.

Simon Deakin is Professor of Law and Fellow of Peterhouse, University of Cambridge.

Linda Dickens is Professor of Industrial Relations at Warwick Business School, University of Warwick.

Paul Edwards is Professor of Employment Relations at the Birmingham Business School, University of Birmingham. He was formerly Professor of Industrial Relations at the University of Warwick, where his research for his chapter in this volume was conducted, some of it as a Senior Fellow of the Advanced Institute of Management Research.

Sir Bob Hepple QC, FBA, is Emeritus Master of Clare College and Emeritus Professor of Law, University of Cambridge.

Christopher McCrudden is Professor of Human Rights and Equality Law, Queens University Belfast; Leverhulme Major Research Fellow (2011–14); William W Cook Global Professor of Law, University of Michigan Law School (on leave) and a former member of the Northern Ireland Procurement Implementation Team and the Procurement Board of Northern Ireland.

Colm McLaughlin is Lecturer in Industrial Relations and Human Resources at UCD School of Business.

Gillian Morris is a barrister at Matrix Chambers and an Honorary Professor, Warwick Business School, University of Warwick.

John Purcell is an Associate Fellow of the Industrial Relations Research Unit, Warwick Business School, University of Warwick.

Steve Tombs is Professor of Sociology at Liverpool John Moores University.

David Whyte is Reader in Sociology at the University of Liverpool.

1

Introduction—Making Employment Rights Effective: Issues of Enforcement and Compliance

LINDA DICKENS

BACKGROUND AND RATIONALE

DESPITE THE PROLIFERATION of statutory employment rights there is continued widespread experience of unfairness in British workplaces. The reasons for this are many and complex, but part of the explanation is that the development of a more comprehensive role for legislation has not been accompanied by any strategic consideration of the mechanisms, institutions and processes for rights enforcement. In focusing on issues of enforcement and compliance, this volume illuminates how they might contribute to making employment rights effective—by which is meant giving substantive effect to formal rights, reducing the likelihood of adverse treatment and promoting fairer workplaces.

Over the past 40 or so years Britain has experienced dramatic change in the rôle of legal regulation of the employment relationship. The so-called voluntarist system, which characterised British industrial relations for most of the twentieth century, has gone. At its heart was a policy of relative legal abstention, with primacy of, and support for, regulation through collective bargaining. Today, in contrast, protection at work rests less on collective organisation than on individual legal rights, the number of which has expanded considerably since the 1970s, partly through domestic policy and partly through the influence of the European Union. The main thrust of enforcement in Britain rests on individuals asserting their statutory rights, if necessary by making a claim at an employment tribunal (ET). ETs were first given jurisdiction over employer/employee disputes in the mid-1960s and early 1970s when statutory rights were enacted relating to redundancy and unfair dismissal. There is some agency enforcement in Britain but, as statutory protections developed (for example in relation to sex, race and other forms of discrimination; gender pay equality;

time-off and leave; 'work-life balance'; and protections for part-time workers, among others), ETs became the expedient—if not necessarily the most appropriate—enforcement option for handling the ever increasing numbers of rights.

There is a growing consensus that, although these specialised bodies compare favourably with the ordinary courts on many measures, there are problems for all parties with the existing system of rights enforcement centring on the ETs—although the definition of the precise problems, and thus the proposed solutions, varies. Government consultations and official reviews conducted at different times (including one being undertaken at the time of writing) have focused mainly on the efficient operation of the system and reform measures aimed at cutting costs, and attempting to reduce the number of cases coming to ETs, rather than exploring the appropriateness and effectiveness of potential different forms of rights enforcement in terms of achieving social objectives (eg BIS 2011; Gaymer 2009; Employment Department 1994). Some concerns about the ET system are widely shared, but often the reform 'solutions' run counter to making employment rights effective by narrowing their scope, making it harder for workers to exercise rights and more difficult and costly to access justice and to secure appropriate remedies, while at the same time providing limited encouragement to employers to address workplace issues which give rise to legal claims. There has been little official questioning of the efficacy of relying on the 'victim complains', self-service approach, which the ETs embody, despite weaknesses in the nature, application, enforcement and limited impact of the increasing number of individual employment rights which research has revealed—weaknesses which are exacerbated by the changing nature of employment, the labour market and employment relations.

Survey and other evidence suggests continuing 'unfairness' with widespread experience of problems at work (eg Casebourne et al 2006; Pollert and Charlwood 2009; Fevre et al 2009). The Fair Treatment at Work survey in 2008 found just under a third (29 per cent) of respondents to the survey reported that they had experienced a problem at work in the two years prior to the survey interview (Fevre et al 2009) and it has been argued that such surveys (drawing on perceptions) often fail to capture the extent of certain types of unlawful treatment (Fevre et al 2011). Over 28,000 claims of breach of employment rights were upheld by ETs between 1 April 2010 and 31 March 2011. Ministry of Justice statistics show that a further 25,500 were settled through Acas conciliation, others being settled privately or withdrawn. As discussed below, surveys of different kinds indicate that only a very small proportion of workers who experience problems at work, including those involving a potential breach of legal rights, actually go to ETs, so the tribunal figures for cases where an employment rights breach is found are likely to understate considerably the extent of unfairness or adverse treatment being experienced.

Although current policy debate presents the 'problem' as too many cases being brought to ETs, it could be argued that in terms of addressing adverse treatment at work, there are too few cases. The proportion of justiciable disputes going to ETs was estimated in 2001 at between 15–25 per cent (DTI 2001). The Gibbons review noted that rates of employment litigation in Britain are relatively low, with only 0.4 per cent of the working population submitting a claim in 2002, compared to 1.5 per cent in Germany for example (Gibbons 2007: 15). The 2008 Fair Treatment at Work survey showed that only three per cent of employees who report experiencing a problem at work actually go on to register an ET claim, and the profile of ET claimants differs from the profile of those who report experiencing workplace problems (Fevre et al 2009). While some problems may be resolved without need of an ET claim, the relatively low proportion of problems being brought to tribunals also undoubtedly reflects the nature of the enforcement system which calls for a knowledge of rights and how to assert them, and the capacity and willingness to do so. Awareness of rights is not evenly distributed. It has been found to vary by personal and job characteristics. The better informed are those relatively advantaged in the labour market: white, male, better qualified, white-collar employees and those in permanent full-time jobs with written employment particulars (Meager et al 2002; Casebourne et al 2006). Such workers, however, are least likely to report experiencing violations of their rights (Pollert 2005: 222–26). Even where knowledge of rights does exist, people may work in contexts where they are reluctant or fearful to exercise them, fearing reprisal (see for example Mitchell 2009). Further, those experiencing adverse treatment may lack the capacity or support necessary to bring a legal claim (Pollert and Charlwood 2009).

Problems at work, and perceptions of adverse treatment, extend beyond areas covered by employment rights (Bewley and Forth 2010) and statutory employment rights constitute only one, incomplete, mechanism for delivering fairer workplaces. Nonetheless legal rights can play an important role in this, and so the nature and effectiveness of enforcement matters—not only in terms of outcomes for those individuals whose rights are infringed but in terms of bringing about change. The enforcement landscape in Britain is the result of historical accident, political convenience and ad hoc responses to particular needs, rather than one informed by a logic of enforcement designed to make employment rights effective—by which I mean ensuring compliance with statutory standards, giving substantive effect to formal rights, reducing the likelihood of adverse treatment and promoting fairer workplaces.

This book developed from a workshop held at the University of Warwick early in 2011, aided by a small grant from Warwick Business School. It was attended by a group of scholars from different disciplines whose current and recent research I thought could inform debate by critically exploring potential alternative, additional approaches to enforcement through ETs and other drivers for securing compliance, and by illuminating the way in which employment rights interact with organisational and workplace contexts. In combining contributions from labour lawyers, sociologists, and employment relations scholars the aim was to provide an overall richer consideration than might be provided within the separate disciplines. Contributors were encouraged to consider audiences beyond their own discipline in writing and revising their chapters, both in terms of style (eg minimising the detailed case citation and statute referencing common in legal texts) and in the need to explain various concepts which might be familiar in some fields but not others.

The book deals generally with 'Britain' unless otherwise stated and where legal differences or separate systems exist within Britain, it deals with England and Wales. The law is as at 30 November 2011.

STRUCTURE AND CONTENT

In chapter two, Gillian Morris provides a broad overview of the development, range and nature of statutory employment rights and the current mechanisms for enforcement, particularly the nature and operation of ETs, to provide a context for the subsequent chapters. Chapter three looks briefly at the tribunal reform agenda before considering in detail an aspect of it, namely a greater emphasis on alternative dispute resolution (ADR). Current provision for, and conceptualisation of, arbitration, conciliation and mediation in the context of the ETs are critically examined. In the chapter I argue that there is potential for ADR to make a wider contribution in terms of improving workplaces rather than simply reducing tribunal case loads.

The following two chapters turn to a consideration of rights enforcement through agencies and inspectorates. This approach is relatively underused in Britain but there is long-standing agency enforcement in the area of equality, and of health and safety—the areas which provide the basis for consideration in two chapters in this book. In chapter four Bob Hepple describes and reflects on the different approaches to rights enforcement taken by different agencies and at different times in the area of workplace equality, and highlights the unrealised potential of recent legislative and institutional developments. Health and safety at work is an area which is not usually discussed as part of labour law, and also tends to fall outside mainstream industrial relations considerations. However, the critical review of how agency enforcement of health and safety legislation has fared under the 'better regulation' agenda provided in chapter five by Steve Tombs and David Whyte, helps in understanding factors which may influence the effectiveness or otherwise of agency enforcement, and is of relevance to a consideration of 'reflexive regulation', something also addressed in chapters four and seven.

Chapters six and seven contribute to a consideration of alternative, non-judicial approaches to achieving the desired policy outcomes behind individual employment rights such as the use of procurement/supply chains, and levers such as corporate social responsibility (CSR). In chapter six Christopher McCrudden looks at the use and potential of public procurement as a strategy which can deliver fairness in the workplace, drawing particularly on the experience of public procurement in Northern Ireland to assess achievements and identify the factors which help to determine its effectiveness. In chapter seven Simon Deakin, Colm McLaughlin and Dominic Chai draw on their original research to explore various 'reflexive' legal mechanisms to encourage employers to address the gender pay gap and gender inequalities. Although focussed on a particular area of employment rights, their contribution, like others, has a broader relevance: comparing the modes of working of different regulatory techniques, assessing the effectiveness of different mechanisms in the public and private sectors, and considering the potential, and limitations, of CSR and shareholder pressure based on the logic of the business case for fairer workplaces.

The organisational context within which rights fall to be implemented is an important consideration in terms of compliance and rights' likely impact on practice (Dickens and Hall 2006: 349–51). Small firms are often depicted as particularly problematic in terms of employment rights. In chapter eight Paul Edwards looks at employment rights and practice in small firms, drawing on research in this sector to demonstrate a more complex and varied picture, with response and impact varying according to the nature of the law and the kind of firm concerned. In chapter nine, the nature of and explanations for variation among medium and large organisations in attitudes towards, and compliance with, employment rights is explored by John Purcell. He considers the management of employment rights, locating it within the context of business strategy and different preferred approaches to managing employees, and discusses the role of line management and the human resource management function in the implementation of employment rights. Such factors influence the extent and way in which rights in the statute book are translated into practice and given substance in the workplace. In chapter ten Trevor Colling discusses the role of trade unions in making employment rights effective. He explores issues arising from the shift from social regulation, that is regulation through collective bargaining, as the main source of protection at work, to legal regulation through individual employment rights, and provides detailed consideration of the changing relationship of, and interaction between, these two systems of regulation.

In the final chapter, I discuss the reluctance of successive governments to address strategically the issues of effective enforcement in terms of securing compliance and delivering fairness. I draw on the other contributions to this volume to consider the potential for reducing the likelihood of adverse treatment offered by placing greater emphasis on agency enforcement and inspection and encouraging the use of other regulatory and non-regulatory measures, and by utilising the regulatory capacity of non-state actors. There are no straightforward universal solutions and currently the alternative approaches display their own weaknesses. In chapter eleven, however, I argue that, were the necessary political will to emerge, such approaches could be used to encourage proactive, structural employer action to deliver fairer workplaces. In combination they have the potential to help translate formal rights in the statute book into real, substantive rights in the workplace; to reduce the likelihood of adverse treatment and so make employment rights effective.

BIBLIOGRAPHY

BIS (2011) *Resolving Workplace Disputes: A Consultation* (London, Department for Business Innovation and Skills).

Bewley, H and Forth, J (2010) *Vulnerability and Adverse Treatment in the Workplace* (London, BIS).

Casebourne, J, Regan, J, Neathey, F and Tuohy, S (2006*) Employment Rights at Work: Survey of Employers 2005*, Employment Relations Research Series (London, Department of Employment).

Dickens, L and Hall, M (2006) 'Fairness – up to a Point:Assessing the Impact of New Labour's Employment Legislation' 16 *Human Resource Management Journal* 338–56.

DTI (2001) *Routes to Resolution* (London, HMSO).

Employment Department (1994) *Resolving Employment Disputes: Options for Reform*, Cmnd 2707 (London, HMSO).

Fevre, R, Nichols T, Prior, G and Rutherford, I (2009) *Fair Treatment at Work Report: Findings of the 2008 Survey* (London, BIS).

Fevre, R, Grainger, H and Brewer, R (2011) 'Discrimination and Unfair Treatment in the Workplace' 49 issue supplement s2 *British Journal of Industrial Relations* 207–35.

Gaymer, J (2006) 'The Employment Tribunals System Taskforce' in L Dickens and A Neal (eds), *The Changing Institutional Face of British Employment Relations* (The Hague, Kluwer).

Gibbons, M (2007) *Better Dispute Resolution. A Review of Employment Dispute Resolution in Great Britain* (London, Department of Trade and Industry).

Meager, N, Tyers, C, Perryman, S, Rick, J and Willison, R (2002) *Awareness, Knowledge and Exercise of Individual Rights*, Employment Relations Research Series No 15 (London, DTI and IES).

Mitchell, D (2009) *Citizens Advice Client Research Final Report*, Employment Relations Research Series, No 99 (London, BERR).

Pollert, A (2005) 'The Unorganised Worker: The Decline in Collectivism and New Hurdles to Individual Employment Rights' 34 *Industrial Law Journal* 217–38.

Pollert, A and Charlwood, A (2009) 'The Vulnerable Worker in Britain and Problems at Work' 23 *Work Employment and Society* 343–62.

2

The Development of Statutory Employment Rights in Britain and Enforcement Mechanisms

GILLIAN S MORRIS

T HIS CHAPTER CONTAINS a broad overview of the development, range and nature of statutory employment rights and the current mechanisms for their enforcement. As such, it does not discuss in detail the content of these rights (see generally Deakin and Morris 2012) or the reasons for their introduction (see Davies and Freedland 1993, 2007). Rather the aim is to provide a context for the chapters which follow. The enforcement mechanisms themselves divide into those which are based on individual complaints that a right has been breached and more proactive mechanisms of protection through a licensing or inspectorate model or other forms of administrative enforcement.

THE DEVELOPMENT, NATURE AND RANGE OF STATUTORY EMPLOYMENT RIGHTS

Statutory employment rights covering the workforce as a whole were introduced only recently in Britain. The legal relationship between employer and worker in British law is based on an individual contract, enforceable through the same courts which enforce other types of contract. Historically, the brake on the exploitation of workers which a 'freedom of contract' model could produce came not from legislation but from collective bargaining. In major industries key terms of the employment relationship, such as pay, hours and holidays, were derived from collective agreements between employers or employers' associations and trade unions, whose provisions were then incorporated into individual contracts. From the end of the nineteenth century, and more actively from the end of the First World War, it became government policy to support collective bargaining as the preferred method of determining terms and conditions of employment, including in its own role as employer (Fredman and Morris 1989). The trade union movement supported this preference for 'voluntarily-determined' rather than statutory standards, which was combined with a reliance on voluntary procedures for dispute settlement negotiated by the collective parties rather than resorting to litigation. Substantive statutory regulation of the employment relationship was essentially confined to matters which collective bargaining did not in practice cover, such as health and safety, or sectors or groups of workers which were difficult to organise or otherwise outside the reach of collective bargaining. Thus, special provision was made for the working hours of women and children and from 1909 there was a statutory scheme for minimum rates of pay (and subsequently other terms of employment) to be set by trade boards (later called wages councils) in sectors where the absence of collective bargaining left workers vulnerable to exploitation.

The residual role of statute as a source of regulation has been transformed over the past 50 years. The process began modestly, with the introduction of the right to a written statement of employment terms and minimum notice periods in 1963. 1965 saw the introduction of statutory redundancy payments for no-fault economic job loss, followed by a broader range of individual rights in 1971, most notably the right not to be unfairly dismissed. The 1970s also brought the right to equal pay for men and women and individual rights in the areas of sex and race discrimination; maternity; and membership and non-membership of, and participation in, trade unions. The 1979–97 Conservative governments sought to deregulate the labour market both by weakening trade unions and relaxing or removing statutory standards; the powers of the long-standing wages councils, for example, were curtailed and eventually abolished. However, there were limits to the deregulatory strategy: obligations resulting from membership of the European Community (now the European Union) required new or extended statutory rights, such as rights on transfer of a business and a broader scope for equal pay. Protection against disability discrimination was introduced following domestic pressure. The advent of a Labour government in 1997 brought more fundamental reforms, the most notable being the introduction of a national minimum wage to which the trade union movement had dropped its historical opposition. Further EU obligations also produced important changes, particularly general restrictions on working time; rights for part-time workers and those working under fixed-term contracts; rights to non-discrimination on a much wider range of grounds, including age; and 'family-friendly' rights. New rights for agency workers, again required by EU law, were introduced by the Conservative–Liberal Coalition Government which took office in 2010.

The major areas covered by the multiplicity of statutory rights which now govern the employment relationship include those listed in the table below (Dickens and Hall 2010: 304).

Table 1. Individual statutory employment rights

---

(1) Statutory employment rights in place in 1997 include:
— a minimum period of notice of termination;
— a statement of the principal terms and conditions of the contract of employment and of discipline and dismissal procedures;
— an itemised pay statement;
— a statement of the reason for dismissal;
— protection against unfair dismissal;
— protection against discrimination on grounds of race, sex and disability;
— time off work for ante-natal care;
— maternity leave and pay;
— return to work after leave for childbirth;
— time off work for various public and trade union duties;
— equal pay and other contractual terms as between men and women;
— redundancy payments;
— protection against dismissal or action short of dismissal on grounds of trade union membership, non-membership or union activity;
— preservation of acquired rights on the transfer of undertakings;
(2) Statutory employment rights introduced since 1997 include:
— the national minimum wage;
— protection against dismissal or detriment for 'whistleblowing';
— the right to be accompanied in grievance and disciplinary hearings;
— statutory limits on working time;
— paid annual leave;
— parental leave;
— time off for family emergencies;
— the right to request flexible working;
— paternity leave and pay;
— adoption leave and pay;
— equal treatment for part-time workers;
— protection for fixed-term employees;
— protection against discrimination on grounds of age, religion or belief and sexual orientation.
(3) Statutory employment rights introduced since 2010 include:
— protection for agency workers

Source: Dickens and Hall 2010: 304.

The significance of statutory rights as a source of employment protection in Britain was enhanced by the radical decline in the coverage of collective bargaining since the early 1980s (Brown 2010). The proportion of employees covered by collective agreements fell from 64 per cent in 1984 to 41 per cent by 1998 in workplaces with 25 or more employees (Cully et al 1999: 242; Kersley et al 2006: 185). Collective bargaining is now largely confined to the public sector; the 2004 Workplace Employment Relations Survey found that it was used in only 14 per cent of private sector workplaces (Kersley et al 2006: 179–81). Moreover the range of issues over which bargaining took place has also shrunk (Brown and Oxenbridge 2004: 70). Thus, far from being an adjunct to collective bargaining, statutory minimum standards are now for many workers the main source of protection in relation to fundamental terms, such as pay, hours and holidays. They are also particularly important in relation to discipline, termination of employment and equality.

This book is concerned primarily with the mechanisms of enforcing employment rights rather than their substantive content. However there are certain important features of statutory employment rights which are integral to enforcement and compliance. The first is the technical complexity of many of these rights, which can make it difficult for workers who have no access to specialist advice to claim them and potentially poses problems for employers seeking clarity about their obligations. Moreover, the incremental approach to legislation has meant that rights are located in a wide variety of statutes and secondary legislation rather than being collected in a single document; indeed, the relevant provisions governing a specific right may themselves be scattered among different legislative instruments. The second important feature is the partial nature of their coverage and consequential difficulties in determining whether or not an individual is covered by them. Many significant rights, notably those available on termination of employment, are confined to 'employees', although others, including the National Minimum Wage, limits on working time, and protection against discrimination, apply to the wider category of 'workers'. An 'employee' is an 'individual who has entered into or works under ... a contract of employment'; 'contract of employment' is, in turn, defined, as 'a contract of service or apprenticeship'. The term 'worker' is not identically defined in every statute, but usually refers to an individual

> who has entered into or works under (or, where the employment has ceased, worked under) (a) a contract of employment, or (b) any other contract ... whereby the individual undertakes to do or perform personally any work or services for another party to the contract whose status is not by virtue of the contract that of a client or customer of any profession or undertaking carried on by the individual.

In very broad terms, the category of 'employees' was traditionally intended to distinguish dependent or subordinate labour, subject to the employer's direction and control, from more independent or autonomous workers.

However, this form of demarcation has proved increasingly difficult to apply (Deakin and Morris 2012: paras 3.18 *et seq*). Historically, the case law adapted to allow highly skilled workers employed by a single employer to be classed as 'employees', despite their ability to exercise professional discretion, but it has proved much less able to accommodate individuals who are in a high degree of economic dependence but may lack other formal attributes of a contract of employment. There is a particular problem in relation to 'casual' workers who are offered work only when it becomes available because of the (contentious) insistence by the courts that there should be subsisting mutual obligations between the parties in the form of a requirement to work and to offer work in order for a contract of employment to exist. This has the effect of excluding those in precarious work relationships who may be most in need of protection. In the National Minimum Wage Act 1998, specific provision was made for homeworkers, whose status may otherwise have been uncertain, as well as for 'workers' generally. However this approach has not been adopted widely, nor was the opportunity taken by the government to change the scope of application of pre-existing rights, which remains ill-matched to patterns of employment in the contemporary labour market (Dickens 2004; Leighton and Wynn 2011). Indeed, even where legislation does extend to 'workers' the courts have recently emphasised the need for there to be an element of direction from the recipient of work or services to distinguish 'workers' from independent businesses, an approach which risks unduly narrowing the scope of protection. In summary, therefore, although on one view the rights listed in Table 1 could be said to be sufficiently comprehensive to constitute, in essence, a labour code, they are much less universal and coherent in their application than such a description would suggest. A further limitation on the coverage of many rights is the requirement for an employee to have worked for the employer for a minimum period of time; to claim unfair dismissal, for example, at the time of writing the employee requires one, and from April 2012 will require two, years' 'continuous employment' (with specified exceptions, such as dismissal on grounds of union membership and whistleblowing). This excludes those on short-term contracts and may encourage employers to shed staff before they qualify to claim.

Practical guidance on conduct in many areas covered by statutory rights is contained in codes of practice. These are issued, variously, by the Secretary of State, the Advisory Conciliation and Arbitration Service (Acas), the Equality and Human Rights Commission (EHRC) and the Health and Safety Commission (now merged with the Health and Safety Executive: HSE). Those currently in force which are particularly relevant to individual rights are those issued by Acas in the areas of Disciplinary and Grievance Procedures (revised in 2009) and Time Off for Trade Union Duties and Activities (revised in 2010) and those issued by the EHRC and its predecessor bodies in relation to discrimination and equal pay.

Breach of a code of practice does not of itself make an individual liable to legal proceedings but the codes are admissible in evidence before an ET (those issued by the EHRC and the Secretary of State are also admissible before the courts) and must be taken into account where relevant. In the past, codes were intended actively to promote good employment practice rather than merely codifying existing practices (an aim which the tripartite Acas was well-suited to fulfil), and research showed that they could have a significant impact in the workplace (Dickens et al 1985). It is notable, however, that the latest version of the Acas Code on Disciplinary and Grievance Procedures is considerably briefer and narrower in range than its predecessors, with much of the material which was previously in the code (such as details on drawing up disciplinary rules and procedures) now appearing in a non-statutory guide (Acas 2009). This approach was linked to a new provision, discussed later in this chapter, allowing ETs to adjust awards to successful claimants in the event of non-compliance with the code by either employer or employee. However, there is a risk that transferring provisions to the guide may lead to a weakening in substantive employee protection both in the workplace and, eventually, in case law.

ENFORCING STATUTORY RIGHTS BY INDIVIDUAL CLAIMS

In general, statutory employment rights in Britain are enforced by individuals taking cases to ETs, which were first established in 1964 under the name 'industrial tribunals'. ETs sit in a variety of locations around Great Britain. Unlike the ordinary courts, ETs are tripartite bodies, composed of a legally qualified chair (since 2008, known as an 'Employment Judge') and two lay members drawn from separate panels of employer and employee representatives, all of whom are appointed by the Lord Chancellor. The lay members do not sit as representatives of their respective 'sides' but, rather, make an independent judgment on the merits of the case. Although the Employment Judge controls the conduct of the hearing, the lay members can also intervene and each party has one vote. In practice the vast majority of decisions are unanimous (Meeran 2006: 132; Corby and Latreille 2011: 16).

Appeals from ETs on points of law are heard by the Employment Appeal Tribunal (EAT), also (at the time of writing) a tripartite body composed of a more senior judge and members with special knowledge or experience of industrial relations. Again the lay members may outvote the judge but, as in ETs, majority decisions are very rare (Corby and Latreille 2011: 26). Subsequent appeals may be made, with leave, to the Court of Appeal (or Court of Session in Scotland) and thence to the Supreme Court, both of which are courts within the general legal system. Thus, although there is recognition of the specialist nature of employment law at the lower tiers of the system, the most authoritative interpretations of the law come from non-specialist appellate courts; the system of precedent means that ETs are bound by decisions of the EAT which, in turn, is bound by decisions of the higher courts. British employment law therefore lacks the autonomy which characterises legal systems where the final appeal is to a specialist court. Appeals from ETs lie only on a point of law, which requires the appellant to establish that the ET misdirected itself in law or misapplied the law; that there was no evidence to support a particular conclusion or finding of fact; that the decision was 'perverse'; or that it was obviously wrong. In many cases, such as whether the individual is an 'employee' or whether an employer acted reasonably in dismissing the claimant, it is not always clear whether the matter should be characterised as a question of law or of fact. Classifying a matter as a question of fact means that different ETs may reach differing decisions without those decisions being open to appeal even if the situations before them were the same or very similar.

As the first section of this chapter indicated, many areas of the law with which ETs now have to deal are highly technical; the difficulty of their task may be compounded if EU law is relevant to interpreting the provisions with which they are concerned. Equality law is an area of particular complexity, and cases in this area may involve sensitive factual scenarios. Although an attempt is made to include at least one woman on an ET for sex discrimination cases, and for race discrimination cases a member with experience and training in such cases, it has been argued that specialist tribunals, or a separate division within the ET system, would be able to deal more justly and efficiently with cases relating to equality law, especially given the expanded range of grounds upon which discrimination claims may now be based.

Individuals may be represented in ETs and the EAT by the person of their choice, as well as representing themselves; unlike the ordinary courts, there is no requirement for representation to be by a lawyer. There is no provision for state-funded legal aid for those bringing or responding to ET claims in England and Wales, regardless of the complexity of the case (although the Court of Justice of the European Union has recently upheld a right to legal aid for the vindication of EU law rights, which may require the position to be reviewed for cases where EU rights are at issue). Legal aid for representation in ETs where specified criteria are satisfied is available in Scotland and is available for EAT proceedings and proceedings in the higher courts throughout Great Britain. Despite the absence of legal aid for ET proceedings in England and Wales, the most common source of advice for both claimants and employers is a lawyer and in cases where parties are represented at a hearing this usually takes the form of legal representation (Peters et al 2010: ch 5).

THE OPERATION OF ETs

The caseload of ETs has increased exponentially in the past 20 years or so. In 1989–90 there were 34,697 applications; by 1993–94, this had more than doubled to 71,661. By 2010–11 there were 218,100 claims and 382,400 jurisdictional claims, meaning that many claims covered more than one statutory right (unfair dismissal and discrimination, for example). Table 2 below shows the number and nature of the claims submitted over the past three years.

The absence of any provision for 'class actions' to be brought on behalf of a group of workers, and the need for individuals to protect their own position by registering a claim within the appropriate time limit, means that the figures may be inflated by multiple claims against the same employer, as shown by the working time claims in 2010–11 (84,000 were resubmitted multiple claims against an employer or small number of employers). Multiple claims also commonly occur in the area of equal pay. Of the remaining claims in 2010–11, 28 per cent were for unfair dismissal, breach of contract and redundancy and 19 per cent were for unauthorised deductions.

In 1968, a Royal Commission on Trade Unions and Employers' Associations expressed the view that 'labour tribunals' should provide an 'easily accessible, speedy, informal and inexpensive procedure' for the settlement of disputes (Donovan 1968: para 578). These aims remain the touchstone for assessing the performance of ETs today but they have become increasingly difficult to realise. In 1994 the Employment Department proposed reforms to the tribunal system 'with a view to identifying any changes which would help ... to cope with an increasing volume and complexity of cases with reduced delays, while containing demands on public expenditure' (ED 1994: para 1.1). Since then, a succession of reforms has been proposed, which have varied in their detail but shared the same central objective: that of reducing the number of cases going to tribunals by encouraging parties to resolve disputes by alternative means. The next section of this chapter outlines how ETs currently operate under the headings of bringing a claim and the conduct of proceedings. It then discusses sanctions and remedies. The account which follows draws on Deakin and Morris (2012: paras 2.16–20). For a detailed description of tribunal practice and procedure, see Harvey (1972, as updated: div P1).

Bringing a Claim

An individual wishing to apply to an ET completes a claim form which requires personal details and details of the respondent, together with the details of the claim. There are tight time limits for bringing claims compared with claims in the ordinary courts; in general, claims must be brought within three months of the act complained of (with provision for extension

Table 2. Claims Accepted by Employment Tribunals 1 April 2010–31 March 2011

	2008–09	2009–10	Apr 10 to Mar 11 2010–11
Total Claims Accepted[1]	151,000	236,100	218,100
Total Claims Initially Rejected[2]	10,600	4,100	1,400
Of the total, those that were resubmitted and subsequently accepted	2,900	1,300	210
Of the total, those that were resubmitted and not accepted or never resubmitted	7,700	2,800	1,100
Jurisdiction Mix of claims accepted			
NATURE OF CLAIM	**2008–09**	**2009–10**	**2010–11**
Unfair dismissal	52,700	57,400	47,900
Unauthorised deductions (Formerly Wages Act)	33,800	75,500	71,300
Breach of contract	32,800	42,400	34,600
Sex discrimination	18,600	18,200	18,300
Working Time Directive[3]	24,000	95,200	114,100
Redundancy pay	10,800	19,000	16,000
Disability discrimination	6,600	7,500	7,200
Redundancy—failure to inform and consult	11,400	7,500	7,400
Equal pay	45,700	37,400	34,600
Race discrimination	5,000	5,700	5,000
Written statement of terms and conditions	3,900	4,700	4,000
Written statement of reasons for dismissal	1,100	1,100	930
Written pay statement	1,100	1,400	1,300
Transfer of an undertaking—failure to inform and consult	1,300	1,800	1,900
Suffer a detriment/unfair dismissal—pregnancy	1,800	1,900	1,900
Part Time Workers Regulations	660	530	1,600
National minimum wage	600	500	520
Discrimination on grounds of Religion or Belief	830	1,000	880
Discrimination on grounds of Sexual Orientation	600	710	640
Age Discrimination	3,800	5,200	6,800
Others	9,300	8,100	5,500
Total	**266,500**	**392,800**	**382,400**

Source: MOJ & Tribunals Service 2011: 7.

[1] A claim may be brought under more than one jurisdiction or subsequently amended or clarified in the course of proceedings but will be counted only once.

[2] The figures from 2009–10 reflect the repeal of the pre-existing statutory three step procedures for dealing with discipline, dismissal and grievance issues, set out in the Employment Act 2002 on 6th April 2009.

[3] These figures include approximately 84,000 resubmitted multiple claims in 2010–11.

if it was not 'reasonably practicable' for the claim to be presented in time, a difficult test to satisfy). Once accepted by the tribunal a copy of the claim is sent to the employer who has 28 days to enter a response stating whether it intends to resist the claim and, if so, on what grounds. These forms are then copied to Acas, whose conciliation officers have a duty for most types of claim to attempt to promote a settlement between the parties without the need for a tribunal hearing. As discussed by Dickens in the following chapter, in practice a significant proportion of cases are settled by Acas conciliation or withdrawn (in 2010–11, 29 per cent and 32 per cent respectively of the jurisdictional claims received by ETs (MOJ 2011: 5)). Settlement under the auspices of Acas bars the case being heard. Cases may also be settled by means of a 'compromise agreement' where the claimant has received independent advice as to the meaning of the agreement from a qualified lawyer or other specified persons certified or authorised by an independent trade union or advice centre. An Acas scheme which came into effect in 2001 for the resolution of unfair dismissal disputes (and subsequently disputes over flexible working requests) by confidential binding arbitration, which it was hoped would offer a less legalistic and more informal option than ETs, has been used extremely rarely (Dickens, this volume). Since April 2009, in a further effort to resolve claims before they reach tribunals, Acas has been empowered to offer a voluntary pre-claim conciliation service which, in 2010–11, dealt with around 16,700 jurisdictional claims, of which nearly 8,000 were resolved (Acas 2011: 41). The Coalition Government has recently announced its intention to require parties to submit details of all claims to Acas prior to making an ET claim; they will then be offered the opportunity of early conciliation, although either party will be free to reject this offer (BIS 2011a: para 61).

Other measures are aimed at requiring parties to attempt to settle their disputes internally prior to submitting an ET claim. Since April 2009 there has been provision for ETs to adjust an award to a successful claimant by up to 25 per cent either way in the event of an employee or employer 'unreasonably' failing to comply with a 'relevant code of practice', a definition which currently applies to the Acas Code on Disciplinary and Grievance Procedures referred to earlier in this chapter. The provisions of the code which relate to grievances are relatively brief and recognise that what is reasonable will depend on all the circumstances, including the employer's size and resources. In outline, they require an employee to raise a matter with the employer formally in writing if it cannot be resolved informally; the employer to arrange a formal meeting at which the employee can explain the grievance; a written response from the employer; and an opportunity for the employee to appeal. The provision for adjustment of an award for failure to comply with the code applies to a wide range of jurisdictions, including equal pay and discrimination; unfair dismissal; claims relating to working time; unauthorised deductions from pay; and the National

Minimum Wage. At the time of writing the extent to which the power to adjust awards is being used by ETs is not known. This provision replaced a short-lived requirement introduced in 2004 for claimants (generally) to institute a statutory grievance procedure before presenting a tribunal claim (Deakin and Morris 2005, paras 2.21–26), a requirement which was highly controversial (Hepple and Morris 2002; Sanders 2009) and itself the source of substantial litigation.

Tribunals may screen out claims at a 'pre-hearing review' (PHR), an interim hearing conducted by an Employment Judge alone (unless a party requests a three-member ET and the judge agrees that specified criteria are met). Oral or written representations or evidence, as well as the claim form and response, may be considered. Preliminary issues, such as whether the tribunal has jurisdiction to hear the case (whether the employee has the requisite period of service, for example) may be determined at a PHR and, if appropriate, a claim may be struck out at this stage. In addition, if it appears that the contentions put forward by a party in relation to a particular matter have 'little reasonable prospect of success' (which may be determined without evidence being heard), that party may be required to pay a deposit of up to £500 as a condition of being permitted to continue to take part in the proceedings relating to the matter in question. In determining whether a deposit should be ordered, and the amount, account must be taken of a party's means. As well as being at risk of losing their deposit if they continue with the matter, the party concerned is put on notice that they may be liable for another party's costs (if legally represented) or preparation time (if not so represented) if they subsequently lose the case on the grounds identified at the PHR. Even if no deposit is required, costs orders may be ordered by an ET following the proceedings in favour of each legally-represented party if in bringing or conducting the proceedings another party has acted 'vexatiously, abusively, disruptively or otherwise unreasonably' or the bringing or conducting of the proceedings was 'misconceived' (which includes 'having no reasonable prospect of success'). There is also provision in specified circumstances for 'preparation-time' orders to be made in favour of non-legally-represented parties. At the time of writing, costs and preparation-time orders are subject to a maximum of £10,000 (although the parties may agree a higher costs order). In deciding whether to make a costs or preparation-time order, and in setting the amount, an ET may (but is not required to) have regard to a party's ability to pay.

In practice the powers of tribunals to award costs have been little used; over the past three years they have been awarded to an average of 315 respondents and 107 claimants (Tribunals Service 2009; MOJ 2010, 2011: table 12. The figures for preparation-time orders are not given.) This suggests that, contrary to anecdote, the number of unmeritorious claims is few. Nevertheless, the threat of a costs award may constitute a considerable deterrent to a claimant, as may the risk of losing a deposit. Moreover, cases which appear unarguable to Employment Judges may, if pursued to the higher tiers of the legal system, change the law; a challenge to differential retirement ages for men and women in the 1980s is a notable example. Despite this, the Coalition Government has recently announced that the limits on deposits and costs orders will double to £1,000 and £20,000 respectively (BIS 2011b: para 80). It has also decided to introduce fees to bring an ET claim (and to appeal to the EAT) although at the time of writing the structure of the charging regime is subject to consultation.

The Conduct of Proceedings

Employment Judges are empowered to give directions on any matter arising in connection with proceedings, including requiring a party to give additional information; the provision and exchange of witness statements; the disclosure of documents; and the attendance of witnesses. Failure to comply with a direction or requirement may result in the claim or response being struck out. In discrimination cases for which the merits hearing is expected to take three days or more, the Employment Judge will advise the parties of the possibility of judicial mediation, although research on a judicial mediation pilot conducted between June 2006 and March 2007 showed no statistically significant impact on settlement rates (Boon et al 2011).

For cases that proceed to a hearing, Employment Judges are required, so far as appears appropriate, to avoid formality in the conduct of proceedings and the rules of evidence governing the ordinary courts, such as the hearsay rule, do not apply. The proceedings are adversarial rather than investigatory, with each party having to present or prove its case and bear responsibility for calling witnesses, although tribunals are mandated to make appropriate inquiries of parties or witnesses to clarify the issues. Appearing at a tribunal is likely to be a stressful experience, particularly for a non-represented party.

Although ETs are tripartite bodies, since 1993 there has been an increasing number of jurisdictions (in addition to PHRs) where an Employment Judge may sit alone. They currently include disputes over entitlement to redundancy payments; claims for holiday pay under the Working Time Regulations; and complaints relating to the written statement of employment particulars, as well as any other cases where the parties consent to this. The Coalition Government has recently announced that Employment Judges should be permitted to hear unfair dismissal cases alone, although (as with other jurisdictions) it will be open to them to choose otherwise. The Government made this decision on grounds of cost despite opposition from many consultees who pointed out that unfair dismissal cases often revolve around factual questions where the experience of lay members may be particularly relevant (BIS, 2011a: paras 116–17) and evidence that the majority of Employment Judges consider that lay members add value in unfair dismissal cases (Corby and Latreille 2011: 12).

Reasons must be given for all tribunal judgments, although these need be oral only unless a party requests written reasons or written reasons are requested by the EAT. In 2010/11, 2,048 appeals were made to the EAT but only 363 reached a full hearing, the remainder having been filtered out by the EAT at a preliminary stage or withdrawn. Of those 363, 91 were allowed and 103 were allowed and remitted to the same or another tribunal (MOJ 2011: tables 13–16). Radical reforms in case management were introduced in 2002–04 (Burton 2005). All appeals to the EAT are sifted by a judge (or by the registrar with an appeal to a judge) to determine the most effective management of the case. The sift may result in the appeal being stayed (with a final date by which the papers must be restored for further consideration); struck out (for example, if it discloses no reasonable grounds for bringing the appeal); sent to a full hearing; or (where the judge is in doubt as to arguability on the papers) sent to a preliminary hearing. An appeal from an Employment Judge sitting alone will normally be heard by an EAT judge alone unless he or she directs to the contrary; to date other appeals have been heard by the judge and lay members.[4] EAT judges show less support for the participation of lay members than Employment Judges but a majority consider that they add value in unfair dismissal and discrimination cases (Corby and Latreille 2011: 20). Nevertheless the Coalition Government has announced a radical departure from the tripartite principle; the default constitution of the EAT will henceforth be the judge alone in all cases unless he or she directs that members should also sit (BIS 2011a: para 119).

Sanctions and Remedies in ETs

Most claims heard by ETs do not succeed (an average of 13 per cent of cases were successful in the period April 2008–March 2011: Tribunals Service 2009; MOJ 2010, 2011: table 2). If a claim is upheld, the remedy which can be granted in relation to that claim will be specified in the individual statute. In general, remedies consist of financial compensation. ETs can order reinstatement or re-engagement of an unfairly dismissed employee but in practice this is very rarely done. In 2010/11 in only eight out of 4,200 unfair dismissal claims upheld at a tribunal hearing was reinstatement or re-engagement ordered (MOJ 2011: table 3) and this is not an atypical figure. Research has shown several reasons for this, including a failure by the claimant to request re-employment with the employer and

---

[4] Usually two, one drawn from each side of industry, but there is provision for four. With the consent of the parties the EAT judge may sit with one or three members.

the reluctance of tribunals to make such orders; whether it is 'practicable' for the employer to comply with such an order is a factor specified in the legislation and tribunals have seen employer opposition as highly relevant to practicability (Dickens et al 1981). Even if a 're-employment' order is made, if the employer fails to implement it the only option is additional financial compensation (which can be defeated if the employer shows at this stage that compliance with the order was not 'practicable'). This is a notable contrast with the ordinary courts, where non-compliance with an order constitutes contempt of court, punishable by an unlimited fine and/ or imprisonment. In the context of a successful discrimination claim, ETs may make a recommendation that the respondent takes specified steps to obviate or reduce the adverse effect of any matter to which the proceedings relate on the claimant or (significantly) on any other person but, once again, the only remedy if the employer fails to comply with the recommendation is financial compensation (see also Hepple, this volume).

ETs have no power to grant injunctive relief to an individual claimant to prevent an act occurring, although in very limited circumstances they can order 'interim relief' to maintain an employee in his or her employment pending the hearing of an unfair dismissal claim (if the employer objects to re-employing the dismissed employee, this takes the form of continuation of the contract for the purposes of pay and benefits and continuity of employment). These circumstances include where the dismissed employee is claiming that the principal reason for dismissal is one which relates to trade union membership or activities; acting in other specified representative functions; making a 'protected disclosure' under the whistleblowing provisions; or exercising the right to be accompanied (or accompanying another worker) at a grievance or disciplinary hearing or meeting. The tribunal must be satisfied that at the full hearing such a claim is 'likely' to be upheld. It seems probable that if interim relief were more widely available the effectiveness of the unfair dismissal jurisdiction in preserving employment would be much greater in that the tribunal would be ordering the continuation of the existing position rather than reintroducing the claimant to a workplace he or she has left.

In the majority of cases there is a statutory limit on the amount of compensation which may be awarded. In the case of unfair dismissal the award is divided into two elements: the basic award, based on age and length of service (subject to a maximum of £12,000 at the time of writing), and the compensatory award, whose maximum currently stands at £68,400. (These figures are uprated in line with RPI inflation on an annual basis.) In practice the median award is very considerably lower than this: between April 2008 and March 2011 the average median award was £4,588. In discrimination cases there is no statutory maximum but, again, median awards are relatively low. (Tribunals Service 2009; MOJ 2010 2011: tables 5–11).

Tribunals have no power to enforce their money judgments; if an award is not paid, enforcement action must be taken through the county court (or civil courts in Scotland). Until 2010 the initiative for taking enforcement action lay solely with the claimant. Research published in 2009 found that, of 1,002 claimants who had been awarded a monetary payment between January 2007 and April 2008, 53 per cent had been paid in full, eight per cent in part, and 39 per cent had received nothing. Of those who had not received payment, only a minority had initiated county court proceedings, the 'hassle', time involved, expense, and lack of awareness of this option being cited as reasons for not doing so (Adams et al 2009). As from April 2010 a 'fast track' scheme has been available, enabling a successful claimant to ask a High Court Enforcement Officer to commence proceedings in the county court on the claimant's behalf and to seize and sell the employer's goods if payment is not made. Costs of enforcement are added to the employer's debt. In addition, the details of any enforcement action are added to a publicly-available Register of Judgments, Orders, Fines and Tribunal Decisions which may affect an employer's ability to obtain credit, as well as attracting unwelcome press attention.

INSTITUTIONAL MODES OF ENFORCEMENT

ETs represent a mode of enforcement which relies on individuals bringing claims that their rights have been infringed. There are specific areas within the British system in which a more proactive approach to enforcement has been adopted. They can be divided broadly into the licensing; inspectorate; and administrative enforcement modes although as the overview below makes clear, the agencies involved have functions which overlap these categories. The chapter concludes with a brief description of the Pay and Work Rights Helpline which aims to assist those with queries and concerns about compliance in specific areas for which government agencies are responsible.

Licensing

The Gangmasters Licensing Authority (GLA) was established in 2005 to curb the exploitation of workers in the agricultural, horticultural, shellfish gathering and associated processing and packaging industries. From the late 1990s the Labour Government had recognised that considerable informality and abusive practices were found in these sectors, but the catalyst which led to the formation of the GLA was the death of 23 Chinese cockle pickers in 2004. Since 2006 it has been an offence, punishable by a maximum 10 years in prison and a fine, to act as a labour provider ('gangmaster') or to use labour to provide a service in these industries without a licence. It is also an offence to obstruct GLA officers in the course of their duties; to falsify documents; and to use workers or services from an unlicensed provider unless (in outline) 'reasonable steps' were taken to establish that the gangmaster had a valid licence. There is a public register of licence-holders (available online) and users can record their search of the register. As of 31 March 2011 more than 1,230 licences have been issued.

In order to obtain and retain a licence, gangmasters must comply with a wide range of conditions. These include requirements to provide workers with specified terms of employment in writing; to keep proper records; to ensure that workers have suitable accommodation if they work away from home; and restrictions on detrimental action if workers propose to leave the gangmaster. Licence-holders are subject to compliance inspections, which may be random or based on risk-assessment or intelligence; the GLA has recently appointed Regional Field Intelligence Officers to operate at grassroots level. It also works closely with other government departments and agencies such as HMRC (Her Majesty's Revenue and Customs). In addition, workers and third parties are encouraged to report (anonymously if they choose) any breach of standards to the GLA. The GLA describes its approach to compliance as 'proportionate ... concerned with identifying the more persistent and systematic exploitation of workers rather than concentrating on isolated non-compliances, unless such a non-compliance is "critical" in its own right' (GLA 2009a: 5). All inspections are listed on the GLA website. At the time of writing more than 150 licences have been revoked by the GLA.

The GLA is sponsored by the Department for Environment, Food and Rural Affairs (DEFRA) and its activities are supervised by a board whose members include industry and worker representatives. Board meetings are held in public and the GLA generally seems to operate in a highly transparent fashion. An independent review of its operation in 2008 concluded that licensing had been an appropriate tool to regulate labour providers and that the GLA was an 'effective and efficient regulator' (GLA 2009b: 9).

Many of the gangmasters licensed by the GLA operate in sectors outside food production and it has been argued that the licensing model should be extended to cover labour providers more widely. In 1973 legislation was enacted requiring all temporary work agencies and recruitment agencies to be licensed. In 1995, however, this was replaced by a power for the Secretary of State to seek a prohibition order for up to 10 years in an ET where an individual has committed misconduct or is otherwise unsuitable to operate an agency. Compliance with regulations governing the conduct of employment agencies is enforced by the Employment Agency Standards Inspectorate (EAS) whose powers are much more limited than the GLA's (Wynn 2009). It investigates individual complaints and conducts targeted investigations (BIS 2010a: 14) but lacks the broader remit that a licensing regime provides.

Inspectorates and Administrative Agencies

There is no general labour inspectorate in Britain. However, there are three bodies which have specific powers of investigation and enforcement in the area of employment rights: the Equality and Human Rights Commission (EHRC); the Health and Safety Executive (HSE); and HMRC in relation to the minimum wage. The powers of the EHRC are analysed in detail by Hepple later in this volume. The enforcement strategy of the HSE is discussed later in this volume by Tombs and Whyte and this chapter therefore outlines its specific powers only briefly. Enforcement by HMRC, which is not covered elsewhere in this volume, is discussed in greater detail below.

Health and Safety Executive (HSE)

The HSE is a non-departmental body sponsored by the Department for Work and Pensions which regulates work-related health and safety in Britain in partnership with local authorities. It has a chair and between seven and 11 members, all of whom are appointed by the Secretary of State. Organisations representing employers and employees respectively must be consulted prior to the appointment of three members each; organisations representing local authorities prior to the appointment of one; and up to four other members may be appointed after consultation with the Scottish or Welsh ministers or other organisations.

The HSE investigates specific incidents and complaints in relation to health and safety matters and also conducts targeted inspections of industries and workplaces where it perceives there is the greatest risk of accidents and ill-health. Individual inspectors can be given very extensive powers, including entering premises and requiring them to be left undisturbed pending investigation or examination; requiring articles or substances to be dismantled; and requiring individuals to answer questions and sign a declaration that their answers are true. It is an offence intentionally to obstruct inspectors in the performance of their functions, or to make false statements or keep false records. Inspectors may issue two forms of enforcement notice. An 'improvement notice' requiring specified contraventions to be remedied within a specified period may be served if an inspector considers that an individual is contravening any statutory provisions, or has done so and is likely to do so again. A 'prohibition notice' may be served if an inspector considers that activities involve, or will involve, a risk of 'serious personal injury'; it directs that the activities should not be carried on unless specified matters have been remedied. Both forms of notice are subject to appeal to an ET, which may, for the purpose of such proceedings, appoint assessors. The ET may cancel, affirm or modify the notice. It is a criminal offence, punishable by a maximum term of two years' imprisonment, an unlimited fine or both, to contravene an improvement or prohibition notice.

This form of enforcement has been adopted in the area of employment rights in relation to limits on weekly working time and night work, in respect of which HSE and local authority inspectors may issue improvement and prohibition notices where breaches of these limits are discovered.

HMRC

The legislation introducing the National Minimum Wage (NMW), which came into force in April 1999, provides for the obligations imposed on employers to be enforced by 'officers' appointed by the Secretary of State of BIS. Rather than establishing a separate agency, officers of HMRC, who deal with tax matters, were contracted to undertake this task and a number of dedicated compliance teams were established throughout the UK together with a central team. Enforcement is initiated either by a complaint from workers or third parties (via a telephone 'hotline' or otherwise) or as a result of risk profiling, including targeted enforcement in key low-paying sectors (BIS 2011b: 2.2.1). The enforcement provisions were strengthened by the Labour Government from April 2009 (Simpson 2009) and officers now have wide powers to inspect premises and documents and to remove documents for copying together with powers of arrest. The tripartite Low Pay Commission (LPC), which reviews NMW rates, also monitors and makes recommendations on enforcement. In March 2010 the Labour Government published a new compliance strategy which moved away from a 'one-size-fits-all' approach to enforcement towards the prioritisation of resources (dealing with some employers by letter, for example, rather than a personal visit) and greater information sharing and joint working with other agencies such as the GLA and the EAS (BIS 2010). The NMW teams in HMRC have also forged greater links with other parts of HMRC, such as the Hidden Economy Group to facilitate joined-up working, and a Dynamic Response Team to target areas where migrant labour is being used to undercut legitimate employers (LPC 2011: 4.77–83).

HMRC's primary focus is the recovery of arrears on behalf of workers. Officers are empowered to issue a notice of underpayment against an employer who is failing or has failed to comply with the law. This notice requires the employer within 28 days to pay arrears to workers (since 2009, at the current rate rather than the rate applicable at the date of underpayment) together (generally) with a penalty equal to half the total underpayment for all workers covered by the notice (subject to a minimum of £100 and a maximum of £5,000) payable to the Secretary of State. The employer may appeal to an ET against an enforcement notice or any requirement imposed by it. In the event of non-compliance with an enforcement notice, the HMRC officer may pursue payment on behalf of workers in the civil courts or ET, so establishing a debt which is ultimately enforceable by distraint or other measures if the employer still fails to pay.

This approach means that action can be taken on behalf of low-paid, vulnerable workers who may lack the knowledge, skills or time to bring claims on their own behalf or who may fear reprisals if they do so (although there is statutory protection against detriment for enforcing individual rights, individuals may not wish to rely on this). By March 2010 more than £36 million in arrears for over 80,000 workers had been identified by officers (BIS 2010b). In 2009/10 over £4.4 million in arrears (for over 19,000 workers) was identified, with workers receiving an additional £94,000 as a result of the provision for uplift to current rates (BIS/HMRC 2010). More detailed statistics on enforcement are published in the annual LPC reports.

The NMW legislation specifies a number of offences, including refusing or wilfully neglecting to pay the NMW; failing to keep or preserve records; falsifying records; delaying or obstructing a compliance officer; and refusing to answer questions or furnish information or documents when required to do so. In the early years of the NMW it seems that little attention was paid to the possibility of criminal proceedings. In 2006, however, it was agreed that the most serious cases should be subject to criminal investigation and by March 2010 there had been six successful prosecutions covering all the specified offences (BIS 2010b: 2.4, 4.8). Since 2009, prosecutions may be brought in the crown court where tougher penalties are available, although current policy continues to focus on civil powers (BIS 2011b: 4.1.3). Despite the higher cost of criminal investigations, the LPC (supported by the Confederation of British Industry) has urged the Government to increase the number of prosecutions and to publicise them widely to act as a deterrent (LPC 2011: 4.62). In 2011 a new 'name and shame' scheme was introduced, whereby employers who have failed to comply with their obligations will be named in a BIS press notice so potentially exposing them to adverse consumer pressure. However the criteria for naming employers (who will have the opportunity to make representations against this) are tightly drawn and may prove to be unduly restrictive (BIS 2011b: 5.2–5.5; LPC 2011: 4.56).

The Coalition Government has continued the Labour Government's avowed commitment to robust enforcement of the NMW although the LPC has expressed concern that public sector cuts have the potential to jeopardise the progress made (LPC 2011: 4.67–72). There are also concerns that the economic situation may further increase the 'informal' economy where non-compliance with the NMW is likely to be greatest. Because much of the 'informal' economy is 'hidden', and because of the technicalities of the NMW regime (which allows an offset for accommodation, for example) it is difficult to measure the extent of non-compliance accurately. Nevertheless the NMW is one area where, to date, a proactive model of enforcement appears to have met with some success. The Revenue's experience in dealing with employers 'who take chances on tax matters' has proved to be valuable (Brown 2006: 68), as has the oversight provided by the independent LPC.

The Pay and Work Rights Helpline

In 2009 a Pay and Work Rights Helpline was introduced to enable workers and others (on an anonymous basis if they so choose) to raise queries and report concerns relating to the NMW, agricultural minimum wage,[5] working time, gangmasters and employment agencies with a single point of contact. In its first year of operation the Helpline dealt with more than 73,000 calls, two-thirds of which were from workers and 16 per cent from employers (the remainder being third parties or unknown). The Helpline resolved 48 per cent of calls and directed 4,500 to enforcement agencies; the remainder were signposted to Acas or another organisation. 32 per cent of calls related to the NMW or HMRC. A survey of callers found a high level of caller satisfaction (Rutherford and Achur 2010). Although only the first step in the enforcement process, the Helpline provides a welcome contribution to assisting compliance with the limited range of employment rights with which it is concerned.

BIBLIOGRAPHY

Acas (Advisory Conciliation and Arbitration Service) (2011) *Annual Report 2010–11.*
Acas Guide (2009) *Discipline and Grievances at Work* (London).
Adams, L, Moore, A, Gore, K and Browne, J (2009) *Research into Enforcement of Employment Tribunal Awards in England and Wales* (London, Ministry of Justice).
BIS (Department for Business Innovation and Skills) (2010a) *Employment Agency Standards (EAS) Inspectorate: Annual Report 2009–10.*
—— (2010b) *National Minimum Wage Compliance Strategy* (London, BIS).
—— (2011a) *Resolving Workplace Disputes: Government Response to the Consultation* (London, BIS).
—— (2011b) *National Minimum Wage: Policy on HM Revenue & Customs Enforcement, Prosecutions and Naming Employers who Flout National Minimum Wage Law* (London, BIS).
BIS in association with HMRC (2010) *Delivering Results: National Minimum Wage Compliance.*
Boon, A, Urwin, P and Karuk, V (2011) 'What Difference Does it Make? Facilitative Judicial Mediation of Discrimination Cases in Employment Tribunals' 40 *Industrial Law Journal* 45–81.
Brown, W (2006) 'The Low Pay Commission' in L Dickens and A Neal (eds), *The Changing Institutional Face of British Employment Relations* (The Netherlands, Kluwer).

---

[5] At the time of writing the minimum wage and other terms of employment for workers employed in agriculture are set by the Agricultural Wages Board (AWB), which consists of eight representatives of workers; eight of employers; and five independent members. Orders of the Board are legally binding and enforced by DEFRA in response to specific complaints of non-compliance. The Coalition Government has announced that the AWB will be abolished once the requisite primary legislation has been enacted.

—— (2010) Negotiation and Collective Bargaining in T Colling and M Terry (eds), *Industrial Relations Theory and Practice* 3rd edn (Chichester, Wiley).

Brown, W and Oxenbridge, S (2004) 'Trade Unions and Collective Bargaining: Law and the Future of Collectivism' in C Barnard, S Deakin and G Morris (eds), *The Future of Labour Law: Liber Amicorum Sir Bob Hepple QC* (Oxford, Hart Publishing).

Burton, M (2005) 'The Employment Appeal Tribunal: October 2002–July 2005' 34 *Industrial Law Journal*, 273–83.

Corby, S and Latreille, PL (2011) *The Role of Lay Members in Employment Rights Cases—Survey Evidence*, www2.gre.ac.uk/about/schools/business/research/centres/weru/publications.

Cully, M, Woodland, S, O'Reilly, A and Dix, G (1999) *Britain at Work. As Depicted by the 1998 Workplace Employment Relations Survey* (London, Routledge).

Davies, P and Freedland, M (1993) *Labour Legislation and Public Policy* (Oxford, Clarendon Press).

Davies, P and Freedland, M (2007) *Towards a More Flexible Labour Market. Labour Legislation and Regulation since the 1990s* (Oxford, Oxford University Press).

Deakin, S and Morris, G (2005) *Labour Law*, 4th edn (Oxford, Hart Publishing).

—— (2012) *Labour Law*, 6th edn (Oxford, Hart Publishing).

Dickens, L (2004) Problems of Fit: Changing Employment and Labour Regulation 42 *British Journal of Industrial Relations* 595–616.

Dickens, L, Hart, M, Jones, M and Weekes, B (1981) 'Re-employment of Unfairly Dismissed Workers: The Lost Remedy' 10 *Industrial Law Journal* 160–75.

Dickens, L and Hall, M (2010) 'The Changing Legal Framework of Employment Relations' in T Colling and M Terry (eds), *Industrial Relations Theory and Practice* 3rd edn (Chichester, Wiley).

Dickens, L, Jones, M, Weeks, B and Hart, M (1985) *Dismissed: A Study of Unfair Dismissal and the Industrial Tribunal System* (Oxford, Blackwell).

Donovan (1968) Royal Commission on Trade Unions and Employers' Associations 1965–1968: *Report*, Cmnd 3623.

ED (1994) *Resolving Employment Rights Disputes—Options for Reform*, Employment Department, Cm 2707.

Fredman, S and Morris, G (1989) *The State as Employer: Labour Law in the Public Services* (Mansell, London).

GLA (2009a) *Licensing Standards*.

—— (2009b) *Annual Review 2008: Executive Summary*.

Harvey (1972) as updated: *Harvey on Industrial Relations and Employment Law* (London, LexisNexis).

Hepple, B and Morris, G (2002) 'The Employment Act 2002 and the Crisis of Individual Employment Rights' 31 *Industrial Law Journal* 245–69.

Kersley, B, Alpin, C, Forth, J, Bryson, A, Bewley, H, Dix, G and Oxenbridge, S (2006) *Inside the Workplace: Findings from the 2004 Workplace Employment Relations Survey* (Abingdon, Routledge).

Leighton, P and Wynn, M (2011) 'Classifying Employment Relationships—More Sliding Doors or a Better Regulatory Framework?' 40 *Industrial Law Journal* 5–44.

LPC (2011) *National Minimum Wage. Low Pay Commission Report 2011*, Cm 8023.

Meeran, G (2006) 'The Employment Tribunals' in L Dickens and AC Neal (eds) *The Changing Institutional Face of British Employment Relations* (The Netherlands, Kluwer Law International).

MOJ (Ministry of Justice) and Tribunals Service (2010) *Employment Tribunal and EAT Statistics 2009–10 (GB)*.

—— (2011) *Employment Tribunal and EAT Statistics 2010–11*.

Peters, M, Seeds, K, Harding, C and Garnett, E (2010) *Findings from the Survey of Employment Tribunal Applications 2008*, EMAR No 107 (London, BIS).

Rutherford, I and Achur, J (2010) *Survey of Pay and Work Rights Helpline Callers*, EMAR No 113 (London, BIS).

Sanders, A (2009) 'Part One of the Employment Act 2008: 'Better' Dispute Resolution?' 38 *Industrial Law Journal* 30–49.

Simpson, B (2009) 'The Employment Act 2008's Amendments to the National Minimum Wage Legislation' *Industrial Law Journal* 38, 57–64.

Tribunals Service (2009) *Employment Tribunal and EAT Statistics (GB) 1 April 2008 to 31 March 2009*.

Wynn, M (2009) 'Regulating Rogues? Employment Agency Enforcement and Sections 15–18 of the Employment Act 2008' 38 *Industrial Law Journal* 64–72.

3

Employment Tribunals and Alternative Dispute Resolution

LINDA DICKENS*

TRIBUNAL REFORM AGENDA

SUCCESSIVE CONSERVATIVE AND Labour governments, and now
the Conservative-led Coalition Government, have shared a diagnosis
of the employment tribunal (ET) 'problem' with reforms focussed
mainly on issues facing the tribunal system in coping with increasing
caseloads, and the cost to the taxpayer in so doing, and also on addressing concerns raised by business. Reform agendas appear to have been less
concerned with how to improve the effectiveness of the system in terms
of giving effect to social policy intentions relating to minimum employment standards and fairness at work. Titles of consultation exercises have
appeared to indicate a wider compass but in practice they did not her-
ald any radical rethinking. For example a 1994 Green Paper was called
Resolving Employment Rights Disputes—Options for Reform but the
terms of reference were 'to review the operation of the Industrial Tribunals
with a view to identifying any changes which would help them cope with
an increasing volume and complexity of cases with reduced delays, whilst
containing demands on public expenditure' (Employment Department
1994: 4). This disjuncture between broad title and main intent can be seen
also in subsequent consultations and taskforces (eg Gaymer 2006). As I
have argued elsewhere (Dickens 2008), more radical rethinking might have
included, for example, whether some of the tribunal jurisdictions more
appropriately might go elsewhere; whether the ET system provides the best
route for all sections of the workforce or whether there should be a greater
role for different kinds of enforcement, rather than relying primarily on
individuals to bring cases to tribunals(a concern of this volume). Further, a
broader, more radical focus might have encompassed consideration of ways
to encourage better management of workplace conflict, of which disputes

* Gill Dix and Gillian Morris provided helpful comments on a draft of this chapter.

and tribunal claims are manifestations (Dix et al 2009), and explored the utility and contribution of workplace employee representation to this end.

Reform 'solutions' have revolved around reducing costs to employers and to the public purse by seeking to improve the efficiency and operation of the tribunal system, including ET case management, and attempting to reduce the number of cases coming to ETs. While some business/employer concerns about the ET system are shared by claimants (for example, cost, delay, complexity and legalism), others tend towards a reform agenda which may run counter to claimant interests by making it harder to exercise rights, access justice and secure appropriate remedies. Certain employer concerns which have helped to drive reform rest on belief and perception not supported by available evidence, as for example the belief that there are large numbers of meritless and vexatious cases being brought to tribunals (BIS 2011a: 140). Some of the most controversial of the latest reform proposals (removal of lay members, introducing a fee-charging mechanism) overtly have cost saving/income generation as their main or a major rationale. That such money saving reforms risk adverse outcomes in terms of fairness and justice is acknowledged, but these cannot be easily monetised and thus appear to carry less weight in the present climate of constrained public resources (BIS 2011a). Past and present reforms seeking to reduce the caseload of tribunals have involved erecting barriers to access (eg lengthening service qualification periods for exercising rights) and introducing disincentives to claimants bringing or pursuing cases (eg increasing the likelihood of costs being awarded and threatened; requiring an 'entry fee').

Reforms of this type continue to be favoured (BIS 2011b) but at the same time a potentially different approach to avoiding the need for a tribunal hearing or a tribunal claim can be seen—one which is concerned less with disincentivising or barring tribunal applications and more with facilitating dispute resolution. Following the failure of an ill-judged attempt in 2002 to encourage early dispute resolution by introducing mandatory grievance and dismissal procedures (see Morris, this volume), there has been renewed attention to forms of alternative dispute resolution (ADR). This chapter considers forms of ADR in the context of the ETs.

ALTERNATIVE DISPUTE RESOLUTION AND THE TRIBUNAL SYSTEM

In the employment relations field the term ADR started to gain currency from the mid-1990s although dispute settlement processes and mechanisms included under this umbrella term, notably conciliation and arbitration, had been around a very long time. Ministerial powers to offer conciliation in employment disputes were set out in the Conciliation Act 1896 and later in the Industrial Courts Act 1919 (Hawes 2000). Within the voluntary system of British industrial relations, which gave primacy to regulation through collective bargaining, these third party processes were seen not as alternatives to resorting to law (since the courts had little remit) but as ways of supporting and facilitating collective bargaining and assisting voluntary resolution of disputes.

Early advocates of arbitration as a potential alternative to ET judicial determination (Dickens et al 1985: ch 9; Rideout 1982a) drew on evidence and experience from arbitration in collective labour relations. In recent debates where experience of ADR is drawn upon it has tended to be from within civil courts (eg Gibbons 2007), where mediation has been encouraged, rather than from employment relations, overlooking perhaps the distinct characteristics of the employment relationship—an indeterminate, incomplete, continuous and open-ended relationship, a blend of contradictory principles concerning control and consent (see for example Sisson 2008).

The 'alternative' in ADR currently is focussed on alternatives to judicial determination in ETs. Ironically, the ETs themselves were at one time viewed as an 'alternative' form of dispute resolution—a better alternative to the ordinary courts. When the unfair dismissal jurisdiction was being conferred in the early 1970s, the tripartite ETs (then called Industrial Tribunals) were seen as a form of ADR offering advantages over the ordinary courts in terms of speed, accessibility (particularly to unrepresented parties), informality, expertise, acceptability, and an ability to pay attention to policy intentions underpinning legislation and facilitating amicable settlement of differences (Dickens et al 1985: 7–8). The tribunals still offer advantages over the ordinary courts but, as Morris notes in her chapter in this volume, ETs today struggle to demonstrate these characteristics, and proposed reforms risk undermining them further.

Since the 1990s, ADR has been presented as a way of reducing the number of ET hearings (eg DTI 2001) and thus saving costs, but the type of intervention favoured has varied. Arbitration as an alternative to judicial determination in the ET was promoted in the 1990s; there was a renewed focus on conciliation in the first decade of this century, and currently mediation is in the spotlight (BIS 2011b). Various reviews of dispute settlement and the ET system have provided an opportunity for strategic engagement with the nature of different ADR processes and mechanisms, such as conciliation, mediation, arbitration and judicial and non-judicial adjudication, and for consideration of what each might offer in the area of statutory employment rights, and what limitations each may have. At each point, the opportunity was not taken. Current discussion of ADR takes the ETs as given; ADR is not being considered strategically as an alternative to the ET system as such, but rather as a tactical way of ameliorating some of the problems within the system and reducing recourse to it. Forms of ADR such as mediation are being encouraged without sufficient attention to definitional dilemmas and ambiguities of process (see below and Dolder 2004). Furthermore, there is little attention to whether, and if so how, ADR might provide a means of generating valuable outcomes beyond solving the individual dispute, thus contributing to making employment rights effective in a wider sense.

I consider first the arbitration alternative scheme, and then the use of conciliation and mediation in relation to the ET system. I argue that locating consideration of ADR within the context of tribunal reform with a particular focus on minimising costs by avoiding tribunal hearings, has influenced the way in which different forms of ADR have been conceptualised and approached, and the ways in which 'success' is evaluated. In turn this reduces their potential impact in terms of making employment rights effective (in the broad sense of delivering fairer workplaces), as opposed to disposing of tribunal claims.

ARBITRATION ALTERNATIVE

An argument began to be made in the 1980s that an arbitral system might be better than judicial determination in the ET. An arbitration system, based on experience in collective employment relations (which included arbitration over individual dismissals when parties treated them as a collective issue), and also on British experience of 'regulated arbitration', that is, that performed within a statutory framework or other external rules (Rideout 1982b), could be distinguished from judicial determination in the ETs in terms of personnel, form, procedure, objectives, outcomes and the nature of the process (Dickens et al 1985). The proposal for arbitration was revived in the early 1990s and actively promoted by Lewis and Clark (1993). But in the 1990s it was the fact that arbitration could also be cheaper to provide, and quicker than a tribunal hearing, that carried most weight with the government at a time when the tribunal system appeared to be unable to cope effectively with increasing caseloads and was requiring increased funding. The resulting 'arbitration alternative', set up by Acas (Advisory, Conciliation and Arbitration Service) under the Employment Rights (Dispute Resolution) Act 1998, started in May 2001 for England and Wales (The ACAS Arbitration Scheme (England and Wales) Order 2001 SI 2001/1185), with Scotland covered from 2004. Originally open only to unfair dismissal claims, the ability to hear claims arising under the flexible working provisions was added in 2003.

Importantly, in terms of the likelihood of delivering the potential advantages, the arbitral alternative is not really an alternative to the ET *system* for resolving employment disputes but, in practice, a voluntary alternative to an ET *hearing* in limited circumstances. It is available only to those who have made an application to the ET or where individuals claim they could make such an application; where the case is 'straightforward', relates only to a permitted jurisdiction (if part of the dispute involves any other jurisdiction that associated aspect has to go to the ET); and does not raise complex legal issues, jurisdictional questions or points of EC law. Entry to the arbitral alternative is via a compromise agreement meeting the statutory requirements, or an Acas conciliated agreement. The main elements of the scheme are that *both* parties have to agree to go to arbitration rather than to an ET, signing an arbitration agreement with standard terms of reference and signing a waiver ending the right to go to a tribunal hearing (and so dispense with its particular features such as cross-examination). The case is heard by a single arbitrator who need not be legally qualified, selected by Acas from its panel of arbitrators chosen for their impartiality, skills, knowledge and employment relations experience, and employed on a fee-paid, case-by-case basis. The arbitrator is required to avoid unnecessary delay or expense and hearings are intended to be non-legalistic and quick (about half a day). The arbitrator will have regard to 'general principles of fairness and good conduct in employment relations' including the relevant Acas Codes of Practice, rather than strict law or legal precedent in making a decision. However, remedies are limited to those available in the ETs (outlined by Morris, this volume). If compensation is awarded, it is based on the ET approach to calculation. Unlike in the ETs, the hearing is not public and the arbitration award is confidential to the parties. The alternative offers finality in that there is no right of appeal and only very limited grounds for challenging an arbitrator's decision (lack of substantive jurisdiction and serious irregularity); the parties agree that the arbitrator's award is final and binding.

The scheme attempts to offer some of the advantages which have been claimed for arbitration (as understood in the British employment context) over judicial determination, for example in terms of less formality/legalism; more flexible procedure, an inquisitorial rather than adversarial approach; the ability of the arbitrator to draw on wider considerations and notions of fairness, and with consistency resting more on how cases are handled rather than on application of case law precedent. However, its narrow remit and close alignment with the tribunal system constrains the extent to which advantages of arbitration may be realised. The distinction is between—on the one hand—arbitration seeking to resolve the particular dispute but with a concern for workable solutions taking account of wider contexts and workplace issues of which the individual dismissal may be a symptom and—on the other hand—judicial determination seeking to determine who is 'right' on the basis of evidence presented and application of legal tests and rules. The fact that remedies under the arbitration scheme are restricted to those available to ETs limits the extent to which arbitration awards are likely to have impacts within the originating organisation broader than the particular claim. Organisational learning or dissemination of lessons from an individual case is also less likely to result from arbitration in the absence of collective representation on the employee side (see also Colling 2004 and this volume). Any potential impact *beyond* the originating organisation is prevented by the private nature of proceedings and confidential nature of the award, features not necessarily present in other instances of regulated arbitration where awards, and the considerations behind them, are published (see, for example, the role of the Central Arbitration Committee in connection with Schedule 11 of the Employment Protection Act and the Fair Wages Resolution, Dickens et al 1985: 284–85; Gouldstone and Morris 2006).

Evaluation of the operation of the arbitration alternative is hampered by the fact it has hardly been used, with only 64 cases in a decade. In practice there appear to be few incentives for parties to opt for this alternative once already in the ET system. Take-up might be higher if it were to be linked to Acas pre-claim conciliation (which occurs before any tribunal claim is made, see below). It might be offered as a quick route to resolution where pre-claim conciliation (PCC) does not lead to withdrawal or settlement of the claim. Currently those who might encourage use of the arbitration alternative have few if any incentives to promote it. Parties are not likely to know about the scheme before engaging with the ET system; having to consider this option may simply add to the problems/stress of unrepresented claimants; legal representatives (increasingly common) are more likely to advise clients to stay with the ET system with which they themselves are familiar and where their particular legal skills are of most value; and Acas conciliators, although potentially important in raising awareness, have little time or opportunity to be proactive in explaining or promoting the Scheme (and are not required to).

The arbitration alternative might be expected to appeal most to union-supported claimants and to unionised organisations more used to this form of dispute settlement. Recently some arbitration agreements have arisen from the settlement of a long-running collective dispute in the airline industry where dismissal claims had been filed (Ewing 2011: 47). However these categories of claimant and representative are under-represented in claims to ETs. The latest Survey of Employment Tribunal Applicants found only nine per cent of claimants received advice or were represented by a trade union following submission of an ET application (Peters et al 2010). The average rate of ET claims per 1,000 employees is lower in unionised workplaces than in non-unionised ones (Dix et al 2009: 198). This indicates something important about circumstances potentially favourable to rights compliance and dispute resolution in the workplace. The rise in applications to ETs coincided with the decline in collective bargaining coverage in the UK economy (Cully et al 1999). An obvious inference is that workplace employee representation and 'voice' arrangements encourage internal solutions to individual employment disputes; an inference supported by more detailed analysis (Burgess et al 2001; Knight and Latreille 2000: 546; Antcliff and Saundry 2009). Brown and his colleagues emphasise the link, suggesting that 'collective procedures are the custodians of individual rights' (2000: 627).

The restriction on jurisdiction (to unfair dismissal and flexibility claims) also reduces the potential take-up of the arbitration alternative scheme. The choice of jurisdiction for arbitration is interesting, given that arbitration has been thought to be particularly well suited to considering polycentric disputes (where an individual case can affect many others) as in the discrimination and equal pay jurisdictions (Hepple 1983: 84). In the previous chapter Morris noted the large number of multiple cases (involving the same employer and the same issue) being brought to ETs, including equal pay cases. This indicates that collective concerns are being pursued in the guise of individual claims. Arbitration would appear well suited to address such issues (Dickens 2007). Indeed for a time, under the Equal Pay Act 1970, discriminatory pay structures and practices could be challenged by reference to the Central Arbitration Committee (CAC)—at the time a hybrid body providing arbitration in collective industrial relations disputes and enforcing certain legal rights (Gouldstone and Morris 2006). This was arguably an institution better suited to handling polycentric disputes, and dealing with workplace and labour market realities, than the tribunals. The CAC's purposive interpretation of its role, however, was not supported by the courts on judicial review and, rather than overcome the effects of this to ensure an effective mechanism for addressing systemic pay inequality, the government repealed the provision in 1986, leaving individual claims as the only legislative option.

The insignificant role of the arbitration alternative in practice means that, in the context of individual statutory rights, ADR is primarily about assisted settlement rather than alternative adjudication. The major form of ADR within the existing system is conciliation. This is discussed first, and then mediation—another form of ADR which is increasing in importance.

CONCILIATION

As noted in the previous chapter, when an application is made to the ET, conciliation is offered by Acas which is state-funded. In broad terms, Acas conciliators discuss the issues of the case with parties, explain the ET process, the law and case law where appropriate, and encourage each party to consider the strengths and weaknesses of its case. They provide both parties with information on the options available to them and pass information between the parties, including details of any offers of settlement. Acas policy is that conciliation officers can help to clarify issues, but they do not give advice. Discussions are confidential; information given to the conciliation officer is not divulged to the other party without permission and what happens in conciliation cannot be used in a tribunal hearing.

This attempt to dispose of cases without judicial determination through conciliation has been a feature of the system since its early days in the 1970s, with the range of jurisdictions where Acas has a statutory duty to offer conciliation expanding over time. There is no doubt that Acas conciliation provides a very cost effective filter, saving hearing days at tribunals (and thus saving public expenditure) and reducing financial and non-financial costs to the parties which would have been incurred in continuing to a tribunal hearing. Acas reports that it saved 78 per cent of the potential hearing days arising from all cases received for individual conciliation in 2010/11 (Acas 2011: 14).[1] Over two-thirds of applications do not reach a full merits hearing by the ET. Ministry of Justice figures show that in 2010–11 (as a proportion of disposed jurisdictional claims) 32 per cent were abandoned or withdrawn, 29 per cent were settled by Acas and 10 per cent struck out without a hearing, leaving only a minority of cases to be determined by a full merits tribunal hearing. These proportions are fairly constant over time.

Acas intervention enhances the probability of settlement both by raising the likelihood of an offer being made and, where made, of its resulting in a settlement (Latreille 2007). Evaluation of conciliation by users is positive, with some four-fifths of users expressing satisfaction with the service (Acas Research et al 2011a; Peters et al 2010: 66). The perceived effectiveness of Acas conciliation in avoiding tribunal hearings is reflected in Acas being given the power to offer pre-claim conciliation (PCC). PCC, in place since 2009, forms part of the changes following the Gibbons review of 2007 and represents proactive promotion of early dispute resolution. The rationale is to resolve at an early stage disputes which would otherwise result in a formal ET claim, thus reducing the potential volume of claims entering the ET system. It is offered in cases where an employee is eligible to submit a tribunal application and intends to do so, and where efforts have been made to resolve the issue via internal procedures and the employer is not insolvent. PCC cases are usually identified through telephone calls to the Acas Helpline, a service which was enhanced and provided with additional resources following the Gibbons review.

Previously, however, Acas had statutory responsibility for dealing with cases where no formal complaint had been made to a tribunal but where such a claim potentially could be made. These were known as non-ET1 cases (the ET1 being the tribunal application form). In the 1980s non-ET1 cases rose to over a third of Acas' total caseload. Nearly all of these were initiated by employers in cases of job termination, commonly where they had reached an agreement with an employee but wanted this to be classed as an Acas conciliated agreement in order to bar a tribunal claim. A changed Acas policy on handling non-ET1 cases (including a refusal simply to rubber-stamp agreements) was put into effect in 1990 (Acas 1991: 45).

---

[1] The nominal PHDS value of cases is based on ETS nominal estimates for hearing durations for cases in different categories—highest for discrimination jurisdictions and lowest for those cases concerning unpaid wages, holiday or redundancy pay for example.

This, and the subsequent provision for compromise agreements preventing recourse to the ET to be reached without Acas involvement, led to a substantial decline in such cases and, prior to the post-Gibbons changes to the Helpline, no systematic arrangements existed for identifying such claims or promoting the facility.

The Acas Helpline itself plays a role in reducing ET applications. In some cases information from an Acas Helpline advisor may lead to a potential tribunal applicant changing her mind about making a claim. In one survey 23 per cent of employee callers to the Helpline considering an ET claim decided against this course of action as a result of their call (Davey and Dix 2011: 18). Where they remain intent on making a claim, callers may be referred to PCC. In its second year of operation (to March 2011) there were just under 18,000 referrals to PCC from the Helpline. Generally the parties agree to engage with the PCC process when it is offered and around half of cases referred are resolved in this way. In terms of avoiding claims entering the ET system PCC has a high rate of success—around 70 per cent of cases did not subsequently lead to the submission of an ET claim (ibid). Acas has estimated that, once staff time and legal costs are factored in, businesses which resolve disputes through PCC save £3,700 on average compared with costs involved once an ET claim has been made. Employees save on average nearly £1,300.

Whether in PCC or in Acas conciliation following an ET claim, settlements reached through conciliation are matters for the parties themselves. Conciliation officers do not offer a view as to the sufficiency or fairness of any settlement judged by any external standard or social policy. The Acas literature presents this as an advantage of conciliation in that it 'leaves the employer and employee in control. In the tribunals the decision is taken out of the parties' hands' (Acas 2009: 5). The information given to the parties makes clear that the conciliator 'will not make a judgment on the case, or the likely outcome of a hearing; advise either the employer or the employee whether or not to accept any proposals for settlement' (ibid: 6). Inputs of this kind, however, may be sought—particularly by unrepresented parties (most often claimants) who expect more support from the conciliation officer, of the kind associated with a professional representative (Acas Research and Evaluation and Infogroup/ORC International 2011: 29) and want the conciliation officer to help redress what they experience as an imbalance of power (see for example Hudson et al 2007: 69 on the experience of those in race discrimination cases). Acas can act as a broker, but what some need is an advisor.

The law recognises that the inequality in the power relationship between employer and employee could be used to prevent workers exercising their rights. Hence, as noted, only certain agreements can stop a case going to a tribunal. The special status accorded to agreements reached when Acas has taken action appeared to suggest that settlements with the involvement of

Acas were intended to be qualitatively different from those reached without Acas. For some early commentators this implied that the involvement of the conciliation officer would 'provide some guarantee as to the fact that the settlement was reasonable and arrived at in a proper fashion' (McIlroy 1980: 180). This view received little support from the courts, however (Dickens 2000) and, as noted in the previous chapter, a wider range of people are now authorised to provide the independent advice necessary to facilitate compromise agreements blocking tribunal action. The privileged status of such agreements appears to reside not in the fact that they are reasonable, just or equitable ones (although they may be), but rather in the fact that the parties are reaching *informed* agreements. The parties should know their legal rights, understand what they are doing and the implications of settlement. The nature of the settlement is then up to them. As currently interpreted, conciliation is not concerned with the quality of settlements, nor the extent to which settlement may support or undermine the social policy objectives behind the legislation. The nature of any settlement obtained—indeed even *whether* any settlement is agreed, as against abandoning the claim—is not part of the formal performance indicators by which the success of conciliation is judged.

The appropriateness of neutral conciliation (where no view is taken as to the appropriateness or fairness of the outcome) in relation to statutory employment rights has been questioned, particularly with respect to the discrimination jurisdictions. There is a conflict between the search for compromise, which is at the centre of conciliation and the pursuit of rights. Conciliation (and also mediation, discussed below) may be viewed as treating an alleged injustice as equivalent to a disagreement between parties (eg McCrudden et al 1991: 193). Where there has been unlawful discrimination then, it has been argued, conciliated compromise cannot be defended since it may compound unlawful behaviour (Graham and Lewis 1985: 62). At the extreme there is an argument against having a conciliation stage, since 'parties might settle while leaving justice undone' (Fiss 1984). Some have argued that in jurisdictions where a particular social policy is being pursued a form of rights-based, committed intervention is required (eg Hunter and Leonard 1997 in the context of sex discrimination). Committed conciliation is that designed to bring about an agreed settlement promoting certain desired substantive ends. In the area of unfair dismissal, for example, this might include procedural justice. In the final section of this chapter I argue that there is potential for conciliation to help make a broader contribution in terms of promoting wider social policy objectives without adopting a rights enforcement stance or jeopardising neutrality (in the sense of lack of bias), but that this is constrained currently.

A potential advantage of conciliation over going to a tribunal is that it increases the chance of avoiding a permanent breakdown of the employment relationship. In practice however, this is not being realised very often, whether through PCC or post-claim conciliation. Although 97 per cent of complaints are brought by current or former employees at the time of application, only a very small proportion (around eight per cent) remain with the employer against whom they complained (Peters et al 2010). Settlement terms are not restricted to statutory remedies, but nonetheless nine out of 10 settled cases across all jurisdictions involve some kind of financial settlement (ibid: 82).

Acas identifies as an advantage of conciliation that it 'resolves the dispute to suit the employer and employee, rather than what the tribunal has the power to award eg 'tribunals cannot order references to be given, or say what they should contain' (Acas 2009: 5). Pre-claim conciliators felt early contact provided a better opportunity to look at resolving the dispute without monetary consideration (Davey and Dix 2011: 28). A reference or an apology may be what is sought by the applicant, or some change in working arrangements, or 'money owed' (eg holiday pay) rather than compensation as such. This illustrates one way in which settlements may be obtained. Once the conciliation officer has unearthed what is motivating the claim and what is really concerning the claimant, this may facilitate settlement, especially where what is sought is less costly to the employer than any possible tribunal remedy. Part of the role of the conciliation officer is to explain the way tribunals operate and what they take into account in deciding claims. This can help in 'bringing realism to the parties' expectations' (Latreille 2007; Dix 2000), a key factor in achieving settlements.

Conciliation takes place in the shadow of the tribunal and parties' perceptions of what might happen at a tribunal hearing and the relative advantages and disadvantages of proceeding (including the financial and non-financial costs) are crucial in determining the likelihood of settling. In conveying information about the nature of tribunal hearings and decision making, applicant success rates, average levels of compensation in successful cases, how similar cases have fared and so on, and discussing the strengths and weaknesses of the case, the conciliation officer can help shape the desire to settle. This is not to say that Acas conciliation officers put pressure on parties to settle; surveys of representatives show the majority say that this is not the case (Harding and Garnet 2011: 33). Rather they marshal and channel pressures towards settlement (or withdrawal) that are present in the system (Dickens 2000: 75–78). Learning of the risk of having to pay the other side's legal costs if they lose their case, for example, appears to weigh particularly with claimants when considering how to proceed. In the 2008 SETA survey (Peters et al 2010: 63–64) half of both claimants and employers recalled Acas conciliation officers explaining this was a possibility. Three-fifths (61 per cent) of claimants found this important when deciding how to proceed with their case compared with just under a half of employers (47 per cent). Claimants who withdrew their application without any settlement were more likely than average to view the possibility of having to pay their employers' legal costs as important in deciding how they proceeded with their case. In practice, as Morris details in chapter two, cost awards are rare.

Settlement is less likely where what is wanted is something conciliation cannot deliver. Conciliation cannot deliver a public hearing, 'a day in court' for the claimant. It cannot provide 'justice' for an employer seeking exoneration from a charge of discrimination, nor for a claimant seeking public affirmation that he or she was unfairly treated. Nor does it deliver a legal ruling or clarification. Conciliation is a form of 'privatised justice'; as such it does not provide a demonstration effect for other employers and workers, nor perform a wider educative function—a limitation in terms of developing fairer workplaces.

Before turning to discuss mediation it is important to note problems of terminology. The distinction between the processes of conciliation and mediation is a blurred one. To some extent the terms are used interchangeably in common discourse and there is no cross-national consistency. For example, what in the UK is called conciliation may be termed mediation in the USA. The same term, for example conciliation, in practice may cover different processes even within a nation state. This may arise from different roles being appropriate in different circumstances, and also because individuals adopt different styles of conciliation, in part reflecting their personal characteristics but also the nature of the case and parties. Dix (2000: 112) characterised these on three continua: reactive–proactive; message bearer–seeking to influence; and passive–forceful.

It is also the case that in general the process of conciliation in ET claims differs significantly from conciliation in collective industrial disputes. For example in the former it is now extremely rare for any meetings with the conciliation officer to take place (this happens in only two per cent of cases); conciliation is conducted mainly through telephone contact. This was not always the position, but increasing caseloads and reduced resources have driven change (Dickens 2000). Where the parties are represented (as they increasingly are) they may have no direct contact with the conciliation officer at all. In collective conciliation, on the other hand, meetings of the parties themselves with the conciliator, separately and jointly, are the norm to explore issues, get each party to understand the other's position, to build trust and to start working towards finding a solution, which may include the conciliation officer making suggestions as to ways forward. Although such a role is potentially open to a conciliation officer in an ET case (Dix 2000) its likelihood is heavily constrained in practice by the resource and representation factors just noted. When contrasted with collective conciliation's emphasis on reconciliation of the parties with a view to the future, conciliation in the ET context appears more an exploration of preparedness to settle or withdraw the claim.

MEDIATION

As with conciliation, the main public policy interest in the use of mediation, another form of confidential ADR, is in helping to reduce the number of claims being made to an ET. Interest was stimulated by the recommendations of the Employment Tribunal and Better Regulation Taskforces in 2003. Colling (2004: 569–70) noted that commercial mediation providers have been proactive in seeking expanded roles in the employment field. Use of mediation was encouraged in the Gibbons review in 2007 and an increased role for it formed part of the latest government consultation on tribunal reform (BIS 2011b).

Like conciliation, mediation is also an umbrella term under which can be found distinct approaches. The theoretical literature makes distinctions between, for example, facilitative mediation and evaluative or directive mediation, and, notably in the US literature, between transformative (concerned with empowering the parties to control both process and outcomes) and problem-solving mediation. Such terminological difficulties and nuanced distinctions have generally not been engaged with or acknowledged in the government consultation documents or public policy debate at the time different processes were being advocated, although evaluations of mediation pilots and discussion of practice have raised these (see, for example, Latreille 2011; Boon et al 2011). In the Gibbons review report, for example, the definition provided for conciliation—'an independent third party helps the people involved in a dispute to resolve their problem. The conciliator is unbiased and will not take either party's side'—could easily be exchanged with that given for mediation—'an independent mediator facilitates an agreement between the disputing parties. The parties to the dispute influence and decide the terms of the settlement' (Gibbons 2007: fig 9).

In practice, in Britain, mediation in the context of tribunal reform and individual disputes has emerged as meaning a facilitative process (encouraging the parties to find their own solution to the issue) rather than evaluative/directive (where the mediator attempts to help solve the problem and may make non-binding recommendations) although, in the sphere of collective dispute settlement, mediation has been seen as directive, a form of non-binding arbitration. Insofar as line managers may be trained in techniques of mediation there is an element of providing skills to improve conflict management for the future, but as an organisational resource rather than empowering the disputing parties as such (an aspect of transformative mediation). The limitations and criticisms of conciliation outlined above apply also (in some cases more so) to mediation (see also Dolder 2004), although the form mediation takes and its context are important.

Mediation is seen currently by policy makers as a technique which may be useful to facilitate the resolution of individual disputes and disagreements within the workplace. It is envisaged as a process which may be implemented before the stage at which PCC would be likely to be offered, although in the discrimination jurisdictions there has been some experimentation with 'judicial mediation' at a later stage, following an ET application (Boon et al 2011). A judicial mediation service was piloted in three regions for discrimination cases starting between June 2006 and March 2007. ET judges, trained by Acas, offered 'facilitative mediation' in cases not part of their own caseload—a process in practice difficult to distinguish from Acas conciliation which was also offered to the parties before assigning a case to mediation. Parties were told that the mediator judge would remain neutral and try to assist the parties in resolving their dispute, would not make a decision about the case, or give an opinion on the merits of the case (ibid 2011: 53). Analysis of the results of the pilot found that the expense of the process was not offset by estimated benefits: compared to a control group there was no significant effect of judicial mediation on rates of settlement; rates of resolution that avoided a hearing; or on overall levels of satisfaction of claimants or employers, and roll-out was not recommended (Urwin et al 2010). Positive feedback from participants in the pilot included valuing the additional authority of an Employment Judge compared to an Acas conciliation officer, and appreciation of the fact that the judicial mediation involved face-to-face meetings, unlike conciliation in practice (if not in principle) in the ET system (ibid: 47). On the basis of qualitative material from the pilot, the researchers felt that judicial mediation potentially offers 'a chance to resolve issues that might otherwise be intractable in discrimination cases' (Boon et al 2001: 80; see also Ridley-Duff and Bennett 2011).

Surveys of employers and case studies (eg Acas 2005; CIPD 2008; Latreille 2011; Williams et al 2011) indicate that mediation in the workplace is seen by employer users as potentially useful in particular for relationship problems and breakdowns; issues of alleged bullying or harassment and for helping to resolve inter-personal conflicts between an employee and line manager. Some of these, if not resolved, could potentially give rise to ET claims, and some employers using it see this as a potential benefit. However, according to a small-scale CIPD survey, most current mediations have no relationship to any threatened or actual tribunal claim (CIPD 2008: 15). A recent poll of private sector businesses found similar results (Williams et al 2011), and a survey of participants and commissioners of Acas mediation in 2010–11 found organisations' assessment of the risks had mediation not taken place focussed more on negative impacts on working relationships and absenteeism than concern about an ET claim (Acas Research and Evaluation 2011). Evidence suggests that mediation may be seen by managers as less suitable for disputes arising from the exercise of managerial authority and discretion, for example disciplinary sanctions (Saundry et al 2011).

Although conciliation in the context of ET claims (both post-claim and PCC) is provided free to users by Acas under its statutory duties; mediation is not. Since 2005 Acas provides mediation (and mediation training) on request but it is a charged-for service, and increasingly there are commercial providers. Mediation may also be provided in-house rather than by external providers. This is more common in the public sector, where it is often written into procedures relating to diversity, harassment and bullying (CIPD 2008: 9), and in private sector organisations with sophisticated HR approaches where provision for mediation is more likely to be viewed as part of a bundle of good employment practice, reflecting a particular employee relations culture or management style (on which see Purcell, this volume). In such contexts there is likely to be a more proactive emphasis on conflict management (strategies designed to identify and prevent workplace problems as part of a comprehensive approach), rather than simply dispute settlement (Saundry et al 2011, Dix and Oxenbridge 2001).

POTENTIAL FOR WIDER IMPACT

Both conciliation and mediation are confidential processes geared towards securing outcomes in individual cases largely detached from the organisational and employment relations contexts within which they emerged. This limits any direct wider impact of the processes in terms of delivering fairer workplaces. In some studies (for example Saundry et al 2011) indirect impact beyond the specific disputes mediated has been identified—for example an improvement in the climate of employment relations—although measuring such indirect impacts is not straightforward. Further, indirect outcomes may be dependent on particular characteristics of the organisations studied—for example, Saundry and his colleagues investigated a highly unionised public sector organisation. An integrated approach, a way of linking individual and systemic change (Sturm and Gadlin 2007, Lipsky et al 2003) is required for mediation provided in-house to feed into organisation learning, the lack of which was a problem noted by some respondents in the CIPD 2008 survey who used mediation.

This is not to deny that some positive wider impacts within the workplace and beyond may result from ADR provided by Acas in the tribunal context. For example, 28 per cent of employers in a survey of PCC cases and 21 per cent involved in post-claim conciliation said the conciliator had provided them with information or advice that would help them avoid a similar problem or claim in the future. Acas' survey of users (Acas Research et al 2011: 57) shows that 26 per cent of employers involved in tribunal cases which were settled through conciliation made a change to policies or procedures as a result of guidance they received. The majority, however, appear to take no such action. Although changes may not necessarily be required in all cases, this lack of action by over 60 per cent of employers nonetheless indicates limited positive impact beyond the individual claim.

Currently such outcomes are not objectives set for Acas conciliation but are more in the nature of fortunate by-products, and arguably their likelihood is reduced by a focus on short term, quantifiable measures of 'success' (hearing days saved) and by constraints on resources. Such constraints, for example, have reduced the opportunities for conciliators to deal directly with parties in person (rather than all contact being by telephone), making any underlying employment relations issues which might give rise to further disputes less likely to be detected, explored or resolved. Among employers surveyed in 2010 (Acas Research et al 2011), those who felt they had received enough contact from Acas conciliators were more likely to make changes to policies and practices than those who did not (41 per cent compared with 14 per cent). The growth in legal representation has also distanced the conciliator from the workplace and the parties. Similarly, any educative or advisory role Acas might play which could prevent similar disputes arising in that organisation is reduced, as is the ability to help generate organisational practices in compliance with statutory rights and duties.

Deeper and wider impacts could be achieved without compromising Acas' conciliation role. Facilitating such outcomes as procedural or policy review and reform would be in keeping with Acas' general mission—to improve organisations and working life through better employment relations—and need not jeopardise the neutrality of conciliation. There could be some separation of process if desired with employers being referred on to Acas advisors to deal with more complex issues, or where a deeper level of involvement was required with a view to improving workplace relations for the longer term. Conciliation in the ET system is rightly valued as a highly cost-effective filter, saving the expense of tribunal hearings. Having this as the only or overriding objective, however, pushes conciliation towards case disposal rather than dispute settlement (in that the case may be settled but the sense and source of grievance remain), and limits any wider impacts.

At the time of writing it appears that changes will be made so that all ET claims will have to go first to Acas for 'early conciliation'. As well as delivering the kind of benefits for the ET system associated currently with PCC, this potentially provides a way for employers to be given the independent, tailored advice they apparently seek, and to do so in a context where they are most likely to heed it and so help to develop fairer workplaces less likely to generate ET claims in the future. Evidence suggests that written guides have relatively little penetration and that offers of a 'health check' to assess and aid compliance are most likely to be accepted by employers when it is offered face-to-face (eg Patel 2011: 4, Shearn et al 2010). Suitably resourced and structured, the provision for early conciliation could provide a gateway to accessing employers with a view to Acas' broader mission. The focus of the intervention (separate from the conciliation itself) would be on improving workplaces not just on tribunal avoidance.

Through both mediation and conciliation within the tribunal system, Acas potentially might act as an 'institutional intermediary' integrating individual and systemic change (Sturm and Gadlin 2007). Indirectly Acas achieves something of this through use of information generated by conciliators and helpline advisors to inform topics on which it can provide general advice and guidance via its website and training provision. But the current conceptualisation of the key purpose of the ADR role in practice, and the resource-limited context within which it is performed, constrains a wider contribution in terms of improving workplace relations or advancing public values in ensuring fairness at work.

BIBLIOGRAPHY

Acas (1991) Annual Report (London, Acas).
—— (2009) *Pre-claim Conciliation Explained* (London, Acas).
—— (2011) *Annual Report 2010–11* (London, Acas).
Acas Research and Evaluation Section (2011) *Mediation 2010/11: Responses from Participants and Commissioners*, Research Paper 12/11 (London, Acas).
Acas Research and Evaluation Section and Infogroup/ORC International (2011) *Service User Perceptions of Acas Conciliation in Employment Tribunal Cases 2010*, Research Paper 02/11 (London, Acas).
Antcliff, V and Saundry, R (2009) 'Accompaniment, Workplace Representation and Disciplinary Outcomes in British Workplaces – Just a Formality?' 47 *British Journal of Industrial Relations* 100–21.
BIS (2011a) *Resolving Workplace Disputes: A Consultation. Impact Assessment* (London, Department for Business Innovation and Skills).
—— (2011b) *Resolving Workplace Disputes: A Consultation* (London, Department for Business Innovation and Skills).
Boon, A, Urwin, P and Karuk, V (2011) 'What Difference does it Make? Facilitative Judicial Mediation of Discrimination Cases in Employment Tribunals' 40 *Industrial Law Journal* 45–81.
Brown, W, Deakin, S, Nash, D and Oxenbridge, S (2000) 'The Employment Contract: From Collective Procedures to Individual Rights' 38 *British Journal of Industrial Relations*, 611–29.
Burgess, S, Propper, C and Wilson, D (2001) *Explaining the Growth in the Number of Applications to Industrial Tribunals 1972–97*, Employment Relations Research Series, No 10 (London, DTI).
CIPD (2008) *Workplace Mediation: How Employers Do It* (London, Chartered Institute of Personnel and Development).
Colling, T (2004) 'No Claim, No Pain? The Privatisation of Dispute Resolution in Britain' 25 *Economic and Industrial Democracy* 555.
Cully, M, Woodland, S, O'Reilly, A and Dix, G (1999) *Britain at Work. As Depicted by the 1998 Workplace Employee Relations Survey* (London, Routledge).
Davey, B and Dix, G (2011) *The Dispute Resolution Regulations Two Years On: The Acas Experience*, Research Paper 07/11 (London, Acas).

Department of Trade and Industry (DTI) (2001) *Routes to Resolution* (London, HMSO).

Dickens, L (2000) 'Doing More with Less: Acas and Individual Conciliation' in W Brown and B Towers (eds), *Employment Relations in Britain: Twenty Five Years of the Advisory Conciliation and Arbitration Service* (Oxford, Blackwell).

—— (2007) The Road is Long: Thirty Years of Equality Legislation in Britain' 45 *British Journal of Industrial Relations* 463–94.

—— (2008) *Legal Regulation, Institutions and Industrial Relations*, Warwick Papers in Industrial Relations no 89 (Warwick, IRRU).

Dickens, L, Jones, M, Weekes, B and Hart, M (1985) *Dismissed: A Study of Unfair Dismissal and the Industrial Tribunal System* (Oxford, Blackwell).

Dix, G (2000) 'Operating with Style: The Work of the Acas Conciliator in Individual Employment Rights Cases' in Brown, W and Towers, B (eds), *Employment Relations in Britain: Twenty Five Years of the Advisory Conciliation and Arbitration Service* (Oxford, Blackwell).

Dix, G, Sisson, K and Forth, J (2009) 'Conflict at Work: The Changing Pattern of Disputes' in Brown, W, Bryson, A, Forth, J and Whitfield, K (eds), *The Evolution of the Modern Workplace* (Cambridge, CUP).

Dix, G and Oxenbridge, S (2004) *Coming to the Table: The Role of Acas in Collective Disputes and Improving Workplace Relationships*, Research Paper 1/04 (London, Acas).

Dolder, C (2004) 'The Contribution of Mediation to Workplace Justice' 33 *Industrial Law Journal* 320–42.

Employment Department (1994) *Resolving Employment Disputes: Options for Reform*, Cmnd 2707 (London, HMSO).

Ewing, K (2011) *Fighting Back: Resisting 'Union-busting' and 'Strike-breaking' in the BA Dispute* (Liverpool, Institute of Employment Rights).

Fiss, DO (1984) 'Against Settlement' 93 *Yale Law Journal* 10–72.

Gaymer, J (2006) 'The Employment Tribunals System Taskforce' in L Dickens and A Neal (eds), *The Changing Institutional Face of British Employment Relations* (The Hague, Kluwer).

Gibbons, M (2007) *Better Dispute Resolution. A Review of Employment Dispute Resolution in Great Britain* (London, Department of Trade and Industry).

Gouldstone, S and Morris, G (2006) 'The Central Arbitration Committee' in L Dickens and A Neal (eds), *The Changing Institutional Face of British Employment Relations* (The Hague, Kluwer).

Graham, C and Lewis, N (1985) *The Role of Acas Conciliation in Equal Pay and Sex Discrimination Cases* (Manchester, Equal Opportunities Commission).

Harding, C and Garnet, E (2011) *SETA Survey of Representatives in Tribunal Cases 2008*, Research Paper 04/11 (London, Acas).

Hawes, WR (2000) 'Setting the Pace or Running Alongside? Acas and the Changing Employment Relationship' in W Brown and B Towers (eds), *Employment Relations in Britain: Twenty Five Years of the Advisory Conciliation and Arbitration Service* (Oxford, Blackwell).

Hepple, B (1983) 'Judging Equal Rights' 36 *Current Legal Problems* 71–90.

Hudson, M, Barnes, H, Brooks, S, Taylor, R (2007) *Race Discrimination Claims: Unrepresented Claimants' and Employers' Views on Acas Conciliation in Employment Tribunal Cases*, Research Paper 04/07 (London, Acas).

Hunter, R and Leonard, A (1997) 'Sex Discrimination and Alternative Dispute Resolution: British Proposals in the Light of International Experience' *Public Law* Summer.

Knight, KG and Latreille, P (2000) 'Discipline, Dismissals and Complaints to Employment Tribunals' 38 *British Journal of Industrial Relations* 533–55.

Latreille, P (2007) *The Settlement of Employment Tribunal Cases: Evidence from SETA 2003*, Employment Relations Research Series 61 (London, Department for Business Enterprise and Regulatory Reform).

—— (2011) *Mediation: A Thematic Review*, Acas Research Paper ref 13/11 (London, Acas).

Lewis, R and Clark, J (1993) *Employment Rights, Industrial Tribunals and Arbitration: The Case for Alternative Dispute Resolution* (London, Institute of Employment Rights).

Lipsky, D, Seeber, R and Fincher, D (2003) *Emerging Systems for Managing Workplace Conflict* (Jossey Bass, San Francisco).

McCrudden, C, Smith, D and Brown, C (1991) *Racial Justice at Work* (London, PSI).

McIlroy, J (1980) 'Conciliation' 9 *Industrial Law Journal* 179–83.

Patel, S (2011) *Research into Employers' Attitudes and Behaviour Towards Compliance with UK National Minimum Wage Legislation*, Employment Relations Research Series 121, (London, BIS).

Peters, M, Seeds, K, Harding, C and Garnett, E (2010) *Findings from the Survey of Employment Tribunals Applications 2008*, Employment Relations Research Series 107 (London, Department for Business Innovation and Skills).

Rideout, R (1982a) 'Arbitration and the Public Interest – Regulation Arbitration' Lord Wedderburn and Murphy, WT (eds), *Labour Law and the Community: Perspectives for the 1980s* (London, Institute of Advanced Legal Studies).

—— (1982b) 'Unfair Dismissal – Tribunal or Arbitration' 15 *Industrial Law Journal* 84–96.

Ridley-Duff, R and Bennett, A (2011) 'Towards Mediation: Developing a Theoretical Framework to Understand Alternative Dispute Resolution' 42 *Industrial Relations Journal* 106–23.

Saundry, R, McArdle, L and Thomas, P (2011) *Transforming Conflict Management in the Public Sector. Mediation, Trade Unions and Partnership in a Primary Care Trust*, Research Paper 01/11 (London, Acas).

Shearn K, Knight, B and Matharoo, AK (2010) *Evaluation of the Vulnerable Workers Pilots Year 2 (Final) report*, Employment Relations Research Series 108 (London, BIS).

Sisson, K (2008) *Putting the Record Straight: Industrial Relations and the Employment Relationship*, Warwick Papers in Industrial Relations no 88 (Warwick, IRRU).

Sturm, S and Gadlin, H (2007) 'Conflict Resolution and Systemic Change' *Journal of Dispute Resolution* 1–63.

Urwin, P, Karuk, V, Latreille, P, Michielsens, E, Page, L, Siara, B, Speckesser, S, Boon, A and Chevalier, P-A (2010) *Evaluating the Use of Judicial Mediation in Employment Tribunals*, Ministry of Justice Research Series 7/10 (London, MoJ).

Williams, M and Acas Research and Evaluation Section (2011) *Workplace Conflict Management Awareness and Use of the Acas Code of Practice and Workplace Mediation – A Poll of Business*, Research Paper 08/11 (London, Acas).

4

Agency Enforcement of Workplace Equality

BOB HEPPLE

INTRODUCTION

THERE IS OVER 40 years' experience in the UK of enforcing equality law at the workplace through the use of specialist equality commissions. When considering their role it must be remembered that equality at work is only one of their concerns. The commissions also have extensive functions in respect of public and private services, housing, education and other areas.

The first of these non-departmental public bodies (NDPB) was the Race Relations Board (RRB), established by the Race Relations Act (RRA) 1965 to deal with racial discrimination in public places and, subsequently, under the Race Relations Act (RRA) 1968, racial discrimination in employment, housing and services. The second was the Equal Opportunities Commission (EOC), established under the Sex Discrimination Act (SDA) in 1975 to deal with gender equality, including equal pay and equal treatment of women and men in employment. The EOC was the model for a new Commission for Racial Equality (CRE) which replaced the RRB in 1976. The third was the Disability Rights Commission (DRC) set up in 1999 to deal with disability discrimination under the Disability Discrimination Act (DDA) 1995. The Equality Act (EA) 2006 replaced all these bodies, from 1 October 2007, with a single Equality and Human Rights Commission (EHRC) which, in addition to race, gender and disability, also has powers in respect of inequalities because of age, sexual orientation, pregnancy and maternity, gender reassignment, marriage and civil partnership, and religion or belief. These are all described by the Equality Act (EA) 2010 as 'protected characteristics'.

The EA 2010, replacing all earlier anti-discrimination legislation, strengthens and harmonises the prohibition of discrimination and harassment because of any of these characteristics. It also extends and clarifies the law on positive action. Potentially most important of all, the Act contains a new single public sector equality duty applying to all protected characteristics, replacing earlier public sector duties in respect of race (2000), disability (2006) and sex

(2007). The new duty, in force since 1 April 2011, requires public authorities, when exercising their powers, to have 'due regard' to the need to eliminate discrimination, advance equality of opportunity, and foster good relations between various groups. There is, however, no equivalent duty in the private sector, despite longstanding proposals from the EOC, Trades Union Congress (TUC) and others for a duty on employers to conduct employment equity and equal pay audits (see generally on the EA 2010, Hepple 2011a). In Northern Ireland, since 1989, there have been innovative and largely successful legal duties on private and public sector employers to ensure that both Catholic and Protestant communities have 'fair participation in employment'. These duties were initially enforced by the Fair Employment Commission (FEC) whose role was taken over by the Equality Commission for Northern Ireland (ECNI) from 2000 (Heath et al 2009).

North American models of administrative enforcement of anti-discrimination legislation were highly influential in the decision to use such bodies (Hepple 1970; Lester and Bindman 1972; Street Report 1967). The main advantages were thought to be that strategic action in the public interest would be more likely to change organisational behaviour than ordinary adversarial civil and criminal proceedings, and that a specialised expert body which was independent of government would be free from political pressures and could also investigate compliance by government departments. The commissions have used a variety of methods to achieve their objectives of reducing prejudice and discrimination and promoting equality. This chapter, using McCrudden's (2007) categorisation, will examine the development of four regulatory approaches:

1. *Enforced collective regulation.* This leaves it to collective parties (employers and unions) to resolve complaints about discrimination through their own voluntary procedures. The independent agency acts in a non-coercive way, does not require changes in the organisation, but simply takes over the investigation and resolution of the individual complaint if voluntary procedures fail or are non-existent.
2. *Command and control regulation* by an independent agency which sets the standards that organisations are required to meet, and enforces them through investigations and legal proceedings.
3. *Responsive or reflexive regulation.* This approach (also called 'enforced self-regulation') is based on the idea that the regulators need to be responsive to the motivations, customs and structures of those who are being regulated. This involves providing incentives to organisations to undertake internal scrutiny and to engage with interest groups. The role of the agency is that of providing information and advice and negotiating change, with deterrent sanctions available as a last resort when voluntary methods fail.
4. *Assisting individual enforcement.* In addition to any of the above approaches the agency has powers to assist individuals to enforce their rights.

ENFORCED COLLECTIVE REGULATION (1968–76)

The RRB, when first established by the RRA 1965 to deal with racial discrimination in public places, was given power to investigate complaints through local conciliation committees. If the committee failed to settle a complaint by conciliation, it reported to the Board; if the Board found that there had been discrimination and it would be likely to continue it could refer the matter to the Attorney-General who could then bring proceedings for an injunction. In practice, this never happened.

When the RRA was extended to employment in 1968, the main responsibility for enforcement was put in the hands of voluntary procedures in some 40 industries with the RRB as only a backstop. The RRA 1968 retained the two-tier enforcement mechanism of local conciliation committees and the RRB, but the Board itself (rather than the Attorney-General) could now bring proceedings in specially designated county courts if conciliation failed. In the employment field complaints had to be made to the Department of Employment and Productivity (DEP) which had to send them to suitable industrial dispute procedures. Only when these had been exhausted, or no such procedure existed, did the RRB have any jurisdiction to deal with the complaint. This cumbersome and ineffective procedure was a compromise by the Labour Government with the TUC and CBI who claimed that legal enforcement would undermine the tradition of industrial relations voluntarism (Hepple 1970 175–201). The procedure failed to achieve either justice for individual victims or to change patterns of racial discrimination for two main reasons. First, the expectation that reliance on voluntary procedures would stimulate the growth of such procedures to deal with discrimination proved to be illusory. This is not surprising since these procedures were in many cases operated by the very people who were likely to be supportive of discriminatory practices. Secondly, they relied primarily on individual complaints, and the powers of the voluntary bodies and the RRB were extremely limited. The Board had power to initiate investigations without an individual complaint if it suspected an individual had been discriminated against, but this depended on specific information and in practice little use was made of this power (McCrudden 1991).

COMMAND AND CONTROL REGULATION (1976–2006)

The SDA 1975 and the RRA 1976 were major turning points. The RRA 1965 and 1968 were based on the notion of formal equality—treating likes alike. Direct discrimination (treating one person less favourably than another on grounds of race) was prohibited. The Acts of 1975 and 1976 marked the beginning of a transition to substantive equality, or what the EU calls 'full equality in practice'. This was done by introducing the concept of indirect or adverse impact discrimination borrowed from judicial decisions in the USA. This focuses on the disparate impact of an apparently neutral provision or practice (such as job qualifications or word-of-mouth recruitment practices) on members of a disadvantaged group. If such an adverse impact can be proved, it is for the organisation to provide justification for the provision or practice. There were different interpretations of justification under the various Acts until the EA 2010 introduced a single test. There must be proof that the indirectly discriminatory provision is a proportionate means of achieving a legitimate aim (Hepple 2011a, 69–72). The Acts also made specific provision for forms of positive or affirmative action (such as special training) to help disadvantaged people overcome barriers to employment. The EA 2010 has harmonised and extended the circumstances in which positive action may be taken (Hepple 2011a, 128–30). These changes towards substantive equality provided an incentive for organisations to examine their employment practices and to remove barriers to the employment of black and ethnic minority groups and women. An individual complaint of direct or indirect discrimination could push an organisation to undertake an internal review of its employment practices. However, research indicates that the positive effect of individual cases is generally short-lived and can lead to defensive and negative attitudes to change (Hepple et al 2000: app 1). For this reason, the new EOC and CRE were given extensive powers to investigate specific organisations on their own initiative, and to stop directly and indirectly discriminatory practices, backed by deterrent sanctions. This was classic command and control regulation.

There were two types of investigation. First, general inquiries could be carried out, after giving notice, without the commission holding any specific belief that there may have been breaches of the legislation. These inquiries could not be directed against a named organisation and could result only in a report and recommendations. Subpoena notices compelling witnesses could be issued only on the authority of the Secretary of State. The second type of investigation was the 'belief' or 'accusatory' investigation into suspected unlawful acts by a named person; the CRE and EOC had powers to issue subpoenas and, after a hearing, could issue non-discrimination notices to stop discriminatory practices.

The commissions were largely successful in their promotional tasks of setting and raising standards. The principal measures, apart from general publicity, were codes of practice which concentrated on employment processes such as advertising, selection procedures and monitoring. It is clear that a significant number of employers were prompted by the codes to review their practices and to take action that resulted in more opportunities for black and minority ethnic groups, women and disabled persons (Coussey 1992).

However, the commissions were less successful in using their powers of command and control. In the early years, the CRE believed that it could act as an inspectorate and investigate a named organisation, without any prior evidence of unlawful discrimination, either because there was general evidence of inequality in the sector or occupation or because it was a leading company in the sector. The CRE carried out a number of important investigations which showed how discrimination operates and how to deal with it (Coussey 1992). However, this encountered judicial hostility, notably from Lord Denning, the Master of the Rolls, who notoriously compared the CRE's powers to those of the Inquisition.[1] In the 1984 *Prestige* case,[2] the House of Lords held that investigations into named organisations were not permissible unless the Commission had already formed a suspicion that the persons concerned may have committed some unlawful act. In the *Hillingdon* case,[3] the House of Lords turned this into the 'reasonable suspicion' test, saying that

> there should be material before the Commission sufficient to raise in the minds of reasonable men (*sic*), possessed of the experience of covert discrimination that has been acquired by the Commission, a suspicion that there may have been unlawful acts by the named person.[4]

These decisions, coupled with a lack of adequate resources, placed serious restrictions on strategic enforcement, allowing discriminatory practices to continue unchecked. None of the companies involved in investigations before these decisions had equal opportunities policies. The absence of monitoring meant that there were no records of the ethnic origin of applicants and employees, and other evidence was hard to uncover (Coussey 1992). Another nail in the coffin of formal investigations was the Court of Appeal's decision in 1982 in the *Amari Plastics* case that the respondent could challenge the CRE's findings of fact as well as the requirements in a non-discrimination notice to stop discriminatory practices.[5] The courts added to the already elaborate procedural safeguards for respondents, for example by imposing the need to give the named organisation notice of the proposed terms of reference and the opportunity of a hearing even before the investigation started. Lord Denning candidly remarked that the machinery for investigations and the issuing of non-discrimination notices was 'so elaborate and so cumbersome that it is in danger of grinding to a halt.'[6] Not surprisingly, there was a sharp decline in the use of 'belief' or 'accusatory' investigations against named organisations by the CRE. After 1989, the CRE used accusatory investigations only as a last resort when attempts to persuade organisations to change practices had been exhausted.

---

[1] *Social Science Research Council v Nassé* [1979] 1 QB 144 (CA) 172.
[2] *R v Commission for Racial Equality, ex parte Prestige Group Ltd* [1984] ICR 473.
[3] *Hillingdon London Borough Council v Commission for Racial Equality* [1982] AC 779.
[4] Ibid at 791 (Lord Diplock).
[5] *R v Commission for Racial Equality ex parte Amari Plastics* [1982] QB 1194.
[6] Ibid at 1203.

At the time, the usual practice was to negotiate an agreement for changes, and then to suspend the formal investigation while the implementation of the agreement was monitored. This approach paid dividends with major voluntary changes being recorded in organisations such as the RMT Union, the Ministry of Defence (Household Cavalry), the London Borough of Hackney, the Crown Prosecution Service and the Ford Motor Company. The EOC made even less use than the CRE of formal investigations, conducting only 11 from 1977 to 2005, the last of these being in 1995.

The DDA 1995 did not deal with indirect disability discrimination, but did create a positive duty on employers to make reasonable adjustments for specific disabled persons. The DRC was modelled on the EOC and the CRE but its powers to conduct formal investigations were framed in a slightly different way, in effect putting the *Prestige* and *Hillingdon* tests into statutory form, but allowing a non-accusatory investigation into a named person. A useful addition to the powers of the DRC was to provide for 'agreements in lieu of enforcement action'. These were agreements in which the Commission undertook not to take enforcement action in return for the named person undertaking not to commit any unlawful acts and to take positive action as specified in the agreement. If the undertaking was breached the DRC could apply for a court order to enforce it. The DRC also had the power to require a person who committed an unlawful act to prepare an action plan for the purpose of avoiding repetition or continuation of the unlawful act. For example, the plan might set out targets and practical ways in which reasonable adjustments would be made for disabled persons.

Prior to the introduction of public sector equality duties, a limiting feature of the race and sex discrimination legislation was that it relied exclusively on negative duties prohibiting discrimination rather than positive duties to eliminate discrimination and advance equality. The limiting feature of the disability discrimination legislation, before the public sector duty was introduced, was that the duty to make reasonable adjustments applied only to a specific disabled person such as one who applied for a job or was already an employee requesting an adjustment because of their disability. The concept of indirect discrimination was not applied to disability, and there was no general duty to ensure a workplace friendly to disabled people.

More generally, by the turn of the century, after 35 years of agency enforcement, there was still little sense that the majority of organisations had a sustained and coordinated strategy to improve diversity and equal opportunities in the workforce (Hepple et al 2000: 19–20). Such a strategy requires a commitment by managers and workers' representatives to participate in bringing about changes, and a system for measuring progress. The early agencies were devised on the basis of a model of organisations that were hierarchical, vertically integrated and centralised. The top-down rule-making command and control approach depends on individual fault-finding and retrospective investigation of an act alleged to be motivated by an unlawful ground of discrimination. This tends to breed negative, defensive and adversarial responses. However, the reality is that organisations cannot survive in the new globalised economy unless they are flexible and adaptable to market changes and technological innovation. Organisations are flattening their hierarchies, giving more authority to lower-level managers and demanding a high quality workforce, with the active participation of managers, workers and customers or service users. Equality of opportunity at work increasingly depends not simply on avoiding negative discrimination, but on training and improving skills, developing wider social networks, and encouraging adaptability. In that new environment, the traditional command and control approach places too much emphasis on state regulation, and too little on the responsibility of organisations and individuals to generate change.

TOWARDS RESPONSIVE REGULATION (SINCE 2006)

The weaknesses of command and control regulation and individual enforcement led the Cambridge *Independent Review of the Enforcement of UK Anti-Discrimination Legislation* (Hepple et al 2000), using the insights of modern regulatory theory (Ayres and Braithwaite 1992; Hepple 2011b) to design an 'optimal' form of regulation which could help to reduce, if not eliminate, under-representation, exclusion and institutional barriers to equal opportunities. This was described as 'enforced self-regulation', involving three interlocking mechanisms. The first is internal scrutiny by the organisation itself to ensure effective self-regulation. The second is the involvement of interest groups (such as managers, employees and service users) who must be informed, consulted and engaged in the process of change. Third is the commission which should provide the back-up role of assistance and ultimately enforcement where voluntary methods fail. These interlocking mechanisms create a triangular relationship between those regulated, those whose interests are affected, and the commission as the guardian of the public interest. The Cambridge Review argued that this broad strategy needed to be developed in several specific ways: (1) a single commission covering all protected characteristics; (2) a positive duty on public authorities to advance equality; (3) positive duties on private sector employers to achieve employment equity or fair participation; (4) positive duties on employers to introduce pay equity schemes; and (5) the improvement of deterrent sanctions including the use of contract and subsidy compliance.

Only the first two parts of this strategy were embraced in the EA 2006 and the EA 2010. First, the single EHRC was created with more extensive powers than the earlier commissions and with a budget of £70 million in the first year, significantly more than the combined allocations of its predecessors. The outcome of a long struggle to establish this body was said to be 'a statutory body with a powerful mandate, set an inspiring challenge, and equipped with the powers, breadth of functions, independence and internal flexibility of structure to achieve it' (Spencer 2008: 15). The EA 2006 gives the EHRC two powers, largely modelled on those of the DRC; one to conduct an inquiry, and the other to conduct a formal investigation (for details see Hepple 2011a: 151–54). An inquiry can relate to any of the Commission's duties, but leads only to a report and recommendations. These are not legally binding, but a court or tribunal may have regard to a finding, and the Commission may use information or evidence acquired in the course of an inquiry for the purpose of a formal investigation. The Commission has heavily circumscribed powers to obtain information, documents and oral evidence, under judicial control. One of the virtues of a single commission is that the inquiry can cut across strands, for example to investigate possible multiple discrimination. The inquiry may relate to a particular sector. For example, the EHRC has held inquiries into gender equality in the financial services sector, race equality in the construction industry, and the employment of migrant and agency labour in meat and poultry processing. Alternatively, the inquiry may be thematic, for example the EHRC has held one into harassment. The Commission may not use an inquiry to find out whether a named person has committed an unlawful act; it needs to commence a formal investigation (below) for that purpose.

The second power of the EHRC is to conduct a formal investigation. The Commission may do so only if it 'suspects' that the person concerned may have committed an unlawful act. This follows the DRC model and sets a 'threshold test' of 'reasonable belief'. This seems to codify the case law (above), but it has been argued that only if the Commission's decision to investigate is irrational or strongly disproportionate should a court interfere. (O'Cinneide 2007). A single complaint of unlawful conduct is unlikely to suffice as the basis for initiating an investigation, but a series of complaints over time might be sufficient. The suspicion may (but need not) be based on the matters arising in the course of an inquiry (above). There are stringent procedural requirements (Hepple 2011a: 152–53). Named person investigations may lead to an unlawful act notice against which there is a right of appeal to an appropriate court or tribunal. The notice may require the person to prepare an action plan for the purpose of avoiding a repetition or continuation of the unlawful act, and may recommend action to be taken by the person for that purpose. The action plan has to be approved by the Commission, which has power to apply to a county court (in England and Wales) or sheriff (in Scotland) for an order requiring a person to give the Commission a draft or revised action plan. During the period of five years beginning with the date on which the plan comes into force, an order may be sought and granted requiring the person to act in accordance with the action plan or to take specified action for a similar purpose. Failure to comply with an order without reasonable excuse may lead to a fine. The EHRC also has powers to assess compliance with the public sector equality duty (below) and, where it thinks that a public authority has failed to comply with a duty, the power to issue a non-compliance notice.

It can be seen that the EHRC remains largely within the enforcement models of its predecessors. In particular, the opportunity was lost to reverse the *Prestige* and *Hillingdon* tests so as to allow named investigations even in the absence of evidence of unlawful acts. The EHRC could have been given the power to conduct equality audits in the public and private sectors, like the Irish Equality Authority can do, even in the absence of specific evidence of discrimination (O'Cinneide 2007). In Northern Ireland, ECNI is able to use the results of triennial reviews that employers are required to submit relating to representation of Catholic and Protestant communities, as well as their investigatory powers, in order to negotiate agreements designed to remedy under-representation of either community. These are affirmative action agreements which usually require undertakings to change the way they recruit, advertise, promote, and dismiss staff, often setting numerical goals and timetables. Most of the agreements reached have been voluntary but a number are legally enforceable. The voluntary ones usually follow a triennial review, while the legally-binding ones tend to follow a formal investigation. Research (Heath et al 2009) shows that agreements focussing on institutional changes have been more effective in securing progress towards fair employment than lawsuits. Voluntary agreements have been more effective than the legally enforceable ones. The researchers suggest that one explanation for this may be that legally-binding agreements have had to be negotiated where the employers are resistant to change:

> Voluntary agreements where senior staff (with whom agreements are typically negotiated) have been persuaded of the legitimacy of the exercise may thus be more wholeheartedly implemented than are legally enforceable agreements where the leadership of the concern had to be compelled to accept their intervention. (Heath et al 2009)

The research suggests that leadership and commitment from the top of the organisation is crucial for the implementation of reforms.

The failure of the Labour and Coalition Governments to introduce employment equity and pay audits means that there is little incentive in Britain for employers to enter into voluntary agreements with the EHRC. A step in the direction of legally-binding agreements has, however, been made. The 2006 Act gives the EHRC, like the former DRC, the power to make legally-binding agreements in lieu of enforcement. It may do so only if it thinks that the person has committed an unlawful act. The inducements for a person to make such an agreement are that the Commission must undertake not to proceed with a formal investigation or unlawful act notice, and the person is not taken to be admitting to the commission of an unlawful act by reason only of entering into the agreement. If the Commission thinks that a party to an agreement has failed to comply, or is not likely to comply with an undertaking in the agreement, it may apply to a county court (in England and Wales) or sheriff (in Scotland) for an order requiring the person to comply or take such other action as the court may specify.

The Labour Government resisted pressure to give the EHRC and trade unions the right to bring representative (or 'class') actions on behalf of a defined group of persons who would benefit from the litigation. The argument for such actions is that discriminatory practices, like unequal pay, are often systemic. At present each member of the affected group has to bring a separate claim. Although the tribunal may consolidate these and allow 'test' cases to be litigated, each claimant has to be identified at the time action is commenced. The Commission does, however, have a number of powers to bring actions in its own name. If it thinks that a person is likely to commit an unlawful act, it may seek an injunction (England and Wales) or interdict (Scotland) to prevent the person from committing that act. The Commission also has the capacity to institute or intervene in legal proceedings, whether for judicial review or otherwise, if it appears to the Commission that the proceedings are relevant to a matter in connection with which the Commission has a function. Finally, the EA 2010 amends the 2006 Act so as to allow the EHRC to use its enforcement powers, including conducting investigations and applying for an injunction, in a number of situations where individuals may not be able or willing to take action. If the Commission uses its powers this does not affect the entitlement of a person to bring proceedings under the Act. An example would be an advertisement indicating an intention to discriminate. Even if the EHRC takes action, individuals who are discouraged from applying for the job can also bring a claim and seek compensation in their own right. The Commission can act against a suspected discriminatory practice even though it is not aware that any particular individual is affected by it, for example it could take action against an employer believed to be operating an informal policy of excluding people from ethnic minorities, even though it is not aware of any particular individual affected by this policy. The Commission can also use its powers when an employer asks job applicants prohibited enquiries about disability and health. These provisions replace those in earlier enactments relating to discriminatory practices and discriminatory advertisements.

It is too soon to say whether these extensive powers will be effectively used by the EHRC to encourage organisational change, but it is difficult not to be pessimistic. The Coalition Government cut the annual budget of the EHRC to £48.9 million in 2011–12 and this will be reduced to £26 million by 2015, a loss of nearly two-thirds of its initial resources and staffing. This reveals a weakness in the design of the Commission as an NDPB which is not directly accountable to and funded by Parliament, but is vulnerable to executive action in respect of funding and appointments. Moreover, the Government published proposals in March 2011 (Government Equalities Office 2011b) to amend the legislation so as to limit the EHRC to so-called 'core' functions of encouraging good practice, promoting awareness and understanding of equality rights and enforcing them, and a Public Bodies Bill before Parliament at the time of writing proposes to give the Government power to make further changes to its functions. This comes on top of a number of mistakes in the process of setting up the new Commission, as well as management and accounting failures by the Commission itself (Joint Committee on Human Rights 2009–10). The EHRC's draft strategic plan for the period up to 2015 gives relatively low priority to employment issues, mentioning only education and skills training, gender and ethnic career and educational segregation, the gender, ethnic and disability pay gap, unpaid work by carers, and some forms of discrimination and harassment.

The new enforcement powers in the EA 2006 and the EA 2010 still seem locked into command and control regulation. Therefore, one has to turn to the regulations on the public sector equality duty to see how far the other two sides of the triangle of responsive regulation—internal scrutiny by the organisation, and involvement of interest groups—have been achieved. There is a general duty on all public authorities who are listed in a Schedule to the EA 2010 and also on anyone else who exercises public functions (eg operating a private prison). This is a duty to have due regard to the need to eliminate discrimination, harassment, victimisation and any other prohibited conduct, to advance equality of opportunity between persons who share a protected characteristic and those who do not share it, and to foster good relations between groups who share characteristics and those who do not.

In addition, regulations may place specific duties on certain public authorities to enable them to carry out the general equality duty more effectively. The regulations in respect of England[7] approved in October 2011 require only publication by the public body of equality objectives every four years and publication once a year (starting no later than 31 January 2012) of information to demonstrate its compliance with the general duty. This must include information relating to its employees and others affected by its policies and practices. These regulations are a step backwards from the specific duties which applied under earlier legislation. Previously, a public authority's race equality scheme had to state its arrangements for 'consulting' on the likely impact of proposed policies on the promotion of race

---

[7] One of the consequences of devolved powers in respect of the duties, is that the Welsh Assembly has approved separate regulations which have more detailed provision for engagement of stakeholders. At the time of writing, the Scottish Parliament is still considering the matter. A cross-border authority may find itself operating under three separate regimes in Great Britain, and another in Northern Ireland.

equality; those relating to gender required the authority to state the actions it had taken or intended to take to 'consult' relevant employees, service users and others (including trade unions); and those in respect of disability went furthest, requiring the authority to 'involve' in the development of an equality scheme disabled persons who appeared to the authority to have an interest in the way it carries out its functions. Not only is there no duty in the new regulations to publish details of 'engagement' with interest groups, but it is also significant that no duty is imposed on employers to 'engage' with any specific class of representatives, such as recognised trade unions, or equality representatives. There are many thousands of equality representatives appointed and supported by trade unions who give advice and support to members on equality issues in the workplace. Their effectiveness is dependent on the willingness of employers to recognise and consult with them. It has been estimated that only 36 per cent of equality representatives have an employer who automatically consults with them frequently, only 26 per cent of employers negotiate with equality representatives and 22 per cent of employers never involve the representatives (Bacon and Hoque 2009). There is no legal duty to consult these representatives. The Government rejected an amendment to the Equality Bill, promoted by the TUC, to allow these representatives paid time off work to carry out their functions and to receive training. The Government's reason was the familiar one: a lack of sufficient empirical evidence that the time off should come through the law. This contrasts with the regulations which require employers to consult elected representatives of employee safety, and to ensure that they receive training and are given paid time off to perform their functions. Information, dialogue and balanced participation of employees and other interest groups on equality matters are key to effective regulation, but they form no part of the new equality regime.

The justification given by the Coalition Government for limiting the specific duties in England is its commitment to

> reduce burdens and bureaucracy on public bodies, moving away from a process-driven approach to a focus on transparency, in order to free up public bodies to do what is appropriate in their circumstances, to take responsibility for their own performance, and to be held to account by the public. (Government Equalities Office 2011a: para 3)

There certainly was a widely-held perception that the specific duties under race, gender and disability legislation had led some public bodies to focus on paper exercises and a tick-box approach as to whether they had followed the right processes, rather than on whether those processes actually delivered equality improvements. The issue is whether transparency as to objectives and outcomes alone will result in adequate internal scrutiny and voluntary action. There are already reports that some public bodies, in order to make costs savings, are abandoning monitoring and impact assessments and are not consulting interested persons, trade unions and equality representatives, or involving disabled persons.

The Coalition Government maintains that 'challenge from the public will be the key means of holding public bodies to account for their performance on equality' (Government Equalities Office 2011a: para 17). However, the public sector equality duty does not give rise to any enforceable private law rights. It is enforceable only by way of judicial review. Judicial review proceedings may be brought by any person with sufficient interest (including the EHRC or a trade union). Most of the proceedings to date have been brought by non-governmental organisations or individuals challenging the implementation of budget cuts on local authorities and, so far as is known, none has directly affected employment issues. The effects have been limited because the duty imposed on public bodies is only to have 'due regard' to the need to advance equality of opportunity, and not a duty to eliminate unlawful discrimination. After reviewing the case law, Fredman concludes that 'it is unlikely that judicial review on its own is capable of achieving the internal culture change required if equality is truly to be mainstreamed' (Fredman 2011: 424). The usual way of enforcing a specific public sector duty will be by the EHRC using its statutory enforcement power to assess the extent to which a public body has complied with both the general and specific equality duties. In doing so, the Commission must make it clear to the public body the areas to be covered by the assessment and allow the body to make representations. Upon completion of a formal assessment, the Commission may issue a compliance notice. Failure to comply can result in the Commission applying to a court for an order requiring compliance. Failure to comply with the court order is a criminal offence.

The biggest failure to adopt a responsive regulation approach is in relation to the private sector. As already noted, there is no positive duty on private sector employers to advance equality. It seems that, for the foreseeable future, reliance will be placed on voluntary action. The Coalition Government decided not to bring into force a provision in the EA 2010 requiring employers of 250 or more employees to publish gender pay gap information. Instead it is asking employers to sign up voluntarily to the 'Think, Act, Report' campaign undertaking to think about equality and diversity, to act on the findings of their analysis, and to report transparently. This voluntary approach is being pursued despite the Government's own research which shows that the main motivators for action on equal pay are legislation and complaints or legal action by employees (Government Equalities Office 2011c). The EHRC is able to invoke its investigatory powers where the Commission reasonably suspects discrimination, and then seek to negotiate a legally-binding positive action agreement in lieu of enforcement. But in the absence of a legal duty on employers to conduct employment and pay equity audits, there is unlikely to be a sufficient incentive on employers to take positive action to improve employment opportunities for disadvantaged groups and to reduce the pay gap between women and men. In McCrudden's (2007: 265) words, 'the rejection of proposals to introduce compulsory monitoring [as in Northern Ireland] ... [is] the single greatest blow to the likelihood that reflexive regulation will be successful in the British context'.

ASSISTING INDIVIDUAL ENFORCEMENT (SINCE 1976)

Finally, mention must be made of the commissions' role in assisting individual enforcement. Since 1975, anti-discrimination legislation has given individuals the right to complain of unlawful direct and indirect discrimination to industrial (later called employment) tribunals. The usual remedy for individuals is compensation. The problems connected with individual enforcement are discussed elsewhere in this volume by Linda Dickens (see also Dickens 2007). A limiting feature of individual enforcement, even where a commission is involved, is that it is relatively ineffective in bringing about longer-term change in workplaces. While a strong individual case coming at the right time might raise general questions about selection or promotion practices the initial reaction is often to defend the case or, where the paper trail is poor or the procedures were defective, to settle it. Before the EA 2010, the tribunals could make recommendations only in respect of the complainant. The EA 2010 has now given tribunals the power to make recommendations affecting persons other than the complainant (eg about a recruitment process). Potentially this allows an individual case to have a wider impact in encouraging change in the workplace, but there is still no power to compel compliance with such a recommendation. Unless all the affected parties are represented before the tribunal, the employment judge may feel inhibited in making wider recommendations, so it is unlikely that this power will be frequently used.

A link between strategic enforcement by the commissions and enforcement by individuals is the power of the commissions to give assistance to litigants. The three legacy commissions exercised this power in different ways. From an early stage the EOC restricted assistance to cases which raised matters of general principle. Its carefully targeted selected case strategy resulted in several important references to the European Court of Justice (ECJ) and significant extensions of EU law which, in turn, influenced UK developments. The EOC also made use of judicial review proceedings to challenge the failure of the UK Government to implement relevant EU law fully. Before 2003 the CRE received applications for assistance from around one-third of all race discrimination applicants to tribunals and gave assistance in a substantial number of cases which were thought to be 'arguable'. In 2003, the CRE limited assistance to cases which could clarify points of law or create precedents that could affect large numbers of people, that would help to produce legislative change or that would test the new positive duty, introduced in 2000, to promote race equality. After 2003, the CRE would assist only if there was a relatively strong prospect of success. Many cases that might previously have been supported directly by the CRE were taken up by race equality councils, and other bodies receiving grants from the CRE, as well as by trade unions and other non-governmental organisations. The DRC also applied strategic criteria when selecting cases but helped support relatively more claims of discrimination than the other commissions did and secured some notable victories through litigation (Hepple 2011a: 163–66).

The EA 2006 gave the EHRC similar powers to those of its predecessors to provide legal advice and representation, and legal assistance to individuals. The basic criterion for support adopted by the EHRC is whether this will assist the Commission to meet its strategic objectives. In 2009–10 the Commission supported or intervened in 98 strategic legal actions. The draft EHRC strategic plan up to 2015 indicates that the EHRC will continue to move away from routine casework and will focus on strategic cases which are likely a have a widespread impact. Other forms of commission support are disappearing. The Coalition Government has stopped funding the EHRC's helpline which gave information and general advice, and proposes to replace it with a generalist advice service. It is not clear at present how this will differ from Acas' helpline including Equality Direct, a free confidential service designed for small businesses. But it is doubtful whether a generalist service can provide the same expert help in discrimination cases as the EHRC. The Government has also withdrawn support for the EHRC's legal grants programme that provides awards to voluntary organisations, such as race equality councils, to educate individuals about their rights, and makes grants to advice organisations, such as citizens advice bureaux and law centres, to provide legal advice and representation, and training for advisers, caseworkers and lawyers. Civil legal aid is not available for representation in employment tribunals, and is being removed in respect of advice. 'No-win no-fee' conditional fee agreements and damages-based agreements with lawyers are feasible only where there are multiple claimants or in those rare individual cases where there is the reasonable probability of a high compensation award (Hepple 2011a: 163–64).

CONCLUSION

It would be a mistake to view the history of the enforcement of workplace equality as one of trial and error. Each stage of development has been strongly contested. In the early years, employers' organisations and trade unions used their power to retain voluntary enforcement or collective self-regulation. They were in denial about the extent of racial discrimination in employment, and suspicious of legal regulation. A sustained campaign led to the extension of the substantive law from formal race and sex equality (direct discrimination) to substantive equality (indirect discrimination and voluntary positive action and later reasonable adjustments for disabled persons). These were enforced by a combination of individual legal action, and command and control strategic regulation by the commissions. Litigation enabled many individuals to obtain compensation for the hurt and loss caused by unlawful discrimination, and had some effect on human resources management. The commissions were successful in promoting and setting standards, but lack of resources and judicial decisions that tied them up in procedural knots limited their effectiveness in securing organisational change.

The crucial change in Britain has come since 2000 with the enactment of public sector equality duties, now embodied in the Equality Act 2010, applying to all protected characteristics. These mark the beginning of a new stage of transformative and comprehensive equality. Matching this was to be the development of 'responsive' or 'reflexive' regulation, alongside improvements in individual enforcement. The hopes of the reformers have once again been dashed. The Labour and Coalition Governments have refused to go beyond voluntary measures for positive action in the private sector. The specific public sector equality duties have been weakened, and the resources and staffing of the EHRC have been drastically reduced. Support for individual litigants in routine cases is rapidly disappearing. The prospects for transformative change and for access to justice are problematic.

Despite these recent setbacks, there are strong reasons from both theory and practice to believe that the model of reflexive regulation in the longer term holds the key to more effective enforcement of workplace equality. Systems analysis teaches us that law cannot succeed in changing behaviour at the workplace through direct command and control. This is because modern workplaces are not structured hierarchically with law at the apex. There are multiple sub-systems including the legal system, administrative bodies and workplaces. Each sub-system operates autonomously to a greater or lesser extent, and reacts 'reflexively' in its own language and according to its internal logic. So when the workplace receives a command from the legal system to 'advance equality', it filters this through its own internal norms and culture. This may lead to outcomes that differ significantly from the aims of those issuing the legal command. There is what Teubner calls a 'regulatory trilemma': either the legal command is ignored at the workplace; or it damages the ability of the workplace to regulate norms; or it damages the credibility and legitimacy of the legal system itself (Teubner 1987). Teubner's solution is 'reflexive' law that does not seek to impose substantive rules on sub-systems but instead works with the internal dynamics of those systems and coordinates them.

The reflexive model rests on three foundations: strong incentives for internal scrutiny by an organisation; engagement with stakeholders; and an independent enforcement agency which can summon deterrent sanctions where voluntary means fail. As regards the first of these, we have seen that no legislative incentives for internal action exist in the private sector, and that individual complaints may lead only to defensive and short-lived changes. The public sector equality duty is circumscribed and may have been curtailed by the recent regulations on specific duties. This will make it even more difficult than in the past to hold public bodies accountable. The second missing foundation is a duty to 'engage' with employees and other affected parties. The omission of any duty to involve equality representatives in both public and private sectors is perhaps the most serious weakness of all, because it treats employees and those denied opportunities as the passive recipients of equal treatment rather than active participants in the process of achieving change. Finally, this chapter has indicated that although the new EHRC has the potential to provide information and advice and to help negotiate change in organisations, and has the necessary deterrent sanctions, this is likely to be undermined by severe cuts in its resources, the removal of its broader promotional functions, and threats to its independence. A long and difficult struggle for effective reflexive regulation of workplace equality still lies ahead.

BIBLIOGRAPHY

Ayres, I and Braithwaite, J (1992) *Responsive Regulation: Transcending the Deregulation Debate* (Oxford, Oxford University Press).

Bacon, N and Hoque, N (2009) 'TUC Equality Representatives Survey' (London, TUC).

Coussey, M (1992) 'The Effectiveness of Strategic Enforcement in the Race Relations Act 1976' in Hepple, B and Szyszczak, E (eds), *Discrimination: The Limits of Law* (London, Mansell).

Dickens, L (2007) 'The Road is Long: Thirty Years of Equality Legislation in Britain' 45 *British Journal of Industrial Relations* 463–94.

Fredman, S (2011) 'The Public Sector Equality Duty' 40 *Industrial Law Journal* 405–27.

Government Equalities Office (2009) *Equality Bill: Making it Work: Proposals for Specific Duties* (HM Government, GEO).

—— (2011a) *The Public Sector Equality Duty: Reducing Bureaucracy Policy Review Paper* (HM Government, GEO).

—— (2011b) *Building a Fairer Britain: Reform of the Equality and Human Rights Commission* (HM Government, GEO).

—— (2011c) *Voluntary Gender Reporting in Organisations Employing 150–249 Employees,* Research Findings No 2011/3 (HM Government, Home Office).

Heath A, Clifford P, Hamill H, McCrudden, C and Mubarak, R (2009) 'The Enforcement of Fair Employment Law in Northern Ireland: The Effect of Commission Agreements, McBride Agreements and Fair Employment Tribunal Cases' (unpublished paper). For a summary see McCrudden, C (2009) 4 *Equal Rights Review* 7–14.

Hepple, B (1970) *Race, Jobs and the Law in Britain* 2nd edn (Harmondsworth, Penguin Books).

—— (2011a) *Equality: The New Legal Framework* (Oxford, Hart Publishing).

—— (2011b) 'Enforcing Equality Law: Two Steps Forward Two Steps Backwards for Reflexive Regulation' 40 *Industrial Law Journal* 315–35.

Hepple, B, Coussey, M and Choudhury, T (2000) *Equality: A New Framework. Report of the Independent Review of the Enforcement of UK Anti-Discrimination Legislation* (Oxford, Hart Publishing).

Joint Committee on Human Rights (2009–10) *Equality and Human Rights Commission*, 13th Report of Session 2009–10, HL Paper 72, HC Paper 183 (London, The Stationery Office).

Lester, A and Bindman, G (1972) *Race and Law* (Harmondsworth, Penguin).

McCrudden, C et al (1991) *Racial Justice at Work: The Enforcement of the Race Relations Act 1976 in Employment* (London, Policy Studies Institute).

—— (2007) 'Equality Legislation and Reflexive Regulation: A Response to the Discrimination Law Consultation Paper' 36 *Industrial Law Journal* 255–66.

O'Cinneide, C (2007) 'The Commission for Equality and Human Rights: A New Institution for New and Uncertain Times' 36 *Industrial Law Journal* 141–62.

Spencer, S (2008) 'Equality and Human Rights Commission: A Decade in the Making' 79 *Political Quarterly* 6–16.

Street Report: Street, H, Howe, G and Bindman, G (1967) *Anti-Discrimination Legislation* (London, Political and Economic Planning).

Teubner, G (1987) 'Juridification: Concepts, Aspects, Limits, Solutions' in Teubner, G (ed), *Juridification of Social Spheres: A Comparative Analysis of the Areas of Labour, Corporate, Antitrust and Social Welfare* (Berlin, De Gruyter) 3–48.

5

Reshaping Health and Safety Enforcement: Institutionalising Impunity

STEVE TOMBS AND DAVID WHYTE

INTRODUCTION: A 'NATURAL IDENTITY OF INTERESTS'?

IF THERE IS an enduring principle in health and safety law it is that there exists a 'natural identity of interests' between employers and employees. This principle—upon which the western liberal tradition of social regulation is based—can be traced back to early forms of social regulation in the nineteenth century (Tucker 1990; Carson 1985). It is also the principle that formally underpins the Health and Safety at Work etc Act 1974 (1974 Act). The Robens Report, which laid the foundations of the 1974 Act, asserted that: 'there is greater natural identity of interest between "the two sides" in relation to health and safety problems than in most other matters. There is no legitimate scope for "bargaining" on safety and health issues' (Robens 1972: para 66). The 1974 Act established the Health and Safety Executive (HSE) as the national regulator for occupational health and safety (OHS; see also chapter two), responsible for regulating over 800,000 premises across the country. This chapter examines recent trends in regulatory activity conducted by the HSE.

The pervading assumption that underpins the principle of a 'natural identity of interests'—in essence the guiding principle for the bulk of the HSE's work—is that conflict over health and safety in the workplace has, or should have, no place in industrial relations. Health and safety occupies a special status that takes it beyond normal processes of industrial bargaining. Also, and related to this point, because health and safety conditions are removed from the normal business of collective bargaining, they are disconnected from the labour process. Thus, the conditions of work that often have a direct impact upon the labour process such as the intensity of work, changes in systems of work, or even more obvious features such as lack of training, working long hours and so on, are artificially segregated as matters of 'safety' or 'bargaining'. What this principle and 'better regulation', the subject matter of this chapter, have in common is that they both rely upon the idea of 'corporate social responsibility' (CSR). It is with the centrality of this idea to the politics of neo-liberalism that the next section is concerned, before we set out in detail a case study of recent shifts in UK health and safety policy.

NEO-LIBERALISM AND CORPORATE SOCIAL RESPONSIBILITY

The period from the mid-1970s to the present witnessed the emergence of the dominance of 'neo-liberalism', and, its international form, 'globalisation'. In the UK, the deregulation of energy supply markets, the housing market, water, prisons, and a range of other public service functions required a major re-regulation effort and a major transfer of resources from public to private. Moreover, the deregulation of financial services and industrial policies aimed at elevating the financial sector above manufacturing were based upon the idea that neo-liberal globalisation demanded tough policy choices in order to sustain the UK's global competitive advantage. While there was undoubtedly an international convergence of domestic economic and social policy along neo-liberal lines, the effects of 'globalisation-logic' varied from country to country. But it is no surprise to find this globalisation-logic most fully embraced in those countries which had been at the forefront of embracing neo-liberalism, including, notably, the UK. This logic was especially dominant as the Labour Party 'modernised' itself through the 1990s, to the extent that, in office from 1997 onwards, this dominant understanding of globalisation had been 'internalised by New Labour' (Hay and Watson 1998). This was confirmed by the administration's famous pledge to 'accept globalization and work with it' (cited in Holden 1999: 531).

New Labour's self-resignation to neo-liberalism was to be furthered through two key, underlying convictions which underpinned its repositioning as the party of business. The first was that Britain's global economic competitiveness hinged upon the creation of a business-friendly environment through policy reforms. Behind this rationale is an apocryphal fear of capital flight; the idea that over-regulation would result in the displacement of firms to more business-friendly foreign locations. Prime Minister Blair sought to make Britain 'a great place to do business. Labour is now the party for business, the entrepreneur's champion' (1997, cited in Osler 2002: 57). The second was the central conviction that private economic activity is inherently and necessarily better than public sector activity. New Labour bought into a set of neo-liberal claims that proposed, on grounds of economy, efficiency and effectiveness, the private sector as the most appropriate provider of goods and services. The logical consequence of this is that the market can also more effectively deliver regulatory outcomes. From this perspective the regulation of markets and of businesses can best be located in, and achieved through, market rather than government mechanisms.

Key to this is the idea that businesses have the capacity and willingness to regulate themselves. In this sense, there is an intimate, if often obscured, connection between the promotion of a neo-liberal model of regulation and the potential for CSR.

The HSE's own 'version' of social responsibility is entirely consistent with such claims—summed up in the phrase 'win-win'. As HSE Deputy Director General Jonathan Rees has noted, '[s]ensible health and safety management is a key part of effective business management', so that there is the need to recognise and publicise 'the vital contribution that such an approach can have on the performance of businesses as well as on employees' welfare: a true win-win' (HSE 2004). This position is set out in its longstanding and influential document *Successful Health and Safety Management* (HSE 1997) and in a much more recent document, *Leading Health and Safety at Work* (IOD and HSE 2009). Both rely upon highly questionable and flawed arguments, all of which rest on the idea that strong leadership ensures CSR (see James and Walters 1999: ch 2; Davis 2004: chs 2 and 9).

This faith in the social responsibility of business—and in particular of business leaders—continues to dominate both the government and the HSE's regulatory philosophy. It is significant that the HSE document cited above, *Leading Health and Safety at Work*, acted as the key bulwark against the campaign to legislate for positive health and safety obligations on directors (CCA 2007). It is also significant that this document was jointly authored by the HSE and the Institute of Directors (IOD). That said, this faith in voluntarism flies in the face of evidence regarding 'what works'. Thus, in a comprehensive review of the research evidence on what actually generates improved performance in OHS, Davis found that:

> Whilst the weight of international research supports the proposition that legislation, backed by credible enforcement, is the primary driver of corporate commitment to OHS, a number of studies dealing specifically with UK businesses provide confirmatory evidence. These studies have found first, that compliance with the law is the most commonly cited reason for organisations initiating changes to improve OHS management, and that this is true for all sizes of organisations, and second, that the introduction of regulations are generally associated with reported changes in employer practice. (Davis 2004: 21)

For Davis, in her exhaustive meta-review of studies of the levers to compliance with safety law, the only factors consistently identified by UK research to prompt health and safety improvements were the fear of loss of corporate credibility and the need to comply with health and safety legislation.

The empirical inadequacy of claims for CSR in the context of compliance with health and safety law can be highlighted in another quite distinct way: via corporate compliance with the most minimal legal obligation, namely to report a notifiable incident (an injury or 'near-miss') to the HSE under the RIDDOR regulation (the Reporting of Injuries, Diseases and

Dangerous Occurrences Regulations 1995). RIDDOR is the legal requirement according to which duty-holders must report fatalities, major injuries, injuries which are not 'major' but result in over three days away from work, work-related diseases and dangerous occurrences. A Better Regulation Executive and National Audit Office report on the work of the HSE (BRE/NAO 2008) bemoaned the low levels of RIDDOR reporting, a criticism reiterated by the House of Commons Work and Pensions Committee later the same year, when it noted that, 'RIDDOR is not fulfilling its role and HSE is failing in its duties to enforce obligations under the regulations. We call on HSE to urgently address the shortcomings in its data collection' (HOCWPC 2008: 94). It is important here to emphasise that these 'shortcomings' involve widespread violation of a legal requirement placed upon duty-holders, and a fairly minimal one at that. Noting that reporting rates are estimated to vary between 30 and 50 per cent, the BRE/NAO 2008 report interestingly raised this issue of non-compliance, both in terms of the reasons for businesses failing to report, and also in terms of the unequal conditions of competition that such under-reporting creates:

> There is currently a severe underreporting of incidents by businesses under RIDDOR ... This may suggest that the rare number of prosecutions taken for non-reporting has resulted in there being little incentive to report. Businesses expressed the view that firms tend to weigh the risks of reporting against not reporting and frequently decide it is not in the business's interest to report an incident, or they may downplay the seriousness of an incident. As a result, the RIDDOR system is currently more burdensome for those businesses that seek to be fully compliant. (BRE/NAO 2008: 31)

Such levels of basic non-compliance with a minimal legal requirement are not just widespread—they are persistent. It has long been known that significant numbers of reportable injuries and incidences of ill-health are not, in fact, reported. The HSE itself documents the level of this: for example, while there were 131,895 non-fatal injuries to employees reported under RIDDOR in 2008/09 (502.2 per 100,000 employees), the 2009 Labour Force Survey found 246,000 reportable injuries occurred in the same year (at 870 per 100,000 workers) (Tombs and Whyte 2010: 44). Indeed, it is well documented that each category of *non-fatal* injury data maintained under RIDDOR is subject to significant under-reporting (ibid). Although this was highlighted almost 40 years ago by the Robens Committee (Robens 1972: 135 and ch 15) and despite various attempts to improve reporting levels, rates of mandatory reporting have recently been noted as being, again, in decline (Daniels and Marlow 2005). They remain low, perhaps even as low as 30 per cent (Davies, Kemp and Frostick 2007). It is worth pausing to note the significance of the persistence of significant levels of under-reporting—at best half of reportable incidents are actually being reported. For, while this level of under-reporting is frequently noted, it is so well known that it is simply acknowledged, in passing, as if it is, somehow, *normalised*. Therefore, it is worth emphasising here that such levels of under-reporting in fact represent widespread and persistent failures of employers to meet even the most minimal legal requirement, and indeed one which in itself carries with it no cost implications. Thus, on this basis alone, we should be highly sceptical of the likelihood of the socially responsible corporation adequately self-regulating in terms of safety and health law: how can businesses which have failed, over a sustained period, and in spite of a range of regulatory initiatives, even to meet the most basic minimal requirement—that is, to report occupational injury, disease and 'near-misses'—seriously be considered as actually or potentially socially responsible?

There is, of course, voluminous literature on the potential, weaknesses and contradictions of CSR claims, which we do not intend to attempt to review here. Suffice to say, notwithstanding the evidence-base, faith in CSR in general, and in responsible business leadership in particular, has been the basis for—and has facilitated—the drift towards market-based regulatory strategies described in this chapter. It is with a particularly decisive moment in this shift towards market-based regulation that the remainder of this chapter is concerned.

'BETTER' REGULATION

New Labour, undaunted by the lack of any evidence base in support of the potential for CSR, worked hard during 13 years in office to institutionalise and extend the previous governments' deregulation strategies. Elsewhere we have detailed how this was achieved, and how the ground was prepared for perhaps the most far-reaching of all re-regulation initiatives, the Hampton Review and the report it generated (Tombs and Whyte 2010).

In 2004, Gordon Brown, then Chancellor of the Exchequer, appointed the then Chairman of J Sainsbury, Philip Hampton, to lead a wholesale review of business regulation. Hampton was not an uncontroversial appointment. He had been British Gas Group's Financial Director at the time one of the Group's subsidiaries, Transco, caused a gas explosion in Larkhall that killed a family of four. Transco was later fined a record £15 million. The presiding judge noted Transco's 'serious maintenance failure', signalling the centrality of a cost-cutting strategy in the aetiology of the incident. Hampton had also been Finance Director of Lloyds TSB during the period that the Bank was embroiled in a 'stripping' scheme in which it falsified its records to mask transactions from Iranian and Sudanese banking clients in violation of US law. The company agreed to a deferred prosecution settlement with the New York District Attorney's Office (NYDA Office 2009). This settlement cost Lloyds $350 million in fines and forfeiture.

Hampton's report sought to reconstruct the 'regulatory landscape' (Hampton 2005: 76). Having been charged with considering 'the scope for reducing administrative burdens on business by promoting more efficient approaches to regulatory inspection and enforcement without reducing regulatory outcomes', the report, *Reducing Administrative Burdens: Effective Inspection and Enforcement* (Hampton Report), called for more focused inspections, greater emphasis on advice and education and, in general, for removing the 'burden' of inspection from most premises. Most fundamentally, inspections were to be cut by a third across the board, equating to one million fewer inspections. Regulators were to make much more 'use of advice' to business. The principles upon which his proposed system of 'light touch' regulation were to be based were set out as follows:

— Regulators, and the regulatory system as a whole, should use comprehensive risk assessment to concentrate resources on the areas that need them most
— No inspection should take place without a reason
— Regulators should provide authoritative, accessible advice easily and cheaply
— All regulations should be written so that they are easily understood, easily implemented, and easily enforced, and all interested parties should be consulted when they are being drafted
— Businesses should not have to give unnecessary information or give the same piece of information twice
— The few businesses that persistently break regulations should be identified quickly, and face proportionate and meaningful sanctions
— Regulators should recognise that a key element of their activity will be to allow, or even encourage, economic progress and only to intervene when there is a clear case for protection
— Regulators should be accountable for the efficiency and effectiveness of their activities, while remaining independent in the decisions they take
— Regulators should be of the right size and scope, and no new regulator should be created where an existing one can do the work
— When new policies are being developed, explicit consideration should be given to how they can be enforced using existing systems and data to minimise the administrative burden imposed. (ibid: 7)

These proposals were implemented in the Legislative and Regulatory Reform Act in November 2006. The press release accompanying the Act pronounced its aim to 'cut the burden of regulation and embed a light-touch, risk-based approach to regulation ... to improve our status as one of the world's most attractive places to do business' (Cabinet Office 2006). Gordon Brown heralded 'a new, risk-based approach to regulation to break down barriers holding enterprise back'; the 'new' model will entail 'no unjustifiable inspection, form-filling or requirement for information. Not just a light but a limited touch. Instead of routine regulation trying to cover all, the risk based approach targets the necessary few'. According to Brown, this new approach would 'help move us a million miles away from the old belief that business, unregulated, will invariably act irresponsibly' (Brown 2005).

This risk-based approach was developed in the Hampton Report. It had to resolve the tension between the demand to reduce significantly inspectorial scrutiny of companies and the ongoing need to secure compliance with law. It did so through placing a concept of social responsibility at the heart of a somewhat tortuous argument. First, regulatory resources are limited, and indeed are likely to be limited further; because enforcement strategies are resource intensive, regulatory agencies can no longer be expected to maintain current levels of inspection and enforcement. Second, reduced inspection and enforcement do not necessarily lead to less effective regulation; regulation may indeed become *more effective* under conditions of reduced resources. Then, thirdly, this can be achieved if a series of compliance levers is used to secure self-regulated compliance: that is, businesses are likely to be encouraged to act responsibly through more collaborative, responsive forms of regulation.

Moreover, Hampton links, indeed underpins, this line of argument for a further reduction of regulatory activity upon a set of technical claims. Here, his argument turns to what is now loosely referred to as a 'risk-based' approach. This approach relies upon the claim that the most likely offenders can be clearly identified through a series of knowable variables that allow the likelihood of offending to be predicted. In this argument, Hampton severs 'reactive' regulatory activity from 'risk-based' regulation. But therein lies a major contradiction. The Hampton Report's first recommendation is that 'all regulatory activity should be on the basis of a clear, comprehensive risk assessment' which should be based upon 'past performance and potential future risk'. It is conceded at this point that regulation should include 'a small element of random inspection' (Hampton 2005: 33)—even if Hampton tellingly declined to indicate the level of inspection that might be credible (Vickers 2008: 226). Thus, while risk-based regulation is often narrowly cast as a method whereby scarce inspection resources are allocated, it has a wider and increasingly significant impact upon regulators: it helps regulators to 'structure choices across a range of different types of intervention activities, including education and advice' (Black 2010: 186). In other words, the complex and often convoluted logic of risk-based regulation provides a rationale for a shift towards more consensus- or compliance-based strategies which appeal to the cooperation and goodwill of business.

The aim of the risk assessment strategy set out in the Hampton Report is to withdraw regulatory scrutiny from those who had 'earned' their 'autonomy'. Such assumptions about the targets of regulation enable the Hampton Report to endorse enthusiastically twin-track regulation, whereby regulatory interventions are 'targeted at the worst offenders'. But this begs a rather fundamental question: how might the past performance of businesses central to risk calculus be measured in a system where, as we shall see, there is a diminishing chance of the business having been inspected? Hampton's strategy becomes self-defeating. It seeks a reduction in the types of activity most likely to gather useful data for targeted intervention, so that regulation can be based upon targeted intervention.

By accepting the status quo of minimal regulatory resources, the Hampton Report is pushed towards new 'magic bullet' solutions that avoid the most awkward questions of whether regulatory agencies could ever adequately do the job with which they are charged. Indeed, it is rather curious that across its 140 pages of text and seven pages of references that the Hampton Report failed to note the recommendation of the Department for Work and Pensions Select Committee on the work of the HSE that had been reported just a year earlier, namely that the numbers of field inspectors should be doubled (HOCWPC 2008: recommendation 9). This is discussed further below.

CHALLENGING BETTER REGULATION

We now wish to examine some of these claims for better (responsive, smart, targeted, and so on) regulation in the context of HSE strategy and policy, as well as parliamentary commentaries upon these, alongside consideration of both published data and data obtained through a series of Freedom of Information requests to chart the ways in which regulatory enforcement has been repositioned to accommodate neo-liberal, business-friendly values. We do not present these critical qualitative or quantitative analyses in any detail here (see Tombs and Whyte 2010), but we do use these data to raise a series of challenges for advocates of 'better' regulation.

Regulatory Resources

In 2004, the Health and Safety Commission (HSC) formally launched its *Strategy for Workplace Health and Safety in Great Britain to 2010 and Beyond* (HSC 2004). In many respects this was a rather bland document which downplayed formal enforcement, dedicating just two paragraphs of its 17 pages to this issue. This document proved a key index of what appeared to be the emergence of a shift in HSE enforcement practice.

Prospect, the trade union for HSE staff, saw the *Strategy* as framed by a steady decline in funding for the HSE—noting shifts in priorities were undermining the need for a credible presence 'on the beat' (Prospect 2004: para 14). The ongoing underfunding of the HSE, deepened by a further decline in, and a looming crisis of, enforcement was the primary concern of a House of Commons Work and Pensions Select Committee inquiry into *The Work of the Health and Safety Commission and Executive*. Its key findings included a round criticism of the HSE's enforcement strategy:

> The evidence supports the view that it is inspection, backed by enforcement, that is most effective in motivating duty holders to comply with their responsibilities under health and safety law. We therefore recommend that the HSE should not proceed with the proposal to shift resources from inspection and enforcement to fund an increase in education, information and advice. (HOCWPC 2004: para 142)

The Select Committee supported a proposal from Prospect that the number of inspectors in the HSE's Field Operations Directorate should be doubled, and recommended that substantial additional resources were needed to fund this and to reverse the 'low level of incidents investigated and at the low level of proactive inspections' (ibid: 107). Of crucial importance is that this issue was raised at the Select Committee only in evidence presented by Prospect, by other trade unions, by the Hazards Campaign and by the Centre for Corporate Accountability (CCA). The HSE's senior management, in its own evidence, was silent on the issue. Then, in 2007, an officer of the union Prospect again raised the issue of resources, in the starkest possible form, claiming that a lack of resources meant that the HSE 'cannot meet its public expectations to advise, inspect and enforce workplace health and safety'.[1] Still the problem of resourcing the work that the HSE was charged with continued to be either ignored or denied by senior management in the HSE.

Whilst almost all observers of HSE activity—including inspectors themselves—have long argued that the HSE is under-resourced, the HSE's senior management has in fact adopted a very different position. Thus, for example, in early 2010, Rory O'Neill, Editor of Hazards Magazine, followed up a report of a speech in which Geoffrey Podger, the HSE's Chief Executive, appeared to break with recent HSE practice in a reference to the fact that the HSE was 'running out of people'. The HSE's press office immediately denied that the statement referred to a staffing shortfall in the Executive.[2] This state of denial by which the HSE appears to find itself paralysed appears to be a relatively recent phenomenon. In 2003, Bill Callaghan, as then Chair of the HSC, had 'assured the unions that he would make the most compelling case for resources but that whatever the eventual

---

[1] Mike Macdonald, negotiations officer with Prospect, cited at www.hazards.org/enforcement/whodoeshseprotect.htm.

[2] Private communication with R O'Neill, received by Steve Tombs on 2 February 2010.

settlement, HSE would still need to prioritise its activities' (HSC 2003: para 8.1). This statement, made 9 years ago, was to be the last clear argument for more resources from a senior HSE figure. In recent years, senior management at the HSE have publicly resisted calling for extra resources—even when they have been explicitly invited to do so.

Of course, for any organisation, global person numbers and overall levels of financial resource are only part of the story. What matters is what the organisation does. A key criterion in terms of judging the adequacy of resources is how these are utilised, and this is a judgement that in turn reflects any organisation's strategic and operational priorities. At the same time, however, this needs to be considered in the light of the overall resource. Thus, the last decade saw a long debate about the balance between proactive work (often cast as preventative) and investigative (often cast in terms of accountability) work; that is, about the need to balance legal and moral accountability with prevention of future harm, and about the trends in levels of various forms of enforcement activity—a debate which has at times become very heated.

A further House of Commons Work and Pensions Select Committee which met in 2008 highlighted a problem of declining inspection and enforcement that had by then become apparent. Whilst the Committee was broadly supportive of the Hampton Report and the HSE's efforts in reducing the 'administrative burden on businesses' (HOCWPC 2008: 88), at the same time it concluded that the HSE should 'increase its levels of inspection, which we believe will have a significant impact on compliance with health and safety legislation', accepting that this would require 'an increase in the numbers of front-line inspectors' (ibid: 95). However, on this point, the Committee noted the DWP and the HSE's 'obfuscation' and 'total lack of clarity in financial information supplied' (ibid: 95–96), so that the possibility of funding such an increase could not at that point be determined.

Beyond the specific points raised by this detail, three key points need to be emphasised here. First, those doing the on-the-ground enforcement too frequently find their views ignored, and have at times expressed frustration at their seeming increasing inability to do the job they signed up to do; this is one factor contributing to the oft-cited low morale amongst HSE staff in general and inspectors in particular. Second, the distinctions between accountability and prevention are ultimately false ones—all enforcement activity is about prevention, even if it were to seek to achieve this through the most punitive forms of deterrence. Third, there comes a point at which, whatever balances are struck *within* existing resources, however these resources are targeted, it must be apparent to all that as an organisation the HSE does not have adequate resources to do its job, so that the tenacious refusal of its senior management to accept this can only be understood as a measure of the long-term success that neo-liberal ideas and their ideologues, and more specifically 'better' regulation and 'risk-based' strategies, have achieved in securing hegemony in thinking in regulation policy.

Risk-based Targeting

During the course of the last decade, a series of initiatives within the HSE sought to place targeting on a more formalised risk-based model. However, this strategy in effect ushered in earned autonomy by the back door, whilst reducing the discretion that inspection teams have locally on the numbers of inspections undertaken. In 2005, the HSE had launched its Business Plan for 2005–06 and 2007–08 (HSE 2005), central to which was its 'Fit3'—'Fit for Work, Fit for Life, Fit for Tomorrow'—Strategic Delivery Programme, essentially a data gathering process designed to allow the HSE to 'be much more effective in targeting its services to businesses' and to 'have much greater awareness of the kinds of issues businesses face when tackling health and safety issues' (HSE nd). The HSE's Fine Tuning Review, a 'targeting and intelligence project', commenced in September 2006 subsequently 'identified that our current approach to targeting resources is not as good as it needs to be to maximise the impact we expect from our planned proactive activities'(Mallagh 2008: para 4). By 2009, Fit3 had been formally succeeded by a 'segmentation' framework. Fit3 was to provide one focus of a further House of Commons Work and Pensions Inquiry into the work of the HSE, in 2007/08, and this prompted the Committee to conclude that, 'the programme, whilst designed to create an efficient, target-based approach to inspection, is in fact limiting the ability of inspectors to apply their professional judgment on a site by site basis' (HOCWPC 2008: para 120).

The cumulative effect of those efforts has been to reduce further the discretion that inspection teams have on the numbers of inspections undertaken. This targeting strategy is therefore likely to result in 'fewer, but longer and deeper, inspections'.[3] By December 2007, the HSE had formally adopted a position statement on rogue businesses, central to the Hampton Report—that is, those 'persistent offenders' which 'deliberately flout the law and undercut honest business' (Hughes 2007: 6)—to be identified through better intelligence. The flip side of targeting rogues, of course, is the assumption that most businesses can be left, safely, with minimal or no intervention. Thus we find that, by 2008/09, the Field Operations Directorate—the division of HSE which undertakes the bulk of its inspections undertook less than a third of the inspections recorded in 1999/00. In terms of the absolute data, in 1999/00, there were 75,272 such records, compared with 23,004 in 2008/09—so the total number of inspections had fallen by over *two-thirds*. This long term trend is due, according to the HSE, to changes in 'strategies, intervention targeting, internal procedures, guidance and operational information systems'.[4] In particular, the HSE notes

---

[3] *Freedom of Information Request Reference No, p2010020046, 12 April 2010*, page 8 of 8 246.

[4] *Freedom of Information Request Reference No, p2010020046, 12 April 2010*, page 7 of 8.

that as the method of undertaking and recording inspections changed from 2004/05, then data before and after this change are not strictly compatible. However, if we break the period at 2005/06 when the method of recording changed, we still find that: between 1999/00 and 2004/05, inspection records fell by 39 per cent and between 2005/06 and 2008/09 inspection records fell by 26 per cent. In other words, whatever method of recording, whatever the nature of the inspection, the downward trend has continued apace throughout the decade. Even at the end of this period, however, the HSE remained firmly committed to its targeted approach: thus its most recent Business Plan commits it to 'continue with a targeted programme of prevention through inspection' (HSE 2010).

The very premise upon which this 'strategy' was based has been questioned in a Better Regulation Executive and National Audit Office report (BRE/NAO 2008). The report rated the HSE 'highly' in terms of its working within the 'Hampton principles and Macrory characteristics', endorsing the fact that it 'works well with business, including recognising the need to minimise burdens on business' (2008: 5, 12). However, this assessment of the HSE's enforcement activities revealed the fundamental contradiction at the heart of a targeting strategy. The report's central criticism of HSE practice—the first of five 'issues to be addressed'—was the fact that the HSE needed to make 'better use of intelligence' 'in order to improve its targeting of business' (ibid: 7). Now, within the terms of a targeting approach to inspection and enforcement, this is clearly perfectly logical, a crucial requirement. That said, the reasons revealed for the intelligence deficit are significant. The conclusions on the weaknesses in the intelligence underpinning targeted intervention were threefold.

First, the report noted the failure of many businesses even to register their existence with the HSE, leaving the regulator to expend resources even trying to identify premises before their risk could be assessed—yet what is not mentioned is that the requirement to register is a legal one. So what we have here is a targeting strategy, premised on the assumption (above) that most businesses are responsible, undermined by the fact that many business premises remain unregistered—that is, are violating the law. Second, and echoing Prospect's critique of the initiative, the report found that the Fit3 strategy for targeting was being undermined by the focus on high-risk issues, rather than duty-holders' 'past performance and other factors', which it stated were inadequately taken into account (ibid: 21). This aspect of the deficit was attributed to the relative lack of inspections (ibid: 23). Third, the report bemoaned the level of RIDDOR reporting, an issue discussed above. More generally, in the context of these critical comments, the low and declining absolute number of inspections—however 'deep' these may now be—creates a contradiction at the heart of the HSE's strategy that cannot be resolved. Further, as we shall see, absolutely low and rapidly declining levels of investigation into reported incidents represent an inexcusable failure to use 'hard won' data.

Trends in Formal Enforcement Activity

Given the HSE's own framing of its role—its focus upon prevention, the relationships it aims to foster with duty-holders to encourage compliance, its commitment to information and intelligence gathering—then no matter how far the strategy moves towards a risk-based strategy, proactive and preventative inspections must remain central to its work. This much is confirmed in the role that regulatory contacts play in the judgements to be made by inspectors which are central to both its Enforcement Policy Statement and its determination of 'duty-holder factors' which underpin the 'initial enforcement expectation' within its Enforcement Management Model (HSE 2005).

Enforcement action tends to be prompted by two distinct triggers. One is routine inspection work—that is, the majority of cases that prompt an enforcement response come to the attention of the HSE in the course of routine inspection and monitoring work. The other main context in which formal enforcement is prompted follows RIDDOR reports—even though, as we noted above, violation of this legal requirement is both widespread and persistent. RIDDOR reports contribute to a relatively small proportion of enforcement action: typically between a quarter and a third of prosecutions, and between five and seven per cent of enforcement notices, result from such reports. Most enforcement action results from routine inspection. However, while accounting for a minority of enforcement activity, an analysis of HSE enforcement activity in relation to RIDDOR reports allows us to conduct a focussed consideration of the type of regulatory system envisaged in 'better regulation' policy, and more specifically in the Hampton Report, since it offers an opportunity to assess the HSE's enforcement activities on the strategic grounds upon which they are generally justified. Because businesses are legally obliged to submit RIDDOR reports to the HSE, the submission of those reports constitutes an activity that places the onus upon the regulated party to comply 'proactively'. An analysis that focuses upon RIDDOR reports therefore allows us to analyse the type of regulatory activity that might be premised upon something more closely approximating self-regulation.

Investigations are a key element of enforcement activity. Certainly they are the basis upon which any accountability can be derived: only by having investigated the circumstances of any incident can the HSE reach any sensible determination of what kind of action, if any, ranging from the provision of advice through to prosecution, is appropriate in the light of any specific incident. However, *post-hoc* accountability is not the only—or perhaps even the most important—rationale for investigations. As the CCA noted in its evidence to a Select Committee inquiry, investigations have a significant preventative role, that is:

> An important part of any investigation must be to rectify the circumstances that resulted in the harm (or, in the case of a dangerous occurrence, that resulted in the risk of harm) occurring in the first place. At the very least an investigation should ensure that any future risk of a similar incident taking place is very low. The absence of an investigation will mean that a risk of a repeat incident will continue to exist. (CCA 2004)

Over the past decade, investigations of RIDDOR reports have fallen at a much steeper rate than the reports themselves. While there was a decline in RIDDOR reports to the HSE of 23 per cent between 1999/00 and 2008/09,[5] we find during this period that the *proportion* of reports investigated since 1999/2000 has halved. In total, if we look at those RIDDOR reported incidents that are investigated by the HSE, we find that between 1999/00 and 2008/09, there was a 63 per cent decline in numbers of HSE investigations; this is a decline from 11,462 in 1999/00 to 4,272 in 2008/09.

This sharp decline is replicated in further detail in the data on investigation *type*. The HSE continues to investigate 100 per cent of (the limited subset of) employee fatalities reported to it, a constant over the past decade. However, during that decade, we also find that investigations of reported major injuries declined by 55 per cent; of over-three-day injuries by 83 per cent; and of dangerous occurrences by 37 per cent since 1999/2000. By 2008/09, less than one per cent of over-three-day injuries that were reported to the HSE were actually investigated. Less than one in 10 (eight per cent) of reported major injuries were actually investigated. In 2008/09, the HSE did *not* investigate the following: 66 per cent of amputations; 84 per cent of major fractures; 96 per cent of major dislocations; 84 per cent of major concussions and internal injuries; 90 per cent of major lacerations and open wounds; 83 per cent of major contusions; 75 per cent of major burns; and 66 per cent of major poisonings and gassings.

There are two issues we would wish to raise in relation to the significance of such high levels of under-investigation. First, in the case of fatalities and major injuries, one might reasonably expect particular consideration to be given to investigation in order to detect any safety system defects which either caused or contributed to loss of life or major injury. Indeed many specific categories of major injuries noted above correspond very closely

---

[5] Data on RIDDOR reports in this and subsequent tables commence from 1999/2000, not 1997/98 as originally requested of the HSE. The statistical unit noted that 'Data on RIDDOR reports ... are not provided for 1997/98 to 1998/99 as we only hold a partial dataset for the HSE figures for these years due to the transition from our older operational recording systems to their successor' (Freedom of Information Request Reference No p2010020046).

to categories included in the HSE's incident selection criteria—those which determine the incidents, injuries and cases of illness that the HSE inspectors should investigate. Many of those categories are barely investigated, indicating that the HSE currently cannot get close to fulfilling its own performance standards. This is hardly a basis for sound intelligence about offending behaviour. Second, in relation to over-three-day injuries, whilst not to dismiss the effects of any injury, by definition these more minor injuries offer important opportunities for learning in terms of defects in or violations arising out of safety and health systems, and thus, in the HSE's own preventative terms, should form potentially crucial data for the prevention of future, more serious, harm. This point can be made even more strongly, of course, with respect to 'dangerous occurrences'; one of a series of categories of incident defined as where something happens which does not result in a reportable injury, but which clearly could have done. As near misses, these should be treated as key opportunities for learning. These points hold especially in the light of the 'intelligence' deficit to which so many commentators on the HSE's targeting efforts have pointed. In the absence of either robust historic intelligence or the ability to maintain existing levels of intelligence regarding safety and health performance as a function of a dwindling proactive inspectorial resource, it is difficult to see how a risk-based model or any coherent programme of targeted inspections/interventions could be sustained.

If we now shift from HSE inspection and investigation to other formal enforcement action, we again find a decline during the decade under examination. So, on an analysis of the numbers of notices imposed in response to breaches between 1999/2000 and 2008/09, we find a 29 per cent fall in the number of all types of enforcement notice issued over the past decade. There was a 30 per cent fall in improvement notices and 26 per cent fall in prohibition notices. If we examine the data a little more carefully, we can see that the most dramatic fall occurred during the period which *preceded* Hampton, so from their peak during this period, in 2002/03, improvement notices fell by 40 per cent to 2008/09 and prohibition notices fell by 37 per cent. If there were fewer inspections, investigations and notices during the period we might expect to find correspondingly fewer prosecutions. The data confirm that this is indeed the case; between 1999/2000 and 2008/09, HSE prosecutions fell by 48 per cent. This decline also applies to those incidents which we might expect to be most likely to result in prosecution—fatal injuries to workers. Further examination of the data shows that between 1999/2000 and 2006/07 the number of worker deaths that resulted in prosecution by the HSE fell by 39 per cent; from 129 to 79.

All of the above data are consistent with the earlier analyses of inspection and investigation trends in the sense that the period of the most acute decline in the use of enforcement notices and prosecutions is uniformly either between 2001/02 and 2005/06 or between 2002/03 and 2005/06.

This is a period in which already declining levels of enforcement and investigation were forced even lower by the HSC's effort in anticipating the Hampton agenda. Further, and to be clear, this is a period in which responsive regulation has been formally institutionalised. Such data thereby raise the question of whether the enforcement threat that remains after this period of decline is one which is 'credible'. Of course, in some respects this is an unanswerable question, since what is credible is subjective. But two points remain. First, in empirical terms, the levels of decline in enforcement action, coupled with (indeed based upon) similarly declining levels of inspection and investigation, at least point to a diminishing level of credibility. Second, these data undermine the conceptual case for a functioning system based upon the regulatory pyramid. How can one identify a 'credible' threat of enforcement following a collapse in enforcement on this scale, that is, where, over a decade, inspections have fallen by over a third, investigations of reported incidents at work have fallen by a third, and prosecutions have virtually halved? More generally, this evidence mounts a challenge to the hegemony of thinking that assumes a 'credible' threat of enforcement can be sustained under conditions of neo-liberalism. On the contrary, 'better regulation' policies over the past decade or so have quickened the process of institutionalising self-regulation based upon a crude model of CSR.

CONCLUSION

In this chapter we have sought, through a conceptual critique of the construction of the idea of better regulation, as well as an empirical examination of what this has meant in practice in the context of a specific regulator, to address a concrete instance of how state regulation is vulnerable to antagonistic, neo-liberal, business-friendly 'reform'. Implicit within this argument, then, is an assumption regarding the *need for* state regulation. Thus our critique of trends in enforcement is rooted in a claim that a real (credible) threat of enforcement remains the bedrock of *state* regulatory systems. Such a claim, which is, in fact, supported by the empirical literature (eg Davies 2004) is invariably dismissed as idealistic or anachronistic, or is simply ignored in much contemporary literature on regulatory enforcement.

The claims underpinning our argument in this chapter are commonly misread as a defence of enforcement alone as a credible regulatory strategy (eg Braithwaite 2010) through resorting to simplified, binary terms: self-regulation *versus* strict enforcement, or consensus *versus* conflict 'approaches'. This is, of course, a highly unsatisfactory way to conduct a debate about regulation, or indeed about the nature of any state activity. Such a binary approach to the debate can lead nowhere, simply because the question about regulation is never an either/or choice. From our perspective, regulation is a complex process of mediation, one that struggles to negotiate a path between competing social forces. In advanced capitalist societies it is a process which generally seeks to translate class conflict into the language and practice of liberal-democracy. Enforcement, or any other 'reactive' or 'proactive' regulatory activity, has precisely this purpose: it is a means of translating fundamental social conflict into something that can be managed by the state. There can be no illusions about this; no reification of one form of regulatory activity above another as some kind of magic bullet which can tame or sanitise business. But this does not mean that different regulatory strategies cannot have very different material and symbolic significances: regulation is not only shaped by, but *also plays a role in shaping*, the balance of social forces. There is always something to struggle for through regulatory agencies, no matter how captured or emasculated they appear to be by a particular interest or set of interests.

In the specific context of health and safety, research evidence shows that the safest workplaces are those workplaces that have strong trade union representation (James and Walters 2002; Reilly et al 1995; Walters et al 2005). This suggests that the relative strength of workers in the workplace is the key factor in the amelioration of harm to which they may be exposed, often illegally. But to accept this point does not equate to the work of external inspectorates being relatively insignificant. In fact, we might more usefully view collective organisation at the level of the workplace and external regulation as being mutually supportive; as Dickens (1999) has argued, there can be a positive synergy and mutual reinforcement between legal and social regulation. It is a commonplace to note that the lack of law enforcement sends a message to employers that they might endanger workers' lives and livelihoods with greater impunity, but it is less generally noted that this message is also heard by workers and their representatives, if not even more decisively.

If legal standards are by no means the only sets of standards that workers demand, to assert a legal *minima* of standards remains crucial, not least in working environments that are increasingly casualised. It is not only the case that workers at plants or in sectors where safety crimes occur are disproportionately likely to be casualised, sub-contracted and/or increasingly migrant workforces, (Tombs and Whyte 2007; Burnett and Whyte 2010) but it is also the case that those environments are less scrutinised. Finally, workers are disempowered when there is little prospect of the violations of law against them being recognised or taken seriously. In short, the undermining of enforcement strategies undermines the ability of workers to demand that the law is enforced by their employers.

We are not nostalgic in this respect. There has never been a time when workers have been empowered significantly by the regulator. However, as part of the regulatory process, workers' demands for improvements in their working conditions are also demands upon the regulator to enforce the laws that protect them. Just as demands upon management for improvements in working conditions, or demands on government for working hours restrictions, constitute a process of regulation, so do demands upon regulators to enforce the law constitute part of the process of regulation. Where businesses are successful in minimising enforcement, then this is also part of the regulatory process. We are not unrealistic about the rule and role of law. Regulation in capitalist societies always has been one set of mechanisms in the struggle to achieve a 'viable class society' (Carson 1979, 1980). Regulatory systems give shape to the type of class society in which we live. But that is precisely why debates about law enforcement remain paramount, especially in an age in which we have experienced the creeping institutionalisation of impunity for killing and injuring workers.

BIBLIOGRAPHY

Black, J (2010) 'Risk-based Regulation: Choices, Practices and Lessons Being Learnt' in G Bounds and N Malyshev (eds), *Risk and Regulation Policy. Improving the Governance of Risk* (Paris, OECD).

Braithwaite, J (2010) 'Foreword', in Quirk, H, Seddon, T and Smith, G (eds) *Regulation and Criminal Justice: Innovations in Policy and Research* (Cambridge, Cambridge University Press).

BRE/NAO (Better Regulation Executive/National Audit Office) (2008) *Effective Inspection and Enforcement: Implementing the Hampton Vision in the Health and Safety Executive* (London, Better Regulation Executive).

Brown, G (2005) 'A Plan to Lighten the Regulatory Burden on Business', *Financial Times*, 23 May.

Burnett, J and Whyte, D (2010) *The Wages of Fear: Risk, Safety and Undocumented Work* (Leeds and Liverpool Positive Action for Refugees and Asylum Seekers and University of Liverpool).

Cabinet Office (2006) 'New Bill to Enable Delivery of Swift and Efficient Regulatory Reform to Cut Red Tape—Jim Murphy' Cabinet Office News Release, *12 January (London, Cabinet Office Press Office)*, www.egovmonitor.com/node/4164.

Carson, WG (1979) 'The Conventionalization of Early Factory Crime' 7 *International Journal of the Sociology of Law*.

—— (1980) 'Early Factory Inspectors and the Viable Class Society—A Rejoinder' 8 *International Journal of the Sociology of Law*.

—— (1985) 'Hostages to History: Some Aspects of the Occupational Health and Safety Debate in Historical Perspective' in W Creighton and N Cunningham (eds), *The Industrial Relations of Health and Safety* (London, Croom Helm).

CCA (2004) *Memorandum Submitted by the Centre for Corporate Accountability to the Select Committee on Work and Pensions* (February) (London, CCA/UCATT).

—— (2007) *Bringing Justice to the Boardroom. The Case against Voluntary Guidance and in Favour of a Change in the Law to Impose Safety Duties on Directors* (London, CCA/UCATT).

Daniels, C and Marlow, P (2005) *Literature Review on the Reporting of Workplace Injury Trends*, HSL/2005/36 (Buxton, Health and Safety Laboratory).

Davis, C (2004) *Making Companies Safe: What Works?* (London, CCA).

Davies, J, Kemp, G and Frostick, S (2007) *An Investigation of Reporting of Work-place Accidents under RIDDOR using the Merseyside Accident Information Model,* Research Report RR528 (Norwich, HSE Books).

Dickens, L (1999) 'Beyond the Business Case: A Three-pronged Approach to Equality Action' 9 *Human Resource Management Journal* 9–19.

Hampton, P (2005) *Reducing Administrative Burdens: Effective Inspection and Enforcement* (London, HM Treasury/HMSO).

Hay, C and Watson, M (1998) 'The Discourse of Globalisation and the Logic of No Alternative: Rendering the Contingent Necessary in the Downsizing of New Labour's Aspirations for Government' in A Dobson and J Stanyer (eds), *Contemporary Political Studies 1998 Volume II* (Nottingham, Political Studies Association).

HSC (2003) *Minutes HSC/03/M12,* 9 December (London, Health and Safety Executive).

—— (2004) *Strategy for Workplace Health and Safety in Great Britain to 2010 and Beyond,* MISC643 C100 02/04 (London, HSE).

HSE (nd) *HSE Fit3 Survey,* www.hse.gov.uk/contact/faqs/fit3survey.htm.

—— (1997) *Successful Health and Safety Management, HS(G)65(revised)* (Sudbury, HSE Books).

—— (2004) HSE Launches New Business Benefits of Health and Safety Web Pages HSE Press Release E137:04—4 October, www.hse.gov.uk/press/2004/e04137.htm.

—— (2005) Enforcement Management Model Operational Version 3.0, www.hse.gov.uk/enforce/emm.pdf.

—— (2010) *Business Plan 2010/11* (London, HSE).

Holden, C (1999) 'Globalization. Social Exclusion and Labour's New Work Ethic' 19 *Critical Social Policy.*

HOCWPC (House of Commons Work and Pensions Committee) (2004) *The Work of the Health and Safety Commission and Executive. Fourth Report of Session 2003–04. Volume I. HC 456-I* (London, The Stationery Office).

—— (2008) *The Role of the Health and Safety Commission and the Health and Safety Executive in Regulating Workplace Health and Safety. Third Report of Session 2007–08. Volume I. HC 246* (London, The Stationery Office).

Hughes, P (2007) 'Tackling "Rogues"' *Health and Safety Executive Board Paper,* HSE/07/122, 5 December.

IOD and HSE (2009) *Leading Health and Safety at Work: Leadership Actions for Directors and Board Members,* INDG417, 09/09 (Sudbury, HSE Books).

James, P and Walters, D (2002) 'Worker Representation in Health and Safety: Options for Regulatory Reform' 33 *Industrial Relations Journal.*

—— (eds) (1999) *Regulating Health and Safety at Work: The Way Forward* (London, Institute of Employment Rights).

Mallagh, S (2008) 'Fine Tuning Review—Update on Better Segmenting our Market' *Health and Safety Executive Board Paper* HSE/B/08/12, 6 February.

NYDA Office (2009) New York District Attorney's Office New York County News Release, 9 January 2009, www.manhattanda.org/whatsnew/press/2009-01-09.shtml.

Osler, D (2002) *Labour Party Plc. New Labour as a Party of Business* (Edinburgh, Mainstream).

Prospect (2004) Memorandum Submitted by Prospect to the Select Committee on Work and Pensions, www.publications.parliament.uk/pa/cm200304/cmselect/cmworpen/456/456we32.htm.

Reilly, B, Pace, P and Hall, P (1995) 'Unions, Safety Committees and Workplace Injuries' 33 *British Journal of Industrial Relations*.

Robens (1972) *Safety and Health at Work, Report of the Committee 1970–72* Cmnd 5034 (London, HMSO).

Tombs, S and Whyte, D (2007) *Safety Crimes* (Collumpton, Willan).

—— (2010) *Regulatory Surrender: Death, Injury and the Non-enforcement of Law* (London, Institute of Employment Rights).

Tucker, E (1990) *Administering Danger in the Workplace: The Law and Politics of Occupational Health and Safety Legislation in Ontario*, 1850–1914 (Toronto, University of Toronto Press).

Vickers, I (2008) 'Better Regulation and Enterprise: The Case of Environmental Health Risk Regulation in Britain, 29 *Policy Studies*.

Walters, D, Nichols, T, Conner, J, Tasiran, A and Cam, S (2005) *The Role and Effectiveness of Safety Representatives in Influencing Workplace Health and Safety. HSE Research Report 363* (London, HSE Books).

6

Procurement and Fairness in the Workplace

CHRISTOPHER MCCRUDDEN

LOCATING PUBLIC PROCUREMENT

IT WILL BE useful to locate this chapter in the context of the book as a whole. Chapter two considered the growth of employment rights and protections and the main ways they are enforced, with a particular focus on the use of employment tribunals. Recurring criticism of this approach is that it leaves it too much up to individuals to enforce their rights, with questions about how effective individuals are in bringing about structural change through employment tribunals. This approach also appears to put employers into a reactive rather than a proactive mode of thinking.

As noted by Dickens in chapter one, as part of a possible rethink, additional or alternative methods of regulation might be considered. These might include, for example, a greater role for agency enforcement or monitoring of workplaces by a system of labour inspectorates, which might provide an alternative to reliance on an exclusively individualised, private-law model of enforcement. These methods of regulation might encourage employers to take action proactively to deliver fairer workplaces, adopting an organisational and structural focus, rather than focusing on the individual alone. It is at this point that the issue of using public procurement (the power that public sector organisations have to purchase works, goods, and services from the private sector) joins the discussion.

As we shall see in this chapter, public procurement is a potential lever for ensuring greater attention is given to establishing minimum standards and effective employment rights in the workplace. Public sector purchasers may encourage or require private sector employers from whom they buy to adopt a proactive approach to ensuring fairness at work, focusing on organisational changes that the employer could make. This chapter explores whether and how far public procurement does, or could, influence whether—and how much—employment rights have an impact on employer policy and practice. It considers what public procurement offers as a strategy and what factors help to determine its effectiveness.

Arguably, public procurement remains a relatively underused tool for persuading and assisting organisations to comply with statutory standards and deliver fairer workplaces in the United Kingdom, but there is nonetheless some experience of its use. In the context of ensuring equality rights at work, the recent experience of Northern Ireland is particularly apposite. This use of public procurement has recently been given renewed prominence in Britain with the expanded equality duties included in the Equality Act 2010 (McCrudden 2011a). This chapter concentrates, therefore, on how governments presently, or might in the future, use their purchasing power to try to ensure that private sector employers take action to ensure fairness in the workplace. In this context, 'government' includes the state in various forms, including central government, local government, and various public bodies. This is one strand of 'procurement linkages' (McCrudden 2007). The chapter draws on work the author carried out with the International Training Centre of the International Labour Organization, commissioned by the European Commission (ITC/ILO 2008).

DEFINING THE PARAMETERS OF THE CHAPTER

The focus of this chapter is whether and how far *public* procurement is, or could be, a factor that influences whether and how far employment rights have an impact on employer policy and practice towards delivering fairness in the workplace. The use of procurement by *private* sector organisations, that is, the use of their purchasing power to develop fair workplace policies by employers in their supply chain, could provide a similar lever (Deakin and Koukiadaki 2009, 2010). Attention has been given to this also in the context of private sector Corporate Social Responsibility initiatives (McCrudden 2007).

For the purposes of this chapter, the regulatory and legal regime for public sector purchasers is regarded as both a significant extra opportunity (in the case of the public sector equality duties, for example) and a significant additional constraint (in the case of European Union public procurement law), so an approach will be taken that focuses attention on the types of public bodies that fall within the scope of both sets of legal obligations. Nevertheless, the distinction between what is a 'public sector' purchaser and one that is a 'private sector' purchaser is not an easy one to draw, not least because there are several types of organisations that appear to straddle the divide.

The legality of procurement linkages has been a perennial question under EU law, and United Kingdom procurement law, which is largely based on EU law. The EC Treaty and directives dating from the 1970s initially displayed a relatively high level of tolerance towards the domestic use of procurement linkages. From the 1980s to the mid-1990s, however, these linkages received an increasingly hostile reception, particularly from the European Commission. From the mid-1990s, with the 'rediscovery' of linkages at the domestic level in the context of equality and labour issues, the development of 'green procurement', and the advent of Corporate Social Responsibility, EU law began to develop a modus vivendi. A central argument of McCrudden (2007) was that the EU was in the process of creating a way of operating between the economic and social dimensions of public procurement. The EU had progressively given greater domestic regulatory space for procurement linkages as a method of enforcement of (particularly EU) social and environmental policy. In particular, the approach of the European Court of Justice (ECJ) opened up considerable legal space for such linkages, paving the way for a revised legislative approach in 2004.

More recently, however, legal concerns have resurfaced. McCrudden (2011b) argues that there is a problem with the approach that the ECJ took to the resolution of the *Rüffert* case.[1] Although that case involved the relationship between public procurement and posted workers, it is possible that the inclusion of *social (and environmental) linkages* beyond the posted workers context may be called into question under the general Treaty requirements for free movement. If so, then the test of proportionality adopted in *Rüffert* will also apply beyond the posted workers context, and so the big question is whether the use of public procurement linkages is justified as a delivery mechanism where the coverage of the labour (or environmental) condition is limited to the part of the sector in which the procurement contract operates.

The ECJ has risked undermining the coherence of the corpus of EC law relating to procurement linkages, a corpus of law that the ECJ itself partly constructed. On one reading, the ECJ's decision in *Rüffert* tends to indicate that it has considerably rolled back on its previous efforts at helping to construct a workable compromise. The fact that it has done so, however, without mentioning the corpus of pre-existing law on procurement means that we are confronted with two conflicting strands of ECJ judgments on procurement linkages: the older (specifically procurement) judgments of the ECJ, a strand adopted in the interpretation of the directives and the Treaty in the procurement context, versus a newer strand represented in *Rüffert*. Despite this, the European Commission has recently published guidance that takes a broad view of the possibilities of integrating social considerations into public procurement in ways that are compatible with EU law (European Commission 2010).

Leaving aside the legal issues, there is a history of a fraught relationship between fairness at work issues and procurement in the United Kingdom, at least since the latter part of the nineteenth century. Several issues may be

---

[1] Case C-346/06, *Rüffert v Land Niedersachsen* [2008] IRLR 467 (ECJ).

identified: first, *whether* to use procurement as a way of delivering public services, where the issue was the potentially adverse effect on marginalised groups of contracting out such services (an important issue but not the focus of this chapter); second, when procurement is used, how to prevent corruption, discrimination, favouritism, and promote *efficient and effective* procurement (an issue mostly involving access to the opportunity to become a contractor, and the consequent issue of whether the allocation of contracts involved unlawful discrimination (not the focus of this chapter); and third, when procurement is used, how to ensure that it is used to deliver the broad *workplace fairness* agenda of the government and not cut across it (the issue of procurement linkages, which are the focus of this chapter).

VARIETIES OF WORKPLACE FAIRNESS
ADDRESSED BY PROCUREMENT

We need, first, to define more precisely what is encompassed by the idea of 'fairness at work'. We could adopt a relatively narrow conception of the idea, and restrict its meaning simply to individual employment rights, but that seems to me to be too narrow. Instead, I have adopted a relatively broad conception because to do otherwise would miss some of the more important indirect effects of the use of public procurement in the work context. Here is a non-exhaustive list of examples of the use of public procurement to reinforce fairness at work objectives, together with some examples.

Promoting Employment Opportunities

The first set of examples may be grouped under the idea of promoting employment opportunities and includes: promotion of youth employment, promotion of employment of persons from disadvantaged groups, promotion of employment opportunities for the long-term unemployed, promotion of employment for old-age unemployed (older workers), promotion of on-the-job skill development programmes including for persons with disabilities. Examples include, in Northern Ireland, the Health Estates Investment Group contract documentation for the South West Hospital at Enniskillen (CPDNI, Sustainability Case Studies).

An interesting approach has been to insert specific obligations regarding apprenticeships and utilising the unemployed into the contract. For example, the DFP Properties Division is responsible for reactive maintenance, planned preventative maintenance and minor works on over 1000 government occupied properties across Northern Ireland; the properties are either owned or leased by over 60 public sector organisations. Property management framework agreements were awarded in February 2010 to H & J Martin

Limited to provide a comprehensive maintenance service to the DFP Properties Division and its clients. A social objective provision requires H & J Martin to provide employment opportunities for up to 14 unemployed persons. The company has also committed to maintaining 35 apprentice-ships over the four-year life of the agreements (CPDNI 2010: 16).

Decent Work

The second set of examples may be grouped under the theme of decent work and includes the promotion of labour rights in such areas as: the pro-vision of social security and benefits, working hours, sufficient and equal pay, occupational safety and health, freedom of association, collective bar-gaining, gender equality at work, prohibition of child labour, elimination of forced labour, integration of migrant workers, access to vocational training, and anti-discrimination based on disability, race, ethnic origin, age, sexual orientation or religion.

The 2008 Greater London Authority policy statement included as one of six social and economic 'themes' across which the GLA Group aimed to improve London's sustainability through procurement linkages, the promo-tion of fair employment practices, seeking

> to ensure we move towards a position that, where appropriate, our contractors' staff receive a fair wage reflecting the environment in which they work, and that they enjoy contractual terms which represent reasonable minimum standards and which provide for family friendly, flexible and diverse working environments. (GLA 2008)

In the Northern Ireland Civil Service Security Guarding Services procure-ment, the Central Procurement Directorate (CPDNI) awarded a contract for providing security guarding services which was structured to allow small and medium enterprises, or SMEs, to bid for as much or as little work as they could manage thus ensuring there were no barriers in their bidding for work, and to address low pay (CPDNI 2010: 15). Another example was in the construction contract for the Metropolitan Arts Centre, a new build project in Belfast's Cathedral Quarter. This was awarded to Bowen Mascot, which committed to an approach to health and safety management of the project that incorporated robust safety reporting mechanisms, with reports on weekly site audits to the client as part of a feedback process, and an incentive scheme for site operatives (CPDNI 2010: 17).

Social Inclusion

The third set of examples may be grouped under the theme of supporting social inclusion, for example by means of providing incentives to engage firms employing persons with disabilities, and encouraging access to employment for persons with special needs to enhance their employability. The Department of Finance in Northern Ireland has included an equality clause in all government procurement contracts which requires the contractor to comply with the provisions of the Disability Discrimination Act 1995 and ensure that in the delivery of the services required under the contract the contractor has due regard to the need to promote equality of treatment and opportunity for people with a disabilities. In Northern Ireland contracts, certain 'sheltered' workshops employing disabled workers are able to bid for contracts under the EC procurement thresholds on preferential terms.

Accessibility

The fourth set of examples may be grouped under the theme of promoting accessibility and design for all, for example through mandatory provisions in technical specifications to ensure access by persons with disabilities to public services, public buildings, public transport, and IT applications. According to Waller, Hanson and Sloan (2009), the University of Dundee developed a Web Content Management System (WCMS) procurement project, charged with selecting a WCMS on which the University website would run. Detailed accessibility considerations were written into specification documents, and accessibility assessment played a significant role in the assessment of candidate WCMSs.

Fair and Ethical Trade

The fifth and final set of examples may be grouped under the theme of taking into account fair or ethical trade issues in other countries beyond the public authorities' national market, for example by requiring products purchased to conform to fair trade standards (including employment standards), eg by stipulating use of fair trade labels in tender specifications and conditions of contracts. The 2008 Greater London Authority policy statement (GLA 2008) included ethical sourcing practices as one of six social and economic 'themes' across which the GLA Group aimed to improve London's sustainability through procurement linkages (London Underground 2008; Company Clothing 2007). A contract for the supply of all Northern Ireland Health and Social Care (HSC) uniforms for five years from 1 April 2010 was awarded to Hunter Apparel Solutions Limited. This tender placed considerable emphasis on the importance of sustainability in meeting the HSC's needs, incorporating requirements that the successful bidder would be compliant with the Ethical Trading Initiative (ETI) base code (CPDNI 2010: 13).

WAYS IN WHICH PROCUREMENT ADDRESSES
WORKPLACE FAIRNESS

Having defined what may be included within the rubric of 'fairness of work' policies that have been drawn on in the procurement context, we turn now to consider the differing ways in which procurement addresses these issues. We need to begin with a brief overview of the procurement process itself, and some of the more important values to which public procurement is now expected to conform.

Procurement Values

Public procurement is in essence a question of matching supply and demand, just as with any private procurement procedure, the only difference being that public authorities have to exercise special caution when awarding contracts. This is because they are public entities, funded by taxpayers' money, and subject to specific legal and regulatory requirements as public bodies. This special caution can be translated into three main principles: getting the best value for money, acting fairly, and obeying the law.

Contracting authorities have the responsibility of getting the best value for taxpayers' money for everything they procure. Best value for money does not necessarily mean going only for the cheapest offer. It means that the contracting authority has to get the best deal within the parameters it sets. Value for money does not exclude social considerations.

Acting fairly includes following the principles of the EU internal market, which form the basis for the public procurement directives, and the national legislation based on these directives. The most important of these principles is the principle of equal treatment, which means that all competitors should have an equal opportunity to compete for the contract. For example, the procurement directives time limits set for the receipt of tenders and requests for participation, common rules are provided on technical specifications, and there are provisions prohibiting discrimination against contractors from other Member States. To ensure this level playing field, the principle of transparency must also be applied, so there are requirements concerning the publication of notices and an obligation for contracting authorities to inform the tenderers concerned why their tenders were rejected. These principles, together with more technical requirements, are incorporated into a set of domestic and EU legal requirements on public sector purchasers (McCrudden 2007).

Stages of the Procurement Process

We need also to understand the different stages of the procurement procedure. The general structure of a public procurement procedure is essentially no different from a private one, following roughly the same stages: defining the subject matter of the contract, drawing up the technical specifications and the contractual parameters for the product/work/service, selecting the right candidates to bid, determining the best bid, and managing the performance of the contract. Following the logic of this process, there are at least four basic approaches to how fairness at work issues are currently addressed in public procurement. It is important to understand that these approaches are frequently combined in any one public procurement procedure.

Subject Matter of the Contract and Technical Specifications

The first approach arises where the purchaser decides to include fairness at work criteria in the subject matter of the contract itself, and/or in the tender laying down the technical specifications that must be met by successful contractors. The 'subject matter' of a contract concerns the product, service or work the contracting authority wants to procure. When defining the subject matter of a contract, contracting authorities have great freedom to choose what they wish to procure. There is no reason in principle why achieving any fairness at work standard could not be made the subject matter of a contract. This allows ample scope for including social considerations, provided that this is done without distorting the market, that is, by limiting or hindering access to it.

The process of determining what the subject matter of the contract is will generally result in a basic description of the product, service or work, but it can also take the form of a performance-based definition. In principle, the contracting authority is free to define the subject matter of the contract in any way that meets its needs. Public procurement legislation is not so much concerned with what contracting authorities buy, but mainly with how they buy it. For that reason, none of the procurement directives restricts the subject matter of a contract as such.

An example of this approach is that adopted by the Northern Ireland Central Procurement Directorate. A pilot project provided that, for those projects included in the pilot, it would be an objective of the contract to create opportunities to facilitate the unemployed into work. The 'unemployed' were defined as any persons resident in the EU or any other country covered by the WTO Government Procurement Agreement who were not in paid employment in the three months immediately prior to being employed on the contract. Contractors wishing to be considered for a contract within the pilot study would be required to demonstrate clearly their commitment to the scheme. Tender documentation would require the contractor to provide an 'unemployment utilisation plan'.

The technical specifications that must be met by successful contractors can be divided into two separate categories: class-based criteria, and performance-based criteria. As regards the former, the best example is the operation of set-asides for 'sheltered' workshops. In Northern Ireland contracts, certain workshops employing disabled workers are able to bid for contracts under the EC procurement thresholds on preferential terms. A list of eligible establishments is maintained, the principal one being Ulster Supported Employment Limited (USEL).

An example of a performance-based approach is provided by the Northern Ireland Central Procurement Directorate's Buildsafe NI programme (CPDNI, Buildsafe). Buildsafe NI was established in 2003 as a five-year safety initiative for the construction industry run under the auspices of the Construction Industry Forum Northern Ireland. It was set against the background of 44 deaths and over 500 severely injured people in the previous 10 years. Buildsafe NI brought together the public sector client, the industry, the trade unions and the Health and Safety Executive for Northern Ireland as partnering groups and was taken forward in the context of the existing legal obligations and requirements. In 2011 a new action plan was developed. This included a requirement that all contractors seeking to tender for public sector works contracts must have a health and safety management system certified by a recognised third party.

Exclusion and Disqualification

In the second approach, there is a prohibition on obtaining government contracts as a penalty for previous wrongdoing, or to prevent public bodies contracting with those who are currently failing to achieve a particular standard of fair behaviour. Where this approach is adopted, it is most likely that the tender (or general legislation) will specify that a person will be disqualified from tendering for the contract if they have been found to have failed to comply with social requirements. The point of this use of procurement is, essentially, to add the deprivation of government contracts to the other penalties to which the contractor may be subject. Candidates can be excluded for specific failings, including criminal offences, or failure to comply with social legislation or regulations if this relates to their professional conduct. The exclusion criteria deal with circumstances in which a company can find itself that normally cause contracting authorities not to do any business with it, for example, if the company is bankrupt or has been wound up, has committed serious professional misconduct, or has not paid taxes or social security contributions.

A Northern Ireland example is the Fair Employment and Treatment Order 1998, which prohibits discrimination on grounds of religion and politics. This legislation introduced a system that uses the withdrawal of access to government contracts and grants as a final sanction against an employer which was acting contrary to the provisions of the legislation in a recalcitrant way. The legislation imposed significant duties on employers to take 'affirmative action' where the employer's workforce did not accord 'fair participation' to both religious communities in Northern Ireland. The legislation provided that both government contracts and government grants may be withdrawn in cases where the respondent was deemed to be 'in default', thus placing contract compliance on a statutory footing. An employer was regarded as 'in default', for example, where the employer had failed within the time allowed to serve a monitoring return and he or she had been convicted of an offence in respect of that failure, or where the employer had failed to comply with an order of the Fair Employment Tribunal (for example to engage in 'affirmative action') and a penalty has been imposed (Fee and Erridge 1989).

Pre-qualification questionnaires can also provide a format to assess economic and financial standing and technical or professional ability. An example is provided by the approach taken by the West Midlands Local Authorities' West Midlands Common Standard (West Midlands Forum 1998). This requires service providers to demonstrate that they comply with non-discrimination requirements in employment legislation. The approach adopted distinguished between different contractors based on their size, requiring smaller firms to do less than larger firms. The levels of the standard become more demanding depending on the number of staff employed by the firm.

Award of the Contract

The form in which a third approach can be found in practice is where the public body takes conformity to certain standards of fairness into account as an award criterion. This approach differs enormously, however, between different programmes. One example is provided by the Northern Ireland pilot project referred to earlier, which encouraged employers to recruit and train people who had been unemployed for at least three months. Bidders for these contracts had to provide an employment plan with proposals on utilising the unemployed and evidence that they could implement their proposals (CPDNI: nd). In the event of two or more tenders being judged by the contracting authority to be equal, the assessment of the plan would be taken into consideration to decide the award of the contract. It would be a matter for the individual contracting authority to determine the definition of when two bids were equal, in order to justify taking the plan into account at the award stage. For guidance purposes, however, where the award criterion for the contract was 'most economically advantageous', it was recommended that this should be deemed to have occurred where one or more tenders were within two points, in the overall scoring matrix (reflecting quality and price scores, scored out of 100), of the tender receiving the highest overall score. Where the award criterion for the contract was 'lowest price', then it would be when one or more tenders were within one per cent of the lowest satisfactory tender.

Contract Conditions

The fourth approach focuses its attention on the stage *after* the contract has been awarded. It requires whoever is awarded the contract to comply with certain conditions in carrying out the contract once it is awarded. In this approach there is no attempt to build the ability of the contractor to comply with such conditions into the award of the contract. This model presents all contractors with the same requirement to which the contractor must sign up. Contract conditions set out how the contract should be performed. Writing the requirements for fairness at work standards into the contract makes the authority's expectations clear.

The Transport for London (TfL) East London Line Extension Project provides an example (EDF Seminar Series 2006). In 2004, TfL put together a five-year £10 billion investment programme to fund large-scale construction projects including the East London Line extension, the Crossrail project, the Thames Gateway bridge, and other developments linked to the 2012 Olympic and Paralympic Games (GLA Economics 2007: para 3.5). Equality and inclusion were regarded as being at the heart of that programme and integral to it.

The first project was known as the East London line extension. The contracts were valued at £500 million for the provision of the main works and £350 million for the rolling stock and train servicing agreement. In terms of the transport benefits, the aim was to create links between East London and the City of London, taking pressure off London Bridge, to stimulate the East End of London. It also aimed to link the Underground with the orbital railway and was a key component of TfL's overall transport plan for the Olympics. In the summer of 2006, Bombardier was awarded the contract for the rolling stock and train services agreement, and in October 2006 a Balfour Beatty-Carillion Joint Venture was awarded the main works construction contract. A policy decision was taken to try to bring benefit to the communities that the line extension was going to serve. It is a diverse community, culturally and economically, so the aim was to have an impact on some of the issues that those communities were facing. Four commitments were to be required from the contractors: to have an equality policy, to have a training plan, to demonstrate how they were going to engage with the communities they were going to be serving, and to have a plan around how they were going to diversify their supply base. These requirements were incorporated in the invitation to tender and contract conditions for two procurements within the project: the provision of main works, and the rolling stock and train servicing agreement.

PROCUREMENT AS A STRATEGY FOR SHAPING
WORKPLACE FAIRNESS?

There are several potential benefits for the public sector procuring body in ensuring the integration of fair workplace issues into public procurement.

Assisting Compliance with Social Law

Integrating fair workplace issues into public procurement contributes to enhancing legal and policy compliance with national and international legal commitments. There is growing concern that traditional mechanisms of securing social justice and social cohesion are not adequate. Orthodox legal methods of combatting discrimination in employment, for example, have proved to be of limited effectiveness. The power of using procurement lies in the employer's economic interest in obtaining business from public authorities. Linking social issues to procurement seeks to use this economic interest for the promotion of social policy objectives, usually in addition to the use of other regulatory approaches. The use of procurement is not usually the sole or even the primary method adopted to enforce social standards. More frequently, it is but one of several other methods that reinforce each other.

Demonstrating Socially-Responsive Governance

Integrating fair workplace issues into public procurement may contribute to enhanced compliance with broader community values and needs (as it responds to the growing public demand for governments to be socially responsible in their operations). Governments award public contracts on behalf of the communities that they serve. It is not unreasonable that these communities expect that public contracts should go to contractors who do not violate the basic norms of that community. The award of public contracts is not simply an economic activity by the administration in which the contracting authority can consider itself simply as equivalent to a private sector organisation. It is unacceptable that government should allow those acting in its place to behave in ways in which government itself would not wish or be permitted to act, and in this context some contracting authorities have considered it an act of good government that social considerations should enter into the award of government contracts. Those acting with government financing should at least uphold the norms that government would be held to, acting directly. Public procurement not only represents huge spending power, which directly contributes to the fulfillment of social priorities and objectives, but also gives a signal to the market and to the general public in favour of social responsibility, and therefore influences and contributes to shaping choices and behaviours of suppliers and consumers.

Addressing Concerns about Markets

Extensive changes are occurring in the delivery of public services, in part under pressure from global economic developments. These involve a combination of privatisation and contracting out. These contractual methods came to be seen by some as important instruments of deregulation. Procuring services from the private sector has distributional consequences for employees and consumers that need to be taken into account in the procurement process. An important example of this is contracting out the delivery of services that have previously been delivered by government itself through its own directly employed workforce to private sector service deliverers employing workers not in public employment. Where procurement is thought likely to lead to a reduction in social standards, then, linkage between procurement and social policy is justified to limit or control the perceived damage. The role of public procurement in some contexts, therefore, is to reinsert public values into a contractual context that might otherwise underestimate them.

More Effective Delivery of the Fairness at Work Agenda

Evidence from other countries indicates that the integration of fair workplace issues into public procurement may produce beneficial results, in the sense that it may be an effective tool in delivering the results sought (McCrudden 2007). Unfortunately, little empirical research has been carried out in the United Kingdom on this issue. One of the relatively few systematic attempts to measure the impact of such initiatives was conducted in Northern Ireland and involved an assessment of the pilot project discussed earlier. It will be remembered that the aim of the pilot was to encourage employers to recruit and train people who had been unemployed for at least three months to work on contracts with government departments, their agencies, NDPBs (non-departmental public bodies) and public corporations. Using a model found to be acceptable by the ECJ, in the event of two or more tenders being judged equal in the identification of the most economically advantageous tender the tenderers' proposals for addressing long term unemployment was taken into consideration to decide the award of the contract (CPDNI: 2004).

As part of this pilot, the School of Policy Studies, University of Ulster at Jordanstown was commissioned to report on the implementation of this model and its effects. In particular, it was asked to consider the economic costs, the legal risks, and the effectiveness of the model adopted. The Final Evaluation Report (CPDNI 2005) on the pilot was reassuring: extra costs resulting from these requirements were minimal, there were no legal challenges, and the pilot led to an increase in the numbers of unemployed people hired to undertake the public contracts.

The NI Pilot was also chosen as one of six case studies for further analysis under a study (SQW 2006) commissioned by the Department for Environment, Food and Rural Affairs (DEFRA). The aim of this study was 'to deliver peer reviewed robust evidence of a cost benefit analysis of a sample of sustainable public procurement initiatives to evaluate their efficacy as a policy tool'. The cost benefit analysis of the pilot shows a gross present value of the benefits of employing the previously unemployed amounted to £264,785 while the gross present value of costs amounted to £167,615, at a 3.5 per cent discount rate. The pilot therefore generated a social gain with a net present value of £97,170 and a benefit/cost ratio of 1.58. Under certain conditions, then, it appears that public procurement may be a useful tool in practice.

WHAT IS NEEDED FOR PROCUREMENT TO BE AN EFFECTIVE TOOL?

This section addresses the key elements that appear to be relevant for procurement to become an effective tool in shaping workplace fairness. Given the relatively limited amount of rigorous empirical research that is available, the elements identified are based primarily on my experience. It would be useful for future research to test the relevance of these factors more rigorously.

Sufficient Reason

In the United Kingdom, the primary reason why procurement has been focused on by public sector bodies in recent years as a potential tool for achieving greater workplace fairness seems to have been as a result of the legal obligations stemming from the public sector equality duties. In addition, following the introduction of the statutory duty on sustainable development, relevant public authorities must, in exercising their functions, act in the way considered best to contribute to the achievement of sustainable development, except to the extent that any such action is not reasonably practicable in all the circumstances of the case. It has been the equality duty that has been the more effective of these in driving procurement linkages in the workplace context.

The public sector equality duties introduced in the 2010 Act (McCrudden 2011a) were not the first foray into procurement linkages in Britain. Previous equality legislation beginning early in the decade had introduced public sector equality duties first for race, then disability, and finally gender. In that context, the previous Labour Government encouraged the view that procurement was one of the functions of public authorities to which the equality duties should be applied. In 2008, the Office of Government Commerce, the primary UK source of government policy on the use of public procurement (now the Cabinet Office), published guidance on how to address the equality duties in the context of procurement (Office of Government Commerce, 2008).

The new Equality Act 2010 does not apply to Northern Ireland, and the equality legislation therefore remains as it did prior to that Act. In that jurisdiction, section 75 of the Northern Ireland Act 1998 provides that a public body is required in carrying out its functions relating to Northern Ireland to have 'due regard' to the need to promote equality of opportunity: (a) between persons of different religious belief, political opinion, racial group, age, marital status or sexual orientation; (b) between men and women generally; (c) between persons with a disability and persons without; and (d) between persons with dependants and persons without.

Schedule 9 sets out the processes, including equality schemes and equality impact assessments (EQIAs) by which this aim is to be achieved, but only as a means to this end. In particular, each of the specifically designated public authorities is required to produce an equality scheme. This scheme is required to state the authority's arrangements for assessing its compliance with the duties under section 75 and for consulting on matters to which a duty under that section is likely to be relevant (including details of the persons to be consulted). The scheme must also state the arrangements for assessing and consulting on the likely impact of policies adopted or proposed to be adopted by the authority on the promotion of equality of opportunity, and for monitoring any adverse impact of policies adopted by the authority on the promotion of equality of opportunity. The public authority is required to give details of any consideration given by the authority to measures that might mitigate any adverse impact of that policy on the promotion of equality of opportunity, and alternative policies that might better achieve the promotion of equality of opportunity. As is the case under the British public sector duties, these provisions apply to the procurement function of public authorities in Northern Ireland.

Addressing the Political Logjams

Although, therefore, there is a similar legal imperative to embark on linking procurement with (some) workplace fairness issues, the actual adoption of procurement linkage remains patchy, with Northern Ireland appearing to have adopted such linkages to a significantly greater degree than the rest of the United Kingdom. One important factor appears to have been that political logjams preventing the use of such linkages were addressed systematically and directly in Northern Ireland.

There were several problems in the past in Northern Ireland in developing such linkages, including whether such linkages are legal, under domestic, but particularly European Union law. This involved the need to clarify what can and cannot be done legally. Are such linkages sensible and doable in practical terms? This involved the need to meet civil service resistance, or lethargy, or fear of the unknown. Are such linkages politically advantageous? This involved a need to tackle political ignorance of the possibilities of such linkages. More specifically, a series of additional questions was raised: what extra value (if any) does such linkage bring, and at what cost? Are such linkages consistent with a view of procurement as an economic instrument of the government? Since the late 1990s there have been several attempts to try to resolve these perceived issues with procurement linkages.

From the beginning of the implementation of section 75, the public procurement function of public authorities was regarded as one of the functions to which the equality duty applied. The question was not whether the duty applied, but how best to implement the duty in the procurement context. The beginning of the attempt to implement equality in procurement coincided with a general review of public procurement policy in Northern Ireland. A Procurement Review Implementation Team was set up by the Minister for Finance and Personnel in February 2001 to review both issues simultaneously. This committee reported to the Executive (Procurement Review Implementation Team 2002), which had been given responsibility for local procurement in the Northern Ireland Act 1998 establishing devolved government in Northern Ireland. The Executive approved the Procurement Review Report. On 27 May 2002, the Minister of Finance and Personnel made a Statement to the Assembly (Farren 2002), paving the way for the establishment of the Procurement Board, as the main policy making body, and the Central Procurement Directive (CPD) as the main executive body based in the Department of Finance and Personnel (DFP). Of most importance for the purposes of this chapter, the Executive accepted the recommendations of the Committee regarding the implications of the public sector equality duty for procurement: that equality was a central aspect of the exercise of procurement powers for the future.

The CPD produced a Procurement Policy Guidance Note on the *Integration of Social Considerations into Public Procurement* (CPDNI 2004), which provided an outline of the range of possibilities for integrating social considerations into public procurement in Northern Ireland under the existing procurement rules. Eventually, the Procurement Board joined with the Equality Commission of Northern Ireland to produce guidance, the

Equality and Sustainable Development Guidelines (Equality Commission for Northern Ireland and CPDNI 2008), aimed at policy makers and procurement professionals, on how to integrate equality and sustainable development considerations into the procurement process, while meeting the existing statutory duties in relation to equality of opportunity and sustainable development. The guidance applies to all public sector procurement, including Public–Private Partnership or Private Finance Initiative projects.

Importantly, the guidance was accompanied by a 'Dear Accounting Officer' letter from the Treasury Officer of Accounts (2008) which advised recipients that the guidance should be taken into account when preparing business cases for future public procurements. Whilst a major breakthrough, all the guidelines did was to help Departments and NDPBs engage in procurement linkages, *if they decide to do so*, and the major question in Northern Ireland remains: will public authorities so decide? Each public body, in conjunction with other departments and public bodies, needs to develop concrete linkages into actual procurements.

High Level Political Commitment and Leadership

Leadership is a key element for the success of any strategy seeking to use procurement linkages, not least political leadership. Practice in Northern Ireland suggests that successful organisational strategies reflect the government's social priorities and at the same time explicitly acknowledge the role that procurement plays in contributing to its achievement. Procurement spend each year in Northern Ireland has been estimated as being around £1.7 billion per year (15–20 per cent of NI GDP). The Northern Ireland Government Programme for Government (PfG), Budget, and Investment Strategy (ISNI-2), all endorsed by the Northern Ireland Assembly in January 2008, set out an ambitious economic, social and equality agenda. Public procurement was recognised as one major tool for achieving these goals, involving significant economic muscle, thus giving renewed political support from a new government for what had gone before, and providing a secure political base for new initiatives.

Procurement issues were particularly prominent in the new Investment Strategy for Northern Ireland (ISNI-2 (2008): p 2):

> We will seek opportunities to promote social inclusion and equality of opportunity in the procurement of infrastructure programmes. This will impact through employment plans, by building opportunities for local apprenticeships into major delivery contracts, and through a tendering process that prioritises the most economically advantageous option in this context.

It continued: 'We are encouraging departments ... to take advantage with contractors in each major procurement opportunity to progress the

Executive's wider economic, social and employment objectives'. As a result, in 2010, the Strategic Investment Board produced practical guidance (a 'toolkit') for integrating social benefits into large public procurement contracts (Strategic Investment Board 2010).

An associated development has been the incorporation of procurement linkages in several major urban regeneration projects, namely those in Belfast, and Derry/Londonderry. For example, ILEX (the Derry/ Londonderry urban regeneration authority) will use an estimated 200 plus procurement contracts as a principal vehicle for achieving its regeneration aims. Social benefit clauses are included in all construction and supplies and services procurement contracts as a means of providing employment and training for those furthest removed from the labour market by those companies tendering for these contracts (ILEX 2010: 20).

Incorporating Procurement Linkages in Strategic Planning

Organisations also need to assess the social risks and impacts of their purchasing and supply chain activity. This helps to focus their efforts on the spend categories of greatest concern and on those which can contribute to the achievement of their social targets. The prioritisation of key spending areas based on their social impacts can be reflected in their organisational policy and strategy and can assist in the more effective allocation and use of financial resources, which are often limited. The UK Task Force on Social Considerations in Public Procurement Prioritisation Methodology provides an interesting example of this approach. The Sustainable Procurement Task Force (SPTF) was set up in May 2005 and published its Action Plan in June 2006.

The Action Plan presented the business case for sustainable procurement, recommended actions across six broad areas and provided two tools that can help organisations' progress; the Prioritisation Methodology and the Flexible Framework (FFW). The Prioritisation Methodology is a risk-based approach that helps organisations focus their efforts and resources appropriately. The Task Force identified a set of 'Top 10' spend areas at national level. Each organisation has the opportunity to do the same by applying this methodology, taking into account its own drivers, stakeholders, policies and objectives. Instead of only using expenditure data, the methodology allows organisations to take account of environmental and socio-economic risk, the potential that they have to influence suppliers and the actual scope to improve sustainability. The Flexible Framework is a tool designed to help organisations understand the steps needed at an organisational and process level to improve procurement practice and make sustainable procurement happen.

Putting a policy of procurement linkages into practice will thus require strategic planning: setting priorities when choosing the contracts most suitable. Some contracting authorities have chosen to adopt a coordinated and holistic approach to the integration of social considerations. An example is provided by the Greater London Authority. In June 2006, the GLA Group (consisting of the Greater London Authority, the London Development Agency, Transport for London, the London Fire and Emergency Planning Authority, and the Metropolitan Police Authority) adopted a new Sustainable Procurement Policy to support the Mayor's policies. The term 'Sustainable Procurement' was the term used in this policy statement, but in January 2007 the policy was renamed 'Responsible Procurement' because it had become clear that sustainable procurement is often understood to refer only to environmental issues, and to exclude social ones and the Mayor 'wanted to communicate the importance of both social and environmental objectives'.

The 2008 policy statement (GLA 2008) set the policy in the context of the Greater London Authority Act 1999, which sets out the principal purposes of the GLA as economic development, wealth creation, and social development, within the Greater London area, and improvement of the environment. The policy stated that the GLA has the power to do anything in furtherance of these principal purposes. In exercising these powers, the GLA must do so in ways calculated to promote improvements in the health of Londoners, and in ways calculated to contribute towards the achievement of sustainable development in the United Kingdom. In performing these functions, the GLA must also have regard to the principle that there should be equality of opportunity for all people. The Mayor considered procurement 'as a key opportunity to take forward the delivery of these principal purposes'. According to the 2008 Mayor of London's Responsible Procurement Report, the approach of the GLA Group has been for each member to be responsible for its own operational implementation of the Responsible Procurement Policy. A pan-organisation Steering Group ensured consistency and continuous improvement, supported by a working group to share good practice. Implementation was being taken on a contract-by-contract approach.

Monitoring and Controlling Effective Implementation

Measuring and controlling effective implementation of the inclusion of workplace-related procurement linkages and achievement of the outcome included in contracts involves setting up internal and external control measures. It is clear that the simple inclusion of procurement linkages within the contract by itself is unlikely to achieve the goals sought. Internal measures need to be linked to existing reporting systems, which will have to be adapted in order to take into consideration the objectives stipulated in the social clauses. They need to be linked also to internal auditing procedures and incorporate sanctions for non-compliance with social objectives. External measures may involve auditing of performance by the selected contractor by an independent body. The performance management regime will set the terms for assessing performance and taking action. This could mean rewarding the contractor for good performance, addressing under-performance or working together to enhance delivery. The payment mechanism provides the basis for ensuring that the contractor delivers to the required standard. It can provide financial disincentives for poor performance and incentives for exceeding baseline targets.

Unfortunately, there is little empirical information on this stage of the process. What information there is indicates that, in practice, achieving effective compliance has proven challenging, and can involve significant involvement by the public body letting the contract, requiring innovative methods of compliance assessment and flexibility in reacting to non-compliance. Three examples from Northern Ireland must suffice to illustrate these points, none of them involving workplace issues, but involving the use of procurement to achieve other social goals.

In the first (Equality Commission for Northern Ireland and CPDNI 2008: 127) the issue was whether a road-building contract resulted in a useable road for a group of local residents. The contractor provided a sign with telephone contact numbers for complaints about the road being available for use. The data was collated annually for the public authority. The public authority set up a system to contact the health centre, the local authority community planning forum, and the residents' association once every two years to ask whether access was maintained. As a result of this monitoring, it became clear that the perception was that an underpass connecting the road to the residents was unsafe. Litter was left in it and the lights were not replaced if broken. The public authority discussed this with the contractor as part of monitoring contract performance to improve this. However, the public authority also considered how CCTV in use for traffic monitoring could be extended in use to add value to a community safety initiative.

In the second (ibid: 132), a contract for the delivery of a hospital meals service was in issue. The contract included delivery and service to the wards and patients. The contract stipulated that appropriate meals had to be provided accommodating specific dietary requirements. The contractor had to provide annual monitoring information on the requests for specific meals and any complaints received. The contractor conducted an annual patient satisfaction survey (agreed with the public authority), which asked questions about the meals. This survey was monitored for age, ethnicity and gender. Nevertheless, the public authority had to initiate its own assessment of the meals service following press research into malnutrition amongst inpatients in a geriatric ward. The assessment identified problems with the way the meals were delivered to the wards, as many were not eaten. Through the variation clauses in the contract, the service to the geriatric ward was amended to address the problems identified. The combined evidence triggered contractual variations to improve the service to the geriatric ward by helping patients with feeding.

A third example involves issues closer to the workplace, and pointed to the need to consider how a strategic partnership between various elements of the public service was necessary in order to address the issue, and the potential benefits of developing with contractors a partnering culture to underpin contract management. The example concerned the development of essential skills within the workforce. In the areas of facilities management, security guarding, and cleaning, up to two per cent of the Northern Ireland working population were found to be deficient in certain essential skills such as reading. The CPDNI worked with the Department of Employment and Learning and facilitated discussions with contractors as to what the contractors could do to develop skills in the workforce, using whatever subsidies are available. A voluntary approach was seen as more effective, not least because not being compulsory meant that those who were being benefited were not specifically identified.

THE FUTURE FOR PROCUREMENT BEING USED TO ACHIEVE WORKPLACE FAIRNESS

The Future of Procurement Linkages in Northern Ireland

There remains concern that the full opportunities for procurement linkages are not being fully exploited. In November 2008, the Northern Ireland Assembly's Committee for Finance and Personnel agreed terms of reference for an Inquiry into Public Procurement Policy and Practice in Northern Ireland, including the ways in which the social and economic benefits of procurement could be maximised.

Arising from the Inquiry (Northern Ireland Assembly 2010), the Committee made several findings and recommendations. The Committee sensed (para 244) 'a reticence amongst local commissioners and purchasers to pursue social benefit through procurement'. It recommended the Executive to translate its Programme for Government commitments on the need to integrate social goals into procurement 'into a clear policy directive on procuring social benefit, which sets out the priorities that should be pursued by the Procurement Board, the Centres of Procurement Expertise and individual commissioners and purchasers' (para 245). In the meantime, the Committee recommended (para 247) 'the use of clauses setting quotas for employing apprentices and the long-term unemployed in all suitable public contracts'. The Central Procurement Directorate should, in addition, make 'a rigorous assessment of the social clauses applied in recent construction contracts, with a view to identifying lessons and opportunities for further initiatives in this regard' (para 247). The Committee called on the Department of Finance and Personnel 'to put in place a suitable model for systematically measuring, evaluating and incorporating wider social value considerations within economic appraisals and business cases, and which will inform public procurement processes' (ibid: para 253). The Procurement Board (2010) put in place several initiatives to take these recommendations forward.

Equality Duties and Procurement in Britain

If I am right that a major driver for the modern development of a focus on the use of procurement to achieve workplace fairness in the UK is the public sector equality duty, then the future use is also likely to be significantly affected by the new public sector duties in the Equality Act 2010. Professor Hepple has set out in chapter four (this volume) the structure of the general public sector equality duty in the Equality Act 2010, which replaces these three separate public sector duties with one, and I do not repeat that here.

In addition to these 'general' duties set out in section 149, the Equality Act empowers Ministers of the Crown, Welsh Ministers and Scottish Ministers, by regulation after consulting the Equality and Human Rights Commission, to impose more specific duties on the specified public authorities for the purpose of enabling the 'better performance' by the authorities of their general duties. Section 155 provides that these regulations may require a public authority to 'consider such matters as may be specified from time to time'. The Act explicitly provides that the specific duties may impose duties 'in connection with' its 'public procurement functions' on a public authority, that is a contracting authority within the meaning of Directive 2004/18/EC. A 'public procurement function' means a function the exercise of which is regulated by the Directive.

The Labour Government that was responsible for having introduced the Equality Bill published proposals as to how it intended to implement these provisions after the passage of the legislation. The proposals for the new public sector duty included a detailed section on procurement, and proposed three specific duties for public authorities undertaking procurement activities. After the passage of the Equality Bill, however, there was a General Election in which the Labour Government was defeated and replaced by a Coalition Government of Conservatives and Liberal Democrats. This change of government led to considerable speculation as to how far the new government would be prepared to implement the previous government's approach to the implementation of the Act.

In its August 2010 consultation document on the public sector equality duties (Government Equalities Office 2010: para 5.21), the Coalition

Government indicated its scepticism about the specific procurement duty, stating: 'We do not believe it is necessary to impose burdensome additional processes on public bodies telling them how to conduct their procurement activity: they will be judged on the outcomes that they deliver'. In its response to the consultation (Government Equalities Office 2011: 18), the Coalition Government concluded that it would not include any specific duties for procurement for English public authorities, and would simply leave it to public authorities to apply the general duty to procurement without further elaboration, as was the case prior to the 2010 Act. The general duties were brought into force from April 2011.

The Welsh Assembly Government, in contrast, took a somewhat different approach for authorities under its control. Where a Welsh public authority proposes to enter into a relevant agreement on the basis of an offer which is the most economically advantageous it *must* have 'due regard' as to whether the award criteria should include considerations relevant to its performance of the general equality duty, and where a public authority proposes to stipulate conditions relating to the performance of a relevant agreement it must have due regard to whether the conditions should include considerations relevant to its performance of the general duty (Equality Act 2010 (Statutory Duties) (Wales) Regulations 2011). The situation in Scotland was more complex. When the UK Government decided not to pursue procurement duties, the Scottish Government, mindful of the value of a level playing field, took the same decision. When the Welsh Assembly Government decided to pursue procurement duties, the Scottish Government decided to look again at procurement and to seek views on whether similar duties might be effective in Scotland (Scottish Government 2011).

What, if anything, can the Northern Ireland experience teach us in this context? On the one hand, a lesson is that if the general duty applies to procurement but there is no further clear direction from secondary legislation as to how it is to apply, much time can be spent by, and much aggravation can arise for, public authorities working out what precisely they have to do. It is to the benefit of business for the government to produce an explicit regulatory scheme that says to public bodies what they can and cannot do, and thereby provides a degree of consistency across the board for businesses to be able to react to. Leaving it simply to the public authorities to produce different schemes is a recipe for uncertainty both for businesses and for public bodies, and is also likely to give rise to more litigation to clarify matters, including in the ECJ, which the government is going to have to spend time and money in defending. Leaving the EHRC and the Cabinet Office to bring out Codes of Practice or guidance to clarify matters may not solve this problem because they have no real authority on the procurement issue (EHRC) or the equality issues (Cabinet Office) and in any event all they can do is advise. On this argument, it is in the public interest to have a scheme that provides clarity to businesses and a degree of protection to public authorities as to what exactly the general duty should entail in procurement.

On the other hand, the Northern Ireland experience also demonstrates that there may be something to be said for leaving the general duty to apply without further embellishment, not least because this may encourage greater experimentation among a select group of public authorities, which then become a vanguard that other authorities are encouraged to follow. Given that if the present government had produced a set of specific procurement duties these would be likely to have constituted a ceiling rather than a floor, and that this scheme would be likely to have been minimal in any event, it may be better not to encourage this government to produce a model that public authorities would then, effectively, be forced to adopt. Left to their own devices, some public authorities will come up with quite radical schemes (Lulham 2011), certainly more radical than the present government would put in any specific scheme that it drew up. Paradoxically, then, it may be better to let a thousand flowers bloom than force the government to come up with a scheme that homogenises, and risks resulting in a lower common denominator than may arise without such a scheme.

Judicial Review

An important difference is emerging between the British approach to the enforcement of the equality duties in the procurement context, and that prevalent so far in Northern Ireland. Increasingly, it seems, the courts are likely to be brought into the enforcement of these duties. This may, perhaps, be explained by the apparently more limited support for procurement linkages in the political and bureaucratic system in Britain in comparison with Northern Ireland. Two recent cases illustrate how litigation is now being used in order to kick-start the process of linking procurement with workplace issues.

Public Interest Lawyers v Legal Services Commission [2010] EWHC 3277 (Admin) involved judicial review of the Legal Services Commission (LSC) procurement of legal services in the field of mental health law. The claimant had previously been contracted to provide mental health law services for the LSC. The tender specifications required providers to satisfy prescribed standards, and there was a system under which tenderers self-certified their compliance with these standards. Two legal issues arose that are particularly relevant to this chapter. The first issue was whether the contracting authority had adequately verified whether bidders met the standards set. The court held that it had not; the self-certification system was insufficient to provide the information needed to make a proper assessment and it risked including tenderers who did not satisfy the requirements, and this was unfair to those who had met the standards. The second issue was whether the arrangements were contrary to the public sector disability duty. The court held that they were. The LSC had not undertaken an impact assessment of the effect that the process would have on patients in mental health institutions. In some cases, these patients could be adversely affected by the switch in advisors resulting from the procurement process. The LSC was required to assess whether it could take steps to ameliorate the adverse effects on patients.

Hereward & Foster Ltd v Legal Services Commission [2010] EWHC 3370 (Admin) concerned a judicial review of the award criteria used in the LSC's tender process for contracts in immigration law services. The tender evaluation criteria ranked higher those tenderers who employed an immigration supervisor full-time. The claimant was unsuccessful because the claimant's only immigration supervisor was a woman who worked part-time. The court held that this was a breach of the LSC's public sector equality duty, even though it did not constitute unlawful 'indirect discrimination'. The criterion was introduced after the LSC had carried out its EQIA and the LSC had not reassessed the equality impact in light of the new criterion. (The claimant lost, however, because the claim was brought outside the three-month period for judicial review claims.)

CONCLUSION

Several conclusions are suggested by this discussion. First, considerable progress has been made in addressing the issues that bedevilled discussion of procurement linkages in the past; it is clear that the use of procurement to secure workplace fairness is technically possible and that there is now sufficient evidence on which to conclude that it can be effective, given certain conditions, in integrating workplace fairness issues into the organisation in ways that concentrating on individual litigation seems not to achieve. It is also clear, I suggest, that the process of negotiating and applying procurement linkages opens up opportunities for significant involvement by social actors, such as trade unions.

There are several issues regarding the use of such linkages that give cause for concern. Among these issues, two are of particular relevance for the purposes of this chapter. First, will the opportunity to use procurement actually be taken up in practice, and if not what mechanisms will be available to ensure that the linkages are adopted? Second, will contracts containing social clauses be effectively operationalised, and if not, what mechanisms will be available to ensure the social clauses are effectively monitored and enforced? For the moment, two different approaches appear to be emerging distinguishing the evolving British approach from the Northern Ireland experience. In the latter, a primarily political and bureaucratic route has been adopted, which nevertheless has been seen as having delivered significantly less than it might. In contrast, the emerging approach in Britain seems to be about to place considerably greater weight on litigation as the means of securing the effective linkage of procurement with social issues. Will it deliver any more? This is, as yet, uncertain but if it does the irony of the emerging British approach should not be lost: that whilst some at least see procurement linkages as an alternative to litigation, making the system effective may yet require it.

BIBLIOGRAPHY

Company Clothing (2007) 'Ethical Driving Force', *Company Clothing*, April.

CPDNI (2004) Procurement Policy Guidance Notes, Procurement Guidance Note 03/04—*Integration of Social Considerations into Public Procurement* (CPDNI, Belfast), www.dfpni.gov.uk/index/procurement-2/cpd/cpd-policy-and-legislation/content__cpd__policy_procurement_guidance_notes/content_cpd_procurement_guidance_notes_pgn_03_-_04.htm.

—— (2005) *Pilot Project on Utilising the Unemployed in Public Contracts: Final Evaluation Report*, September 2005 (CPDNI, Belfast), www.dfpni.gov.uk/index/procurement-2/cpd/cpd-policy-and-legislation/content_-_cpd_utilising_the_unemployed_in_public_contracts_gateway_page/unemployed_in_construction.pdf.

—— (nd) *Pilot Project on Utilising the Unemployed in Public Contracts: Case Study* (CPDNI, Belfast), www.dfpni.gov.uk/index/procurement-2/cpd/cpd-policy-and-legislation/content_cpd_utilising_the_unemployed_in_public_contracts_gateway_page.htm.

—— Sustainability Case Studies (nd), www.dfpni.gov.uk/index/procurement-2/cpd/cpd-policy-and-legislation/cpd-sustainability/content_-_cpd_sustainability_case_studies.htm.

—— (2010) *Annual Report to the Procurement Board*, 2009–2010 (CPDNI, Belfast).

—— Buildsafe (nd), www.dfpni.gov.uk/index/procurement-2/cpd/cpd-policy-and-legislation/content_-_cpd_policy_framework_for_construction_procurement/buildsafe-ni.htm.

Deakin, S and Koukiadaki, A (2009) Governance Processes, Labour-Management Partnership and Employee Voice in the Construction of Heathrow Terminal 5, 38 *Industrial Law Journal* (2009) 365.

—— (2010) Reflexive Approaches to Corporate Governance: The Case of Heathrow Terminal 5 in O De Schutter and J Lenoble (eds), *Reflexive Governance: Redefining the Public Interest in a Pluralist World* (Hart, Oxford).

DFP (nd) Northern Ireland Department of Finance and Personnel, Disability Action Plan (Department of Finance and Personnel, Belfast), www.dfpni.gov.uk/disability_action_plan.version_2_pdf.pdf.

EDF Seminar Series (2006) Can Procurement be used to Promote Equality? Lessons from Experiences at Home and Abroad: Summary Note of Seminar on Thursday 2nd March 2006, contribution of Valerie Todd (EDF, London), www.edf.org.uk/blog/?p=89.

Equality Commission for Northern Ireland and CPDNI (2008) *Equality and Sustainable Development Guidelines*, www.dfpni.gov.uk/index/procurement-2/

cpd/cpd-policy-and-legislation/cpd-sustainability/content_-_cpd_equality_of_
opportunity_and_sustainable_development_in_public_sector_procurement/
content__cpd_equality_of_opportunity_and_sustainable_development_gateway_
page/equality_of_opportunity_and_sustainable_development_-_full_guidance.pdf.

European Commission (2010) *Buying Social: A Guide to Taking Account of Social Considerations in Public Procurement* (Publications Office of the European Union, Luxembourg), ec.europa.eu/internal_market/publicprocurement/other_ aspects/index_en.htm.

Farren, S (2002) *Public Procurement Policy Statement to the Assembly by Dr Seán Farren, MLA, Minister of Finance and Personnel*, 27 May 2002, www. dfpni.gov.uk/index/procurement-2/cpd/cpd-policy-and-legislation/cpd-review-of-public-procurement-2002/cpd-ministerial-statement-on-the-review-of-public-procurement-2002.pdf.

Fee, R and Erridge, A (1999) Contract Compliance in Canada and Northern Ireland: A Comparative Analysis, *8th International Annual IPSERA Conference* (Belfast, Dublin).

GLA (2008) Mayor of London, *GLA Group Responsible Procurement* (March 2006, updated January 2008) (GLA, London).

GLA Economics (2008) *Women in London's Economy* (GLA, London).

Government Equalities Office (2010) *Equality Act 2010: The Public Sector Equality Duty—Promoting Equality through Transparency—A Consultation* (GEO, London), webarchive.nationalarchives.gov.uk/20110608160754/http:// www.equalities.gov.uk.

—— (2011) *Equality Act 2010: The Public Sector Equality Duty—Promoting Equality through Transparency—Summary of Responses to the Consultation* (GEO, London), webarchive.nationalarchives.gov.uk/20110608160754/http://www.equalities.gov.uk.

ILEX (2010) Regeneration Plan for Derry-Londonderry (ILEX, Derry-Londonderry), www.ilex-urc.com/ILEX/files/53/53f1dd51-3e96-45c1-9a89-96c82016fee1.pdf.

ISNI-2 (2008), Northern Ireland Executive, *Investment Strategy for Northern Ireland 2008–2018* (Northern Ireland Executive, 2008), http://www.sibni.org/ investment_strategy_for_northern_ireland_2008-2018.pdf.

ITC/ILO (2008) *Study on the Incorporation of Social Considerations in Public Procurement* (European Commission, Brussels), ec.europa.eu/social/BlobServlet? docId=1475&langId=en.

London Underground (2008), www.london.gov.uk/rp/casestudies/casestudy08.jsp.

Lulham, J (2011) Transport for London's Approach to Equality and Supplier Diversity Through Procurement, 11 *International Journal of Discrimination and the Law* 99–104.

McCrudden, C (2007) *Buying Social Justice* (OUP, Oxford).

—— (2011a) Procurement and the Public Sector Equality Duty: Lessons for the Implementation of the Equality Act 2010 from Northern Ireland? 11 *International Journal of Discrimination and the Law* 85–98.

—— (2011b) 'The *Rüffert* Case and Public Procurement' in Marise Cremona (ed), *Market Integration and Public Services within the EU* (OUP, Oxford).

Northern Ireland Assembly (2010) Committee for Finance and Personnel, Session 2009/2010, First Report, *Report on the Inquiry into Public Procurement in Northern Ireland*, 10 February 2010, NIA 19/08/09R (NIA, Belfast), www.niassembly.gov.uk/finance/2007mandate/reports/Report_19_08_09R.htm.

Office of Government Commerce (2008) *Make Equality Count* (OGC, London), webarchive.nationalarchives.gov.uk/20110822131357/http://www.ogc.gov.uk.

Procurement Board (2010) *Action Plan in Response to the Committee for Finance and Personnel Inquiry into Public Procurement in Northern Ireland* (Procurement Board, Belfast), www.dfpni.gov.uk/index/procurement-2/cpd/cpd-policy-and-legislation/cpd-policy-documents/cpd-procurement-board-action-plan-in-response-to-inquiry/pb-action-plan-in-response-to-cfp-inquiry-into-public-procurement-in-ni.pdf.

Procurement Review Implementation Team (2002) *A Review of Public Procurement: Findings and Recommendations*, February (Department of Finance and Personnel, Belfast), www.dfpni.gov.uk/pdf-main_report_rev_1_.pdf.

Scottish Government (2011) *Public Sector Equality Duty—Consultation on Public Sector Equality Duty Revised Draft Regulations* (Scottish Government, Edinburgh), www.scotland.gov.uk/Resource/Doc/357629/0120853.pdf.

SQW (2006) *Cost Benefit Analysis of Sustainable Public Procurement*: A Research Report completed for the Department for Environment, Food and Rural Affairs by SQW Ltd, (SQW, Cambridge), randd.defra.gov.uk/Document.aspx?Document=EP01024_4023_FRP.doc.

Strategic Investment Board (2010) *Delivering Social Benefits through Public Procurement: A Toolkit* (SIB, Belfast).

Treasury Officer of Accounts (2008) *Guidance on Equality of Opportunity and Sustainable Development*, DAO (DFP) 05/08, 29 May 2008 (Department of Finance and Personnel, Belfast), www.dfpni.gov.uk/index/procurement-2/cpd/cpd-policy-and-legislation/cpd-sustainability/content_cpd_equality_of_opportunity_and_sustainable_development_in_public_sector_procurement.htm.

Waller, A, Hanson, V and Sloan, D (2009) 'Including Accessibility Within and Beyond Undergraduate Computing Courses' Eleventh International ACM Sigaccess Conference on Computers and Accessibility (Assets 2009) (ACM, Pittsburgh, PA), dl.acm.org/citation.cfm?id=1639670.

West Midlands Forum (1998, revised 2005) *Racial Equality: Common Standards for Council Contracts* (Birmingham City Council et al, Birmingham), wmf-commonstandardforequalities.gov.uk/wmf/portal.nsf/fcontent?readform&docid=SD-BDEX-7DXJDB&contentid=1.001.

7

Gender Inequality and Reflexive Law: The Potential of Different Regulatory Mechanisms

SIMON DEAKIN, COLM MCLAUGHLIN
AND DOMINIC CHAI

INTRODUCTION

I N THIS CHAPTER we look at some of the 'reflexive' legal mechanisms used to encourage employers to address the gender pay gap and gender inequalities more generally in the UK during the 2000s. The Kingsmill review of 2001 argued that improved diversity management would benefit employers by reducing the risks associated with equal pay and sex discrimination litigation, and the costs of staff turnover. Kingsmill implied that a combination of disclosure, reputational effects and shareholder activism would help to drive improved diversity management without the need for new legislative initiatives. The Equality Act 2010, the result of a long process of review of discrimination law which began in the mid-2000s, moved away from a purely voluntarist approach in setting out a number of legislative reforms aimed at increasing the effectiveness of equality law in practice. However, one of the key parts of the Act, its provisions for mandatory disclosure of gender pay inequalities, was put on hold by the Coalition Government after it entered office in 2010. This poses the question of how likely it is that progress on narrowing the pay gap can be made in the absence of greater legal compulsion.

We have a means of assessing the prospects for making equality law more effective from the 'natural experiment' on equal pay audits which has in effect been going on since the early 2000s. Pay audits have been in effect obligatory during this period for public sector employers, while remaining voluntary for private sector ones. The public sector has also been subject to one of the most far-reaching developments in the operation of UK employment law for several decades, namely the huge increase in equal pay litigation which has been triggered by the entry into this field of no-win, no-fee law firms. The greater susceptibility of public sector employers to equal pay claims is, paradoxically, the result of the continuing role played by collective bargaining in that sector and by the requirements of transparency in the reporting of pay structures to which the public sector is subject. These features of the public sector context greatly increase the scope for legal challenges. The private sector, although largely insulated from these pressures, is nevertheless subject to distinctive ones of its own, in the form of shareholder and customer influence based on the logic of the 'business case' for more effective diversity management.

Our analysis is presented as follows. First of all, we set out the principal legal initiatives in this area since 2000. We then outline theoretical considerations on the meaning of reflexive law in the context of equal pay and anti-discrimination legislation. The following sections present our empirical findings: we report on the contrasting experience of pay audits in private sector and public sector firms; we examine the impact of litigation in the public sector; and we assess the experience of shareholder and customer pressure in the private sector.

LEGAL AND POLICY INITIATIVES ADDRESSING THE GENDER PAY GAP IN THE 2000S

35 years after the Equal Pay Act came into effect in the UK there remains a significant gender pay gap. The difference between the median hourly pay of full-time males and females was 10.2 per cent in 2010, while the gap for all employees was 19.8 per cent. In the private sector there is an even wider gap at 19.8 per cent and 27.5 per cent respectively (ONS 2010).

While the pay gap can be partially explained by wider social structures, including occupational segregation, the undervaluation of women's work and the unequal division of family responsibilities, it is generally accepted in policy circles that discriminatory practices by employers also contribute to the ongoing inequality in pay. The assumption is that while some pay discrimination may be deliberate, it is more likely in practice to be systemic, and as such only identifiable through systematic evaluation of payment systems by employers. Following the approach first adopted in Ontario under its 1987 Pay Equity Act (McColgan 1997), the argument for mandatory equal pay audits has increasingly been made in the UK over the last decade. The Equal Pay Taskforce (2001) concluded that as most employers did not consider their pay systems to be discriminatory, they would only conduct an equal pay audit if it were made compulsory.

Compulsion, however, was rejected by the government at this time, and instead Denise Kingsmill was commissioned to examine *non-legislative* proposals for addressing the pay gap and other issues of women's employment (Kingsmill 2001). Given Kingsmill's terms of reference, it was not surprising that her report recommended that firms should be encouraged, rather than required, to undertake equal pay audits. She based her argument for voluntarism on the business case for gender equity. She suggested that the persistent pay gap reflected human capital mismanagement by UK firms. By conducting a pay audit, organisations would not only uncover systemic discrimination if it existed, but would also uncover the causes of the clustering of women in lower levels in the organisational hierarchy and the resulting under-utilisation of women's abilities and experience. Thus, pay audits should lead firms to analyse the barriers to women's advancement, such as promotional structures that favoured long working hours or disadvantaged those with caring responsibilities or who took career breaks. They would also reduce the risks and costs associated with equal pay and sex discrimination litigation, and the costs of recruitment and retention. Finally, they would help bring about a better balanced composition to the workforce, one that would better reflect the companies' consumer bases.

Kingsmill pointed to the increased interest of institutional and individual investors in how effective companies were at managing their non-financial resources, implying that 'reputational effects' and shareholder activism would help drive human capital management reform, which would incorporate better practices around gender equality, including conducting a pay audit. Kingsmill did accept, however, that if it became clear within a few years that the majority of firms were not voluntarily conducting a pay audit then it should be made mandatory.

The issue of compulsory pay audits was also examined by the Women and Work Commission (2006) and the Discrimination Law Review (2007). The former set out the case for and against compulsion, but was unable to reach a consensus on the issue. The latter rejected mandatory pay audits suggesting that the potential costs would outweigh any benefits, and as such would 'contravene better regulation principles' (DCLG 2007: 54).

In order to support the chosen strategy of encouraging employers to undertake equal pay audits voluntarily and tackle gender inequality more broadly, a range of public policy support was implemented throughout the 2000s. For example, various toolkits and codes of practice on conducting equal pay audits were published by the former Equal Opportunities Commission (EOC), award schemes were introduced to reward exemplary employers, and the business case for equality and conducting pay audits was widely promoted through employer networks such as Opportunity Now.

During the same period, pay audits became de facto mandatory in the public sector through the local authorities' National Joint Council pay agreement, the Agenda for Change programme in the NHS and the Civil Service Reward Principles. Additionally, the public sector gender equality duty, which came into force in April 2007, required public bodies to address the causes of the gender pay gap as part of a wider legal obligation to eliminate unlawful sex discrimination and promote gender equality. Part of the logic of compulsion in the public sector was for the public sector to set a 'best practice' standard for private sector employers to emulate. Meanwhile, there was a significant rise in equal pay litigation involving local authorities and a number of cases received widespread media coverage, which highlighted the penalties for employers found to be in breach of the equal pay legislation.

Between the various public policy supports to encourage employers to undertake a pay audit voluntarily and the various governance changes in the public sector, the profile of equal pay audits had significantly increased by the mid-2000s (Neathey et al 2005). Despite this profile, the empirical evidence suggests that it only had a limited impact in influencing private sector organisations to conduct equal pay audits. An EOC commissioned survey conducted in 2005 found that 82 per cent of organisations had not conducted an equal pay audit, did not have one in progress, and did not intend to conduct one (Adams et al 2006). A more recent EHRC survey, limited to large organisations (250 plus), found that only 43 per cent were conducting any gender pay review activity. Of those reporting no pay review activity, the explanation provided by 85 per cent was that there was no need to carry out a pay audit because there was no inequality within their payment systems (Adams et al 2010). These findings confirmed the view of the Equal Pay Task Force in 2001 that, without compulsion, the majority of employers would not voluntarily undertake a pay audit, as they did not think they had any pay equity issues to resolve.

As a result, opinion shifted in favour of regulation, with the Equality Act 2010 containing a mandatory reporting requirement. Initially, this legal reporting measure, which would require organisations with more than 250 employees to report on their gender pay gap, was due to come into effect in 2013 (GEO 2010). However, the new Coalition Government announced in late 2010 that it would not be bringing this section into force, although implementation in the future remains possible as repeal of this section was not proposed.

REFLEXIVE REGULATION AS A RESPONSE TO GENDER INEQUALITY

If the 1980s and early 1990s were periods of deregulation in employment law, the period since the mid-1990s has been characterised by greater innovation and experimentation in regulatory policy, a trend which has influenced legal responses to gender inequality. Regulatory techniques which have been variously referred to as 'responsive' (Ayres and Braithwaite 1992) and 'reflexive' (Teubner 1993) are those which attempt to tailor regulatory mechanisms to particular contexts, in particular by seeking to integrate formal legal devices with self-regulation on the part of societal actors. A possible role for reflexive regulation in the context of discrimination law was identified by the Nuffield Foundation-sponsored review of the enforcement of UK anti-discrimination laws in 2000 (see also Hepple this volume). This work pointed to the limitations of a hard-law approach, which included low success rates for applicants in employment discrimination tribunal hearings and to significant delays in the resolution of litigation (Hepple, Coussey and Chowdhury 2000).

Reflexive regulation offers a critique of voluntarist approaches on the one hand and 'command and control' forms of law on the other. Voluntarist approaches which assume that the interests of business will automatically align themselves with the wider public good are seen as ignoring a range of barriers to this occurring, including externalities and related forms of market failure. The 'command and control' approach, in contrast, is criticised as involving excessive reliance on prescriptive controls. The ineffectiveness of command and control is derived in large part from limits on the capacity of law-makers to predict the consequences of regulatory interventions in the multiple contexts in which they operate. Regulation should aim instead to be reflexive in the sense of both responding, in its form and content, to social contexts, and in triggering a range of responses from social actors which can form the basis for effective self-regulation.

Autopoietic social systems theory provides the foundation for the view that the capacity of the legal system to influence social behaviour is conditioned by its need for internal consistency (Luhmann 1995, 2004; Teubner 1993). The legal system is seen as having its own unique linguistic forms and institutional processes, which translate only partially into the economic and organisational spheres. The more prescriptive a legal rule is in formal terms, the less effective it may be in practice in bringing about the desired outcome. Overly prescriptive law which results in 'juridification' or growing levels of detail and complexity has been recognised to be a particular problem in the employment law field (Simitis 1987).

Experimentation in the form of social legislation has emerged as a response to these dilemmas. A prominent example is the use of so-called 'bargained statutory adjustments' in employment law (Davies and Kilpatrick 2004). Here, legislation sets a default rule on a matter such as working time controls, which social actors can modify through self-regulation, such as collective bargaining between employers and trade unions, if the agreement they make satisfies certain criteria. These criteria could be substantive in nature (for example, setting an absolute upper limit to working hours) or procedural (for example, requiring the trade union to be broadly representative of the relevant workforce). This approach implies that a range of distributive outcomes is possible, and that standards set by law can, within limits, be traded off against other considerations. The result should be to promote diversity of practice, and, on this basis, to stimulate a learning process. Deliberation both within and between organisations is a critical part of the reflexive approach. This can be aided by benchmarking procedures and other 'best practice' dissemination mechanisms, as well as by rules mandating disclosure of current practices by the actors concerned.

Thus the reflexive approach does not at all imply the absence of law. The law has a number of roles to play: setting default conditions which apply in the absence of agreement between social actors; limiting the scope for departure from the default rule through such self-regulation; legitimating the collective actors concerned, by prescribing the conditions under which they are regarded as having the relevant representative capacity; and mandating disclosure of the information needed for meaningful negotiation. Reflexive law is therefore a form of regulation by design, not one based on the notion of law as spontaneous order: the 'frame', or 'the conditions under which a deliberative process may succeed [need to] be identified, and once identified, must be affirmatively created, rather than taken for granted' (De Schutter and Deakin 2005: 3).

A well designed reflexive law is, nevertheless, insufficient on its own to achieve the aims of regulation. For reflexive regulation to be effective in practice, 'bridging institutions' between the legal sub-system and economic and organisational fields must be in place. This means that institutions or mechanisms must be present beyond the legal system in which effective deliberation and participatory decision-making can occur. In the employment relations context these should include, at a minimum, collective bargaining or other employee-based representative mechanisms. Thus reflexive law is by no means individualist in orientation. Where the relevant collective mechanisms do not exist, the law has a capacity-building role to play in enabling them to develop.

Potential limits to the reflexive approach are nevertheless evident in the phenomenon of the 'managerialisation' of law identified by Edelman's studies of the operation of US anti-discrimination legislation (Edelman et al 1999, 2001). These studies highlight the role of HRM (human resource management) professionals in assisting the translation of legal norms into organisational practice (see also Purcell this volume). In the US context, HR managers were able to use the threat of litigation, with the potential for substantial liabilities and wider reputational losses, to persuade employers to adopt a diversity management agenda. They were able to present compliance with the law as part of a wider business case for workplace equality. In this way, 'legal rules [were] filtered through a set of managerial lenses chiefly designed to encourage smooth employment relations and high productivity' (Edelman et al 2001: 1599). As this was happening at a time in the 1980s and 1990s when, in the legal and policy arena, the civil rights agenda which had been initiated in the 1960s was coming under pressure, the advent of diversity management helped to confer a new legitimacy on the goals of the legislation.

At the same time, the metamorphosis of the legally-orientated, civil rights agenda into the practice of diversity management brought with it new dilemmas. The embedding of the diversity agenda in managerial practices had the potential to dilute the social concerns which provided the motivation for the legislation in the first place. The de-radicalisation of the law was also the precondition to its successful institutionalisation at the level of the firm: 'as legal rules are recast in managerial terms, they may be weakened but they are nonetheless more easily incorporated into organizational routines' (Edelman et al 2001: 1633).

Similar tensions are evident in Kirton and Greene's studies of diversity management in the UK. They have looked at the effects of the displacement of equality officers by diversity management specialists with a generalist HRM background during the 2000s. The greater legitimacy enjoyed by diversity managers meant that senior managers were more ready to give them public backing than they had been with equality officers, and that line managers were more prepared to take equality issues seriously. On the other hand, there was a 'considerable risk that if diversity practitioners over-identify with management and management interests, the changes they drive are more likely to serve organisational objectives than improve working lives' (Kirton and Greene 2009: 173; see also Barmes and Ashtiany 2003).

In the process of iteration between the legal system and the organisational field of the workplace, the growing acceptance of a diversity agenda within managerial practice also has potentially negative implications for the way in which the law is designed, interpreted and enforced. Once the aim of the law is seen to be the promotion of organisational efficiency as opposed to the assertion of individual rights, it is in danger of being depoliticised. This issue was raised during the process of deliberation around the Discrimination Law Review of 2007. In part because of concerns over the reflexive turn taken by that review (McCrudden 2007), the Equality Act 2010 emerged as a stronger and more far-reaching measure than had at one stage seemed possible: in addition to the introduction of mandatory reporting on pay inequalities, the Act also widened the scope for positive action in favour of historically disadvantaged groups, and introduced changes to tribunal procedure aimed at enhancing the effectiveness of legal sanctions for discriminatory acts (see GEO 2009). However, as we have seen, the Coalition Government which took office in 2010 deferred, possibly indefinitely, the bringing into force of the Act's provisions on pay disclosure and weakened other aspects (see Hepple this volume and Hepple 2011). The long gestation and incomplete implementation of the 2010 Act highlights the difficulties inherent in applying reflexive methods in the discrimination law field, a context in which conflicting economic interests are clearly visible, and where distributive and deliberative approaches to bargaining often operate in tension with each other. With these issues in mind, we now turn to our empirical evidence.

PAY AUDITS IN PRACTICE: COMPARING THE PUBLIC
AND PRIVATE SECTORS

Our analysis here is based on 40 interviews conducted between late 2007 and early 2010. Our research examined a range of pressures on organisations to address equal pay and gender equalities including corporate governance, the business case, law, unions, employees, and procurement. Here we limit our discussion mainly to the issue of pay audits though we examined other issues of gender inequality as well. At the organisational level, we carried out interviews with eight public sector organisations (six local authorities and two civil service departments), eight private-sector organisations (five listed companies and three professional partnerships), two universities, and two not-for-profit organisations (a housing association and a charity). Here our interviewees were with a mix of HR managers and diversity champions, most of whom occupied senior positions in the relevant organisations. Our sample consisted mostly of organisations which had made a public commitment to greater gender equality, as it proved difficult to get other organisations to participate in the research. As Kirton and Greene (2010) have also found, access to private sector organisations on gender equality issues is problematic because of fears of equal pay litigation and concerns that public statements of commitment to gender equality might be seen to amount to window dressing. We also interviewed five investment/equity funds, a range of union officials at local, regional and national level, one no-win no-fee lawyer involved in equal pay and other national-level stakeholders.

While all of the private sector firms in our study had conducted some form of equal pay analysis, only two had disseminated the results to employees or their representatives, and only one of these was also reporting its pay gap externally. In one case, the relevant union had asked to see the results of an audit but their request had been refused. Grosser and Moon (2008) similarly report that even among the best performing gender diversity companies in their research, the majority do not report information on equal pay audits, and the recent EHRC survey on equal pay activity among large organisations (250 plus) also found that while 43 per cent reported carrying out equal pay activity, of these only 16 per cent reported the results internally and six per cent externally (Adams et al 2010).

A comparison of one private sector and one public sector organisation that were part of our research illustrates the importance of transparency. The private sector firm told us that it had conducted a pay audit in secrecy, and claimed that it had shown there to be no gender discrimination within the firm's payment systems. However, later in the same interview the respondent commented that men engaged in 'harder bargaining' during the interview process than women, to such an extent that a male employee might end up with a starting salary of up to £10,000 more than a woman with similar experience and qualifications.

In contrast, one of the public sector organisations interviewed, which had carried out open and transparent equal pay audits on an annual basis for some years, showed greater awareness of the role played by the recruitment process in building in discriminatory pay structures. This organisation cited a case in which a man and a woman with similar experience had been appointed within the same department at the same time. They had both been offered a starting salary on the same scale point, but the male bargained for a higher starting point, claiming he would not take the job otherwise. Six months later, when it became clear that the female employee's performance was superior, the department came back to the organisation's HR division, looking to raise her salary. The HR division of this organisation was able to use this example, in tandem with the transparent and detailed pay audit, to educate departmental managers about potential gender bias in the appointments process, and its impact on the gender pay gap.

In the first case, the pay audit was conducted in secrecy by management, and as a result was narrow in scope and failed to highlight some potential issues in the appointments process. The outcomes of the appointment process were not perceived to be inequitable, but rather the inevitable outcome of individual bargaining. Additionally, despite the potential litigation risk, it was felt that the organisation could find some way to justify the differences retrospectively if it was ever challenged. The HR manager in this example seemed committed to addressing diversity issues, but her analysis of the equal pay gap and its causes was narrow. In contrast, the pay audit in the public sector organisation was part of a transparent deliberative process that stimulated learning within the organisation around some of the underlying causes of pay inequality. While it was driven by a particularly effective HR department, the inherent transparency of the union-negotiated pay scales made their job easier.

Voluntary pay audits therefore appear to be less effective when there is a lack of transparency. In contrast, those conducted in an open and deliberative way led to a deeper analysis of the causes of the pay gap and related gender issues. Without transparency, the results cannot be assessed or challenged. Where this is the case, there is no deliberation among stakeholders and the end result is likely to be only a partial evaluation of potential discrimination within a company's pay systems, with the analysis conducted from a narrow 'business case' perspective.

Deliberation around the results of a pay audit also has the potential to go beyond simply highlighting discrimination within the pay system. As Kingsmill (2001) noted, highlighting a gender pay gap within an organisation should lead to an exploration of why that gap exists, and thus to an examination of other HR systems, such as promotional structures. Some of the causes of the pay gaps will relate to outside factors, but organisations can take action to mitigate the influence of these factors. One university we interviewed had altered its promotion criteria for academics as a result of the pay audit. In this case the initial audit had found a pay gap between male and female academics, but only across the entire scales and not within different categories. At this point they could have concluded that their pay systems were not discriminatory, in that the causes of the pay gap lay elsewhere. However, they saw the pay audit as a tool for deeper analysis, and by analysing the gender gap by part-time and full-time status, it became clear that working part-time was the major promotion obstacle for female academics and thus a significant contributor to the pay gap. This led the organisation to conduct some qualitative research among part-time staff, which revealed the various pressures around teaching while still needing to achieve the same publication outputs as full-time academics in order to earn promotion. As a result of this process, the university changed its promotion criteria so that academic outputs were weighted on a pro-rata basis. It was hoped that over time this may have some impact on the promotion of female academics, and thus on the gender pay gap within the university.

These cases illustrate some clear benefits for conducting transparent pay audits and allowing meaningful deliberation within an organisation about ways to close any gender pay gap. The diversity manager at a large listed company that did not disclose its pay gap noted, in response to a question about the then expected impact of the Equality Act provisions on disclosure: 'publicly I don't like the transparency, privately I think it can only help'. A key obstacle to public disclosure is, paradoxically, reputational risk. Several respondents noted that there might be legitimate explanations for pay gaps in particular cases, but if only the headline figure were reported, the public would draw negative but arguably unfair conclusions about the organisations concerned. One non-governmental organisation (NGO) we interviewed reported that they had an overall pay gap of 35 per cent between male and female employees, but that the pay gap within each of their two business units was minimal. The NGO felt the overall pay gap could be easily explained. In one of its business units, there were many highly skilled employees, and the gender balance of the staff was roughly equal. In the other business unit, the work was less skilled, the pay lower, and the workforce predominantly female. The NGO was concerned that the headline pay gap figure would be reported in the press without adequate explanation and the conclusion the public might reach would significantly affect the donations it received, which were the primary source of its funding.

A second concern was the potential legal liabilities arising from publishing pay gap data. Several respondents pointed towards the high level of litigation in the public sector as evidence of what organisations could be opening themselves up to. This was also the explanation one respondent gave for having only conducted a pay audit at a high level of generality and not in more detail: 'we haven't done it to that level of detail [and] I don't think we want to ... because [of] what you might find and therefore what it would cost to correct'. Several of our interviewees noted the perverse incentive operating, in that firms that took positive steps to examine their pay systems might then be liable for six years' back pay, whereas taking no action reduced the risk of liability. It was noted, on the other hand, that this was also an argument for mandatory disclosure, as it would open up all firms equally to litigation, and provide an incentive for them to ensure their pay systems were not discriminatory.

Only one of the eight private sector organisations argued for mandatory pay audits. As this respondent noted, conducting a regular pay audit 'gives you comfort that … you are treating people fairly'. This company published the results of its annual pay audit both internally and externally, and had the process externally audited every three years. However, the overall picture emerging from our interviews with private sector firms is that those companies which were not already disclosing their pay structures, either internally or externally, were not going to do so voluntarily. As one HR manager told us, referring to disclosure, 'we would only do it voluntarily if it would show us in a good light … without the law we would never do it'.

EQUAL PAY LITIGATION AND COLLECTIVE BARGAINING IN THE PUBLIC SECTOR

The issue of equal pay among UK local authorities reached crisis proportions in the second half of the 2000s. Some estimates put the liability for back pay in local government at almost £3 billion, and it was thought that an increase of five per cent in the pay bill going forward would be required to ensure compliance with equal pay law (LGE 2006). It was claimed that local authorities would have to cut services and sell off assets in order to meet their equal pay obligations. The employment tribunal system was described by Lord Justice Mummery as 'bursting at the seams' with the sheer volume of cases. The background to the litigation involving local authorities was the 1997 national collective agreement, referred to as the 'single status agreement' (SSA), which was negotiated between the public sector unions and the local authority employers to address historical gender inequalities within the local authority pay systems. The agreement brought together the employment terms and conditions of various groups of workers—what was known as the 'white book' for manual workers and the 'purple book' of the administrative, professional, technical and clerical workers (APT&C)—to form the 'green book', or single spine of terms and conditions. While the SSA was a national agreement with a national pay structure, actual spinal points for different jobs were to be worked out locally through a detailed job evaluation exercise. The most significant inequalities related to the white book for manual workers. A limited job evaluation for the white book had taken place in 1987 but it had ignored the bonus system through which workers in mostly male dominated grades had been receiving historical bonuses of up to 30 per cent that in effect were now part of their basic pay. Hence, there were some clear historical inequalities, as well as potential hidden inequalities that local job evaluation processes were intended to unveil and eradicate. The original pay structures were to apply until after the job evaluation process had been completed, at which point workers would move across to their new scale point in the 'green book'.

Despite the SSA being a significant achievement for the unions which negotiated it, very few agreements were struck at local level over the implementation of single status. No date was set in the 1997 agreement for implementation of single status and there were no penalties for failing to implement the SSA at the local level. The 2004 NJC Pay Implementation Agreement set a deadline of April 2006 for job evaluations to be completed, with the new single status pay structures to be implemented by March 2007. Again, however there were no penalties on the parties for failing to reach agreement by these dates. A small number of local authorities completed the job evaluation process quickly and, as a result, seem to have avoided the back-pay issues which developed at other authorities. Most local authorities took a long time to get the process under way. By the 2007 deadline, estimates reported in the media were that only around half of the almost 400 local authorities within England and Wales had implemented a new single status pay structure, and by the middle of 2009 this figure had still only increased to around two-thirds of local authorities (LGE 2009).

Of the six local authorities we interviewed between late 2008 and early 2010, one had completed the process by 2003, two had adopted a two-phase process and implemented phase one (the lower half of the new single spinal column) and were still working on phase two (although they still had some outstanding legal cases in relation to the implementation of phase one), two authorities were still conducting job evaluations and had yet to implement a new pay structure for any of their green book staff, and one authority had been unable to reach agreement with its unions and had unilaterally imposed a new single status pay structure. Interviews with councils were conducted with senior HR representatives (eg HR managers, pay and reward managers). We also interviewed five union officials from local, regional and national levels, and one no-win, no-fee law firm.

A significant problem in the implementation of the SSA was that employers and unions could not reach agreement about what to do with the results of the pilot studies. Inertia turned to resistance as it became evident that implementation of the job evaluation scheme (JES) would result in some workers facing potential pay cuts (on average, around 20 per cent of council workers are what have been referred to as 'losers'), while other workers would gain from the process (around 40 per cent). Councils could see that one possible impact was a significant increase in the overall wage bill, and many initially tried negotiating on the basis of an overall 'nil cost' settlement, where the additional costs of winners would be offset by reductions for losers. On the union side, it had been assumed that achieving equal pay would be achieved through pay rises for those who were being underpaid, while pay cuts were not something that had been anticipated and nor were they something the unions could sell to their members, particularly as it was not the basis on which they sold 'single status' to them back in 1997. Thus, employers wanted a settlement that would not increase wage costs while unions wanted lifetime pay protection for any workers who would suffer cuts in income as a result of the job evaluation scheme. Negotiations over the JES became fractious and stalled in many local authorities.

The involvement from early 2003 of a Newcastle-based no-win, no-fee law firm was a turning point in this process. Around the same time the period of entitlement for back pay in equal pay cases was increased from two to six years as a result of a series of European law judgments. Prior to the emergence of no-win, no-fee litigation, while there had been some litigation by unions and use of the equal pay questionnaire to get management to the table to negotiate over single status, the issue of back-pay does not appear to have been on the agenda. A local authority we interviewed, which had otherwise fully implemented the JES by 2004, had made no back-pay settlement at all. Another local authority we interviewed had agreed the first phase of the JES with the unions to start in February 2004, and this agreement also contained no back-pay settlement. As the HR manager of this council noted, 'it is hard to believe now but back in 2004 we were in very different territory'. The focus of the negotiation between management and unions up to this point had been about rectifying existing inequalities in the pay structures and dealing with potential 'losers'.

Negotiations between unions and employers over back pay were initially for significantly less than full potential entitlements. As one HR Manager described it, 'it was simply a ... compensatory sum that they would accept in return for giving up their right to make a claim'. Unions argued that in negotiating a deal with management, they had to balance a range of interests. Unions not only wanted back-pay compensation but they also wanted pay protection for losers going forward for a period of time. Some of the early agreements involving the councils we interviewed included pay protection of up to 6 years. Employers claimed they did not have access to unlimited funds and were threatening to outsource services and cut jobs. As one union official put it, 'there is no point us getting our women members X thousand £s in the pocket if they get ... three months' notice and they've got no job to go to'. As back pay had not been an anticipated part of the SSA, no councils had budgeted for it. Initial amounts of back-pay cited to us in the interviews in agreements reached between 2003 and 2005 were capped at around £10,000 per person, with the amount actually paid out based on some form of locally agreed matrix which took account of length of service and hours per week worked. In 2011, settlements were being reached at over three times this amount.

The entry of the no-win, no-fee solicitors had a major impact in large part because of their willingness to support litigation against unions which had negotiated agreements implementing the SSA. In the *Allen v GMB* litigation ([2008] IRLR 690; see Deakin and Morris, 2009: 630), an employment tribunal ruled that the way in which the union arrived at a negotiated collective settlement with the Middlesbrough Metropolitan Borough Council, which had attempted to balance a range of conflicting interests (back pay, pay cuts, and potential job losses through service cuts and outsourcing), constituted indirect sex discrimination against their female members. In balancing the various interests, the tribunal found that the GMB had given undue weight to pay protection for the 'losers'. It recognised that the union had adopted a strategy that would provide 'the least protest from the membership as a whole'. However, the agreed back-pay settlement constituted only 25 per cent of a potential claim by the white book claimants. Moreover, the claimants had not been made aware of this. The tribunal ruling focused on the union's failure to give the women involved adequate advice or to inform them of the extent of the losses they were being asked to bear. The tribunal's finding of indirect sex discrimination was reversed by the EAT but restored by the Court of Appeal. Several thousand further claims were then issued against both the GMB and UNISON, although these were later withdrawn.

There are conflicting views on how far the *Allen* ruling altered the strategy of the unions in dealing with equal pay. The GMB officials involved in the case had, according to a union officer we interviewed, been 'absolutely vilified' in the ruling, and yet had acted in good faith. The *Allen* ruling came as a shock to the unions, but in the local authority sector they responded positively: as a result of the ruling, union systems had been 'enhanced and [made] more robust'. The unions became more cautious in their approach to negotiating settlements, but also more proactive in taking cases of their own against employers. UNISON, for example, had taken more than 40,000 claims to the Employment Tribunal by early 2008 (Jaffe et al 2008). A contrasting view was expressed by a member of the law firm we interviewed:

> unless the unions have an 'on the road to Damascus' moment, they see this as a problem which they have to get round. They don't see it as an issue which they need to pursue on behalf of their female members.

The increased role for litigation, although defended by the no-win, no-fee law firms on the basis of its potential for vindicating the rights of disadvantaged female workers and union members, was seen by unions and employers as having the potential to undermine the effectiveness of the collective bargaining process. As one official put it:

> Everything at the end of the day is a shabby compromise … but it's done on the basis of this is the best we can negotiate; it's not some of you can take it and some of you can't. Once we take a vote on it, it's implemented collectively, that's the whole basis. Why would they bother negotiating with us otherwise?

From the employers' perspective, the prospect of liability for up to six years' back pay was a factor in chilling negotiations. This was seen as contradicting the aim of a more open examination and discussion of pay systems. As we have seen, the high profile of equal pay litigation in the public sector was a reason given by a number of the private sector employers we interviewed for avoiding too close an examination of their own pay systems. Their fears may be justified: according to the member of the law firm we spoke to, 'if there was an actual obligation to publish information, and a right to receive information, in relation to these matters, we would make huge progress' in the private sector.

There is also some evidence that, in the public sector, the cost of back-pay settlements had also slowed down the process of implementing single status. Councils we spoke with talked about the difficulties of meeting the costs within existing budgets and many had held back from reaching agreements hoping that central government might have assisted with funding, particularly given this was an historical issue. In 2007 the government announced that it would not provide additional funding to cover the increased costs associated with equal pay, but it would allow councils to capitalise expenditure (CIPFA 2007).

Finally, there is some evidence that the litigation around the implementation of the SSA had had made it more difficult to reach settlements. Although the scope of the law had become clearer over time, employers continued to fight cases on costs-related grounds, and were using the legal process to delay the resolution of claims. One union official noted:

> everyone is now getting a much clearer picture about what's the scope of the GMF (general material factor) defence, how is it going to work, where is it not going to work, what kind of evidence will stand up to scrutiny in a tribunal, what won't … there is still a huge grey area, but there are a certain number of cases where you think yes that's clearly a case that looks like it's going to succeed. But there isn't always a correlation between the strength of the case and the ferocity with which the employer fights it.

CSR AND SHAREHOLDER PRESSURE IN THE PRIVATE SECTOR

Reflexive mechanisms have been adopted in the area of corporate governance as a way of bringing about change in firm behaviour. As part of the wider CSR agenda, pension funds and other institutional owners have been encouraged to adopt an 'enlightened shareholder value' position by taking a long-term view of their investments and engaging more actively with the social, ethical and environmental (SEE) practices of their investee companies (Myners 2002). To aid this process, pension funds are required to disclose their statement of investment principles (as set out in the 2000 Disclosure Regulations and the 2002 Myners Principles, now incorporated into the Financial Reporting Council's Stewardship Code). The Companies Act 2006 requires boards of large companies to take account of a range of stakeholders, including employees, when managing a firm's financial performance. Thus, firms can legally take a long-term view in adopting human resource management strategies that take account of employee rights and interests, such as gender equalities (Company Law Review 2001; Armour et al 2003).

It was this 'enlightened shareholder value' perspective that influenced Kingsmill's (2001) argument that a combination of shareholder activism and reputational effects would help drive human capital management reform in the area of gender equality, and would thus put pressure on firms to conduct equal pay audits. However, as the research cited earlier showed, the proportion of firms conducting pay audits voluntarily remains small. Additionally, of the private sector firms we interviewed, only one interviewee was aware of any questions being raised by shareholders in relation to gender equality issues. While this resulted in a head office decree for subsidiary organisations to produce a gender diversity policy, this was seen by the subsidiaries as a public relations response to the shareholder concern, with no follow up or monitoring of the policy. This section explores the relationship between shareholder pressure and firm behaviour in this area drawing on our interviews with representatives of SRI (Socially Responsible Investment) funds and union officials as well as an analysis of WERS data. WERS is a survey based on a nationally-representative sample of workplaces in manufacturing and services with five or more employees in Great Britain. It covers both the public and private sectors. We will see that the influence of shareholders is quite minimal in improving gender-related employment rights and other pressures are more significant. For reflexive mechanisms such as shareholder activism to work effectively, more effective disclosure-based regulation is needed.

Evidence of the impact of SRI on employer practice is available from WERS 2004. The 2004 WERS survey made it possible for the first time to study the impact of corporate governance on employment relations by identifying the ownership form and corporate governance structure of the employing organisation. Among other things, WERS 2004 distinguishes between private-sector employers with a stock exchange listing and those without. In relation to equality, WERS enables us to see whether an employer has a gender equality *policy*; whether it *monitors* gender equality in relation to recruitment, promotion and pay; and whether it implements family-friendly *practices* above the level mandated by law. By combining the corporate governance and gender equality data from WERS, we can get a measure of how far listed firms are more likely than others to prioritise gender equality issues in the way that reflexive theory suggests they might. We can also test for other possible influences on gender equality policy and practices: whether a firm has government contracts, and thereby comes under pressure to comply with best practice on gender equality issues (among others); whether it deals directly with the public as consumers (a 'B2C' firm), a possible indicator of its greater sensitivity to reputational issues; whether it subscribes to or otherwise complies with voluntary standards stressing good HR practice on matters including equality, such as Investor in People guidelines; what its ownership structure is (whether it is family-owned and/or foreign-owned); whether it has an employee share- or profit-sharing scheme, a possible indicator of employee empowerment; whether it employs a significant number of female managers; and whether it has a strong union presence. Unfortunately, there is no information in WERS on whether firms have conducted a pay audit, hence the discussion here is on gender equality more generally.

A full analysis of the WERS data is available elsewhere (Deakin, Chai and McLaughlin 2011) and here we briefly summarise our key findings. Around 15 per cent of private-sector workplaces sampled by WERS 2004 belonged to employers with a stock market listing; 26 per cent had government contracts; and 40 per cent dealt directly with members of the public as customers. Around half of all private-sector workplaces had a gender equality policy. However, only 12.5 per cent monitored their recruitment practices from a gender-equality point of view, six per cent monitored promotion, and four per cent monitored pay. When we conducted a bivariate analysis, we found that listed firms were significantly more likely than non-listed ones to have a gender policy and to engage in monitoring of recruitment, promotion and pay. However, some of these differences disappear once we control for other potential influences. We compared the effects of a stock market listing with other external pressures (government contracts, B2C, voluntary standards) while controlling for firm characteristics and the extent of workplace diversity. What we found was that having a stock market listing matters for whether a firm has a gender policy, but that it makes no difference to gender monitoring, and has little impact on family-friendly practices (reduced working for parents, maternity leave and paternity leave are significantly correlated with listing). Of the other external pressures, government contracts do not appear to be significant drivers of equality, but being a B2C firm is significant for both gender policies and monitoring (although less so for family-friendly practices). Firm size (as might be expected) is strongly correlated with the incidence of policy, monitoring and practices (see Edwards, chapter eight this volume). Firms employing a high proportion of female managers are more likely to have a gender policy and to monitor recruitment and promotion, but not pay. In addition, union presence is strongly linked to having a gender policy and to the monitoring of gender equality in recruitment.

In short, the WERS evidence appears to point to some positive effects of a stock market listing in terms of the approach of private sector companies to gender equality. However, these effects are largely confined to gender policies rather than to the monitoring of gender equality outcomes or to the substance of family-friendly practices. One interpretation of this is that a gender equality policy is window dressing for the annual report aimed at (among others) SRI funds. Firms do not need to translate the policy into practice because the level of interest of institutional investors in the area of gender equality is superficial and the presence of a policy ticks the necessary boxes. This interpretation is supported by our interviews with the investment funds, which found that gender equality was not high up the list of social issues that investors raised with them. Among employee issues, child labour, supply chain employment conditions, and health and safety carry the biggest reputational risk. Also, when gender is raised by investors, it is generally in relation to having an equal opportunities policy or the proportion of women on the board, but rarely in relation to equal pay. Despite the publicity in the UK during the 2000s around pay audits, the only question relating to pay audits put to the investment funds we interviewed had come from a trade union official. Most of the investment funds noted that there is a fine line between engaging with companies over important issues and moving into micro-management. As one interviewee noted in response to a question on equal pay audits:

> We have a dividing line or a tenet if you like, thou shalt not micro-manage, [and] that is just too far down. There are limits to what we think we can achieve as corporate owners and although we have here the biggest resource of any fund management company, this is still a finite resource and there are a lot of companies [we invest in] ... So it is our job then to call to account the directors of companies ..., but if we were then to try to get involved in this type of management decision, which is setting pay for employees generally, or quotas for types of employees, it is beyond what I think we should be doing and what I would suspect our clients would want us to do.

Our interview data also suggests that the reputational risk for shareholders that might arise from equal pay litigation may not be significant enough to concern institutional investors, at least not from a purely financial perspective. One union official with responsibility for pensions had raised the question of equal pay audits with six SRI firms in relation to a large public sector contractor. The union official claimed that the contractor had inherited discriminatory pay systems from the public sector and felt there was an equal pay litigation risk in the region of £70 million. The response of one fund manager to this financial risk was that it was too small and 'would have no material impact on the share price; no one would be interested'. Only one of the fund managers took his questions to the company concerned but the union official reported receiving no response.

While gender did not feature significantly as an issue among SRI funds, the picture more broadly is of a limited impact of SRI on the treatment of social, ethical and environmental issues at company level. All of our interviewees noted the growth of SRI over the last decade and could point to examples of where they had filed or supported a shareholder resolution or engaged with firms over specific issues and changed behaviour. Some of these examples related to employment rights. Several of the interviewees cited their involvement in supporting the same resolutions in the US relating to Walmart and to First Group. This is interesting in that it highlights the challenge of bringing about change in very large multinational companies. Given the number of institutional investment funds investing, SRI funds need to be coordinated to have any impact when voting against large mainstream funds which may be less interested in social and ethical issues. One widely reported example of this coordination was when four investment firms from the US and UK—New York City Pension Funds, Illinois State Board of Investment, F&C Asset Management and the UK University Superannuation Scheme—wrote a joint open letter to the chairman of Walmart's audit committee stating it needed to improve its employment practices as they were damaging the share price. This followed a number of embarrassing stories in the media relating to illegal immigrant workers, a class action sex discrimination suit, and cuts to employee healthcare benefits.[1]

However, these appear to be isolated cases; it is clear that the extent of shareholder activism more generally is very limited. SRI remains a niche part of the overall investment market. As one SRI fund told us, 'on the whole people are investing as they have always done. They are not raising issues at company meetings with CEOs; they have issues that affect the share price to discuss—that's the bottom line'. The overall picture that emerged was that many fund managers were not being challenged in relation to social or ethical issues by individual or institutional investors.

The SRI investment firms we interviewed were disappointed about the apparent lack of interest by pension funds and other institutional inves-tors, particularly in the light of developments in disclosure regulation. In the UK, it was anticipated that the Pension Disclosure Regulations would raise awareness of SRI issues for pension fund trustees and lead to greater engagement over social, ethical and environmental investment. The regula-tions require pension funds to report their investment principles and how they are achieving them on an annual basis. However, our interviewees suggested that pension fund trustees are largely conservative, even when they might be overseeing pension funds of NGOs actively engaged in such issues. Additionally, as one interviewee noted, where trustees do have an interest they are not aware of how to use the fund:

> the level of ignorance around how the capital markets and how fund managers, how finance actually works, people might be interested in ethics and being responsible but how you actually progress that through to understand it, it is just too much.

The interviewees were unanimous that the biggest barriers to greater levels of social investment and engagement by pension funds and other institutional

---

[1] news.bbc.co.uk/2/hi/business/4605733.stm.

investors over SEE issues were lack of transparency and quantitative information that third parties can use to make meaningful investment decisions. While pension disclosure rules have led to a significant increase in the number of pension funds drawing up statements about investment principles, the consensus was that the actual impact on practice was questionable; 'a one-off policy statement sits in the drawer or in an investment management agreement signed by two people that probably left the company a couple of years ago'. Without meaningful reporting about how the policy is actually being implemented and what has been achieved, the perception is that most are meaningless statements of intent. However, for pension funds to engage effectively on CSR issues with the companies they invest in, they will also require a commensurate level of transparent, quantitative and regular information to be reported by these companies. As one interviewee put it:

> transparency is a fundamental tenet of responsibility; without transparency you can't have accountability [and] third parties have no way of judging what you have been doing ... In the absence of either civil society institutions or professional bodies that are ranking that transparency, it won't move companies forward, it will become an anodyne boiler plate, the same old 'this is what we said last year it is the same thing this year' type reporting. So you need that evaluation, the analysis of the approach, of the transparency, for it to actually get companies on a conveyor belt to being, if you like, the most responsible.

These findings support the research by Grosser and Moon (2008) into corporate reporting on gender equality. While they found that many 'best practice' companies were reporting on a range of gender indicators, reporting was mostly limited to policy and practices. Only in a small number of cases was there reporting on progress against targets. Moreover, because firms choose what they report on, comparing firm performance on gender performance was not possible. Thus, as a number of our interviewees noted, for disclosure rules to be effective, there need to be key performance indicators developed with an independent verification system so that progress can be monitored and compared across a range of companies. Hence, most of the investor firms we spoke with were not opposed to greater levels of regulation. As one interviewee noted, 'companies operate within a society which itself has laws and rules ... and to suppose that the control of companies can be left entirely to the shareholders as owner seems to me wrong and rather dangerous'. Thus they saw regulation as potentially important, both in assisting institutional activism, and in helping firms understand society's expectations of their behaviour.

CONCLUSION

In this paper we have reviewed evidence on the operation of a range of mechanisms used for making equal pay law in the UK more effective. In the past decade, these have included pay audits and collective bargaining at national and local level in the public sector, and shareholder and customer pressure, based on the logic of the business case for diversity, in the private sector. There has also been a huge increase in litigation against both unions and employers, almost entirely affecting the public sector. This is therefore a rich field in which to compare the modes of working of different regulatory techniques.

We see evidence, firstly, of both the costs and benefits of 'hard law' strategies. The large-scale litigation initiated by no-win, no-fee law firms was defended by them on the basis of the substantive gains it achieved for a group of disadvantaged workers. For unions and employers in the public sector, on the other hand, the litigation process was seen as undermining the effectiveness of collective bargaining as a means of realigning pay structures with the goals of equal pay legislation. In those parts of the public sector most exposed to these legal claims, mandatory pay audits and the resulting public disclosure of pay inequalities had failed to avoid a situation in which the costs of implementing equal pay had increased exponentially, and may have contributed to this situation.

The situation in the private sector is on the face of it very different, but outcomes are equally problematic. Here, collective bargaining has weakened as an influence over pay structures. Pay audits are voluntary and, when they are carried out, are rarely made public. There is comparatively little litigation, in part because of the relative weakness of unions as collective actors in the private sector, and a lack of transparency over pay structures. However, alternative mechanisms for implementing equality law, including shareholder pressure based on the 'business case' for diversity, appear to be failing to have a significant impact on firm behaviour. A growing awareness of the reputational dimension of diversity management has so far been reflected in a greater willingness of private sector firms to agree and disseminate equal opportunities policies, but not to put them into practice.

An emerging conclusion is that there is scope for reflexive solutions of the kind which have not yet been systematically attempted. A reflexive approach does not imply the absence of 'hard law'. Rather, the legal framework has a number of roles to play: inducing efficient disclosure, setting default rules, and encouraging bargaining in the shadow of the law. The current structure of UK equality law arguably fails to provide the kind of structure that is needed. In the absence of a general requirement for mandatory pay audits, disclosure in the private sector is limited and information flows restricted. In the public sector, by contrast, individual litigation has been pursued at the cost of the effective working of the system of collective self-regulation. Victories gained in some high-profile cases have had mixed effects in the wider system. These issues need to be addressed by steps to restore the primacy of collectively-negotiated solutions while enhancing public disclosure of the extent of pay inequalities. This is an approach which, unfortunately, is missing from the Equality Act 2010, at least in the form in which it is being brought into force by the Coalition Government.

BIBLIOGRAPHY

Adams, L, Carter, K and Schäfer, S (2006) *Equal Pay Reviews Survey 2005* (Manchester, Equal Opportunities Commission).

Adams, L, Gore, K and Shury, J (2010) *Gender Pay Gap Reporting Survey 2009* (Manchester, Equality and Human Rights Commission).

Armour, J, Deakin, S and Konzelmann, S (2003) 'Shareholder Primacy and the Trajectory of UK Corporate Governance' 41 *British Journal of Industrial Relations* 531–55.

Ayres, I and Braithwaite, J (1992) *Responsive Regulation: Transcending the Deregulation Debate* (Oxford, OUP).

Barmes, L and Ashtiany, S (2003) 'The Diversity Approach to Achieving Equality: Potential and Pitfalls' 32 *Industrial Law Journal* 274–96.

CIPFA (2007) 'Accounting for Back Pay Provisions Arising from Equal Pay Claims (England and Wales only)' LAAP Bulletin 68, www.cipfa.org.uk/pt/pt_details_l.cfm?news_id=30437.

Company Law Review Committee (2001) *Modern Company Law for a Competitive Economy: Developing the Framework* (London, The Stationery Office).

Davies, P and Kilpatrick, C (2004) 'UK Worker Representation after Single Channel' 33 *Industrial Law Journal* 121–51.

DCLG (2007) *Discrimination Law Review. A Framework for Fairness: Proposals for a Single Equality Bill for Great Britain* (London, Department for Communities and Local Government).

Deakin, S, Chai, D and McLaughlin, C (2011) 'Corporate Governance, Gender Equality, and Family-friendly Practices in British Firms', paper presented to the Regulating for Decent Work Conference, ILO, Geneva, July 2011; CBR working paper series, September 2011, www.cbr.cam.ac.uk.

Deakin, S and Morris, G (2009) *Labour Law* 5th edn (Oxford, Hart Publishing).

De Schutter, O and Deakin, S (2005) 'Introduction: Reflexive Governance and the Dilemmas of Social Regulation' in O De Schutter and S Deakin (eds), *Social Rights and Market Forces: Is the Open Coordination of Employment and Social Policies the Future of Social Europe?* 1–17 (Brussels, Bruylant).

Edelman, L, Uggen, C and Erlanger, H (1999) 'The Endogeneity of Legal Regulation: Grievance Procedures as Rational Myth' 105 *American Journal of Sociology* 406–54.

Edelman, L, Riggs Fuller, S and Mara-Drita, I (2001) 'Diversity Rhetoric and the Managerialization of Law' 106 *American Journal of Sociology* 1589–164.

Equal Pay Task Force (2001) *Just Pay* (Manchester, Equal Opportunities Commission).

GEO (2009) *A Fairer Future: The Equality Bill and Other Action to Make Equality a Reality* (London, Government Equalities Office).

—— (2010) 'Equality Act 2010', www.equalities.gov.uk/equality_act_2010.aspx.

Grosser, K and Moon, J (2008) 'Developments in Company Reporting on Workplace Gender Equality? A Corporate Social Responsibility Perspective' 32 *Accounting Forum* 179–98.

Hepple, B (2011) *Equality: The New Legal Framework* (Oxford, Hart).

Hepple, B, Coussey, M and Chowdhury, T (2000) *Equality: A New Framework. Report of the Independent Review of the Enforcement of UK Anti-Discrimination Legislation* (Oxford, Hart Publishing).

Jaffe, M, McKenna, B and Venner, L (2008) *Equal Pay, Privatisation and Procurement* (Liverpool, The Institute of Employment Rights).

Kingsmill, D (2001) *Review of Women's Employment and Pay* (London, DTI).

Kirton, G and Greene, A (2009) 'The Costs and Opportunities of Doing Diversity Work in Mainstream Organisations' 19 *Human Resource Management Journal* 159–75.

—— (2010) *The Dynamics of Managing Diversity: A Critical Approach* (Oxford, Elsevier).

LGE (2006) *Unblocking the Route to Equal Pay in Local Government* (London, Local Government Employers).

—— (2009) 'LGE Update on Progress on Local Pay Reviews and Equal Pay, July 2009' (London, Local Government Employers), www.lge.gov.uk/lge/aio/2525519.

Luhmann, N (1995) *Social Systems* (Stanford, CA, Stanford University Press).

—— (2004) *Law as a Social System*, trans K Ziegert; F Kastner, R Nobles, D Schiff and R Ziegert (eds) (Oxford, Oxford University Press).

McColgan, A (1997) *Just Wages for Women* (Oxford, Clarendon Press).

McCrudden, C (2007) 'Equality Legislation and Reflexive Regulation: A Response to the Discrimination Law Review's Consultative Paper' 36 *Industrial Law Journal* 255–66.

Myners, P (2001) *Institutional Investment in the UK: A Review* (London, HM Treasury).

Neathey, F, Willison, R, Akroyd, K, Regan, J and Hill, D (2005) *Equal Pay Reviews in Practice* (Manchester, Equal Opportunities Commission).

ONS (2010) 'Full-time Gender Pay Gap Narrows', www.statistics.gov.uk/cci/nugget.asp?id=167.

Simitis, S (1987) 'Juridification of Labour Relations' in G Teubner (ed), *Juridification of Social Spheres* (Berlin, Walter de Gruyter).

Teubner, G (1993) *Law as an Autopoietic System* (Oxford, Blackwell).

Women and Work Commission (2006) *Shaping a Fairer Future* (London, Women and Equality Unit).

8

Employment Rights in Small Firms

PAUL EDWARDS

S MALL FIRMS ILLUSTRATE the issues involved in making employment rights effective in three respects. The first relates simply to
numerical importance. Small firms (defined as those with 1–49
employees) accounted for 34 per cent of private sector employment in 2010
while medium-sized firms (50–249 employees) accounted for a further 14
per cent (BIS 2010). Unless otherwise noted, the reference point in this
chapter is the small firm thus defined. Second, such firms lack many of
the standard mechanisms through which employment rights are commonly
expected to be operationalised. Collective bargaining, for example, is rare.
Analysis of the 2004 Workplace Employment Relations Survey (WERS)
distinguished workplaces owned by small (5–49 employees) and medium-
sized (50–249 employees) companies and compared them to workplaces
owned by larger private sector companies; only twoper cent of employees in
small-firm workplaces, and nine per cent in medium-sized firms, were covered by collective bargaining, compared to a figure of 35per cent in larger
firms (Forth et al 2006: 58). Third, small firms are commonly seen as being
particularly prone to ignore rights. A long-standing fact has been their
disproportionate appearance at Employment Tribunals (ETs).Estimates
from the 2003 Survey of Employment Tribunal Applications show that the
rate of cases per employee in firms with 1–249 employees was twice that
in larger organisations (Saridakis et al 2008: 480). If we look at the 2008
SETA data (Peters et al 2010) and use employment figures for that year, we
find exactly the same ratio. Whether appearance at ETs can be equated with
being a 'bad employer' is not, however, self-evident. Placing the second and
third considerations alongside the numerical importance of the small firm
suggests that the behaviour of this kind of firm will be important for the
overall practice of employment rights.

In this chapter I will argue that the common practice of drawing, from
the second and third facts just listed, the conclusion that small firms are bad
employers, is false. This is done in three stages. First, employment practice
in small firms is outlined. They are not, in general, 'bad employers', and
some reasons are offered as to why they do not fit this stereotype. Second,

the ways in which small firms respond to some specific employment rights are considered and related to the kind of small firm concerned: forms of 'response' or 'impact' vary according to the nature of the law and the kind of firm concerned. We can also address why rights may be seen as irrelevant, as opposed to their being consciously ignored. Third, some specific steps can be suggested for improving the use of rights, in light of the actual practice of the small firm.

NATURE OF EMPLOYMENT RELATIONS IN THE SMALL FIRM

Character of Employment Relations

There are several reasons why employment practice in small firms is hard to assess. First, the starting point is often in terms of a particular theoretical lens such as that of the bad employer. Second, a related issue concerns the implicit explanation: is there something inherent in the size of the firm that leads managers to behave in certain ways, or is size a proxy for something else? If it is something else, then arguments about the size of firms may miss the point. Third, how far are all small firms the same? To the extent that they are not, the fact that some small firms generate many ET cases does not mean that we can generalise about all small firms. If the former group is a subset, what marks it out? The following discussion offers answers to all three sets of questions.

In relation to lenses, debates on the small firm up to the 1970s often equated small size with harmony. This view was famously expressed by the Bolton Committee of 1971, which asserted that small size eases communication problems, allows working rules to be varied to suit each person, and permits a wide variety of roles and experiences (Bolton 1971: 22). Though the implications for employment rights were rarely made explicit, there were at least two: that rights were met through some natural process; and that the informality of the small firm was the functional equivalent of rules in the large firm. Such views have been frequently dismissed (see Ram and Edwards 2010), but they retain force in two very distinct respects. First, policy arguments have been shaped by the perceived needs of small firms and the dangers of imposing rigidity. Second, they are not wholly wrong in analytical terms: there are features of firm size that have effects on employment relations, as discussed below.

A response to these early views was to stress the opposite: the extent of autocracy in the small firm. Most notably, Rainnie (1989), studying the clothing industry, found evidence of low wages and domination of the workplace by the employer. The implication in terms of employment rights would be that the firms needed policing in some way and that stronger mechanisms were needed so that employees could enforce their rights.

Yet the analytical underpinnings of the 'autocracy' view were more subtle: small size could tend towards autocracy but only when other conditions were also present. Curran and Stanworth (1981) had already shown that size did not have determining effects in the workplace: looking at two sectors, they showed that employment relations in small firms had more in common with large firms in the same sector than with other small firms. Goss (1991) developed a very useful framework based on the extent of the employer's and the employee's dependence on each other. The autocracy of the sweatshop could occur where employees were dependent on the employer for jobs but where the employer could easily replace workers, for example where skills were low and interchangeable. In situations of greater mutual dependence other patterns might emerge. For example, parts of the construction industry exemplified 'fraternalism': egalitarian relationships based on low levels of hierarchy and the possibility that the employee could establish his (or, rarely, her) own business, or indeed alternate between independent and employee statuses.

More recent scholarship has sometimes switched between these views. For example, Blyton and Turnbull (2004) carefully discuss different kinds of small firm, but they also conflate small and non-union firms, and in places suggest that small firms tend to be inherently autocratic: 'many small firms are genuinely ignorant of their obligations or else deliberately choose to flout the law' (ibid: 304), and they often suffer high attrition rates as a result (ibid: 302).

The solution lies in several distinctions. First, small firms, like any other firm, have to secure a degree of consent within the work process. It is not the case that they can simply practise autocracy: workers have to be persuaded to attend work and to carry out their tasks in the required way, and trying to secure their consent through force would be very expensive in terms of the costs of supervision and probably only feasible in relation to the most simple of tasks. Studies of conditions likely to promote autocracy have in fact found negotiated order (Ram 1994).

Second, the reason that negotiated consent exists turns on several features of the small firm. Those studied by Ram were Asian-owned clothing firms characterised by two kinds of employer dependence on the employee: some workers had skills that were hard to replace and were thus able to bargain with the employer; others had family or kin relationships that cut across purely economic ties. Family ownership is common in small firms, and familial relations have commonly been found to moderate any tendency towards autocracy (Baines and Wheelock 1998; Ram, Abbas et al 2001). Work organisation in Ram's firms, moreover, was very simple, with little hierarchy and few formal rules. To impose autocracy would mean costs for the employer relating to more direct supervision and the risk of losing valued workers. Studies in the road haulage industry (Marchington et al 2003) and in food manufacturing (Edwards et al 2009) have underlined the combined role of non-Taylorised work systems and personal, if not necessarily family, relationships in moderating autocracy. Face-to-face relationships tend to generate some sense of personal obligation. Small firms also tend to eschew formal systems of monitoring and supervision, which means that there remains a degree of dependence on employees. Many owner-managers are also more concerned with the overall operation of the business than with the details of work organisation, which also creates space for work organisation based on informal principles rather than autocracy.

Third, we can thus say that there is a 'pure' size effect in the sense that being of a certain size has some necessary effects on how firms work (Tsai et al 2007). This effect works mainly through the centrality of face-to-face relationships. The *character* of these relationships is of course variable, but their existence means that the employment relationship has to be managed directly. As a study in China concluded, small firms rely on personal connections and can find the costs of autocracy undesirable; it may be that autocracy is most likely in larger, less personalised, and more Taylorised workplaces (Li and Edwards 2008).

Fourth, the effects of small size will vary according to the specifics of the firms. Small firms can be found throughout the economy, and those in professional services will be very different from low-wage manufacturers. Small firms may on average be more likely than large ones to neglect employment rights, but this average will conceal significant variation. A simple illustration is to take the Workplace Employment Relations Survey (WERS) data and break them down by sector. As detailed in the appendix, this exercise shows substantial variation within the small-firm category. Grievance procedures, for example, are very common in the care homes sector but rare in construction and hotels. In other words, standard systems to allow employment rights to be exercised are much more common among some types of small firm than among others.

Job Quality and Satisfaction with Employment Rights

Images of autocracy suggest very dissatisfied workers. Those of harmony imply complete consent and very high satisfaction. If we see small firms in the above way, the picture becomes more complex and more revealing. Analysis of WERS 2004 produced several surprising facts (Forth et al 2006):

— Small-firm workers were more satisfied with their role in decision-making than were their large-firm counterparts, even though wages were lower.
— Absence and staff turnover rates were not different from those in large firms, suggesting that reported satisfaction was not due to withdrawal

by the dissatisfied, thereby also dismissing the assertion that high staff turnover rates are a feature of all small firms. This result also suggests that small firms are not models of harmony: workers indeed are absent and leave as much as large-firm workers do.

— Work intensity did not vary notably with size of firm. As noted above, many small firms are not Taylorised, with the result that pressures on workers are limited, and may in some respects be less than those in rationalised large firms.

— As against views that small firms are in highly competitive markets, and thus are most likely to practise autocracy in the workplace, small firms did not differ markedly from large ones in relation to overall trading conditions. This may help to explain some of the above points.

— Though equal opportunities practices were less common in small and medium enterprise (SME) workplaces, employees were more likely to think that they were treated fairly and that managers were understanding of family responsibilities. Forth et al (2006: 89) are cautious in interpreting this result which, they point out, could be due to low expectations as much as to better treatment in small firms. This issue is discussed below.

— An overall 'employee needs index' was computed, comprising 22 measures of satisfaction with aspects of the job and views of managers. Scores were clearly better the smaller the size of the firm. These results were confirmed by a multivariate analysis that identified different dimensions of 'need' and showed that a size effect remained even when other factors were controlled (Storey et al 2010).

None of this means that harmony prevails. One aspect of alleged harmony is an absence of a clear divide between manager and worker, together with the sharing of rewards through bonuses and the like. In fact, studies of small firms show a clear divide between the manager and the worker, which is of course underpinned by ownership rights, while profit-sharing schemes tend to be rare (Tsai et al 2007). Employees may on average be relatively satisfied, but the nature of the employment relationship has not dissolved into equality. Indeed, the stark fact of ownership makes the employee-employer divide clearer than it is in large organisations.

As for 'low expectations', this common idea cannot be used to write off the apparent satisfaction of small-firm workers. Some aspects of employment, such as pay and benefits, have a clear metric, and it is likely to be the case that workers in small firms are aware of relatively low rewards and adjust expectations accordingly. But 'fairness' is surely a more absolute measure. It is for example common in small firms that, when work is slack, jobs may be found at the owner's home. It is also the case that workers can observe owner-managers, who often put in much longer hours than the workers themselves and without material reward necessarily being the result. Moreover, where such reward is obtained by owners, it may well be seen as the direct result of personal effort. It is implausible that small-firm workers expect to be treated less reasonably, taking account of the business situation, than do large-firm workers. Detailed ethnographic inquiries do not suggest such a process (Ram 1994; Moule 1998).

Studies specifically directed at employment rights do not suggest that small-firm workers feel that they are disadvantaged. The Employment Rights at Work Survey of 2005 asked about how well employees were informed about their rights and whether they knew where to find relevant information (Casebourne et al 2006). There were no differences according to the measure of size—though, like several employee surveys it used size of workplace, and not employing organisation, as the measure.[1] The successor to this survey, the Fair Treatment at Work Survey of 2008 (see Fevre et al 2009), included a measure of the size of the organisation. There was a clear tendency for the reporting of any kind of 'problem at work' to be *more* common in large than in small organisations (Bewley and Forth 2011: 19).

Harris and Foster (2005) conducted a series of case studies in small firms, looking at family-friendly approaches. They found no principled opposition among managers to such approaches to fairness, though there were concerns about the costs of finding any replacement workers and the possible impact on other workers. Other studies underline the handling of family and similar issues and in an informal manner. A set of case studies from three sectors found that managers generally responded to the need for time off flexibly in light of a worker's needs (Edwards et al 2004). The relevant issues were handled face-to-face, and with an immediate answer. Significantly, a worker who had worked in a large firm specifically valued this approach as compared to the more bureaucratic approach of the large firm. This sense probably underpins the figures in WERS.

Looking at family-friendly practices in SMEs and making comparisons with large firms, Dex and Scheibl (2001: 428) conclude in relation to the SMEs that, 'while entitlements to flexibility were not necessarily on offer to all, there was an *ethical calculus*, acceptable to the majority, which determined who would be granted flexibility' (emphasis added). Though this should not be taken as typical of all SMEs, for the cases were chosen among those already practising some family-friendly activity, it is indicative of an SME approach: informal arrangements can secure substantive results, and there are commonly shared norms of fairness.

---

[1] This is also true of, for example, the Skills Surveys. The rationale is that employees may not know the size of the organisation that they work for. This is, however, an empirical question which can readily be addressed. Employees are surely likely to know whether they work for a small or a large organisation, even if, in the latter case, they are unaware of its overall size. See Edwards (2010) for comment.

Conclusion

The idea of a readily identifiable 'good employer', which tends to be the large firm, is false. Good and bad employment practice can be found across the size range of firms. The idea has survived stubbornly. Blackburn (2007) shows that in the early twentieth century well-known reformers such as Sidney and Beatrice Webb subscribed to it, and they tended to equate sweat-shop conditions with small firms which would eventually be eliminated by larger ones. Blackburn's case study of large firms in low-wage sectors however shows that they were not the good employers of the Webbs. Small firms are not the only 'bad employers'.

SMALL FIRMS AND EMPLOYMENT REGULATION

The second part of the analysis concerns the ways in which small firms respond to legislation. Given the context of informality and the negotiation of order in the small firm, how is legislation understood and what are the prospects for using legislation to promote employment rights?

Impact of Employment Rights

It is commonly argued that small firms oppose legislation aimed at securing employment rights. There might be three reasons for this. First, costs may rise, for example in meeting rights for parental leave. Second, the ability to reach business decisions may be harmed. Third, the administrative costs of compliance may be a burden. Hard evidence to support such apparently commonsense propositions is in fact rare. It is true that numerous surveys purport to give such evidence, and that illustrative arguments can be provided. In relation to the third reason, for example, the Better Regulation Task Force (2002: 5) quotes a caterer and hotelkeeper as having to respond to a stream of different regulations: 'small wonder that we managers of small businesses spend less and less time looking after our clients and more and more time snowed under behind the scenes'. But, as a detailed critique shows, surveys are often conducted by interested parties and use leading questions to generate a desired answer (Westrip 1982).

Independent research has shown more limited effects. In a 1978 survey, Clifton and Tatton-Brown (1979) found that very few small firms (two per cent) cited employment legislation as their main difficulty, though 12 per cent claimed to find some aspect of the legislation troublesome when asked directly about this. Effects on the ability of managers to take decisions were not identified, a result confirmed in later surveys. A survey in 2000 found limited knowledge among managers of individual employment rights

(Blackburn and Hart 2002), though it is not known how this would differ from a random sample of managers in large firms. This survey did not look directly at perceived impact on the firm, though one-third claimed to identify some negative effect. Just what this effect was, and how costly it was, was not, however, assessed. Further analysis of this survey also showed that there was a less than exact relationship between claims of effects within the firm and overall assessments of legislation (Edwards et al 2003: 41).

This last study pursued the point in case study work. It found that managers often had a broad perception that employment legislation must be bad for small firms even though they themselves had no experience of relevant effects. Two examples are informative. A manager of a care home, when telephoned to participate in the study, expressed dislike of the law and promised to show its negative effects. But inquiry within the firm was unable to identify any specific effects in terms of increased costs or constraints on the freedom to manage. And, at a food cooperative, two managers discoursed at length about how managers' hands were tied by legislation. Yet the firm went out of its way to employ people with mental health problems. This practice is likely to have stimulated managerial beliefs that issues of poor performance would arise. If managers had felt that their hands were tied they would surely have minimised, rather than actively encouraged, the risk. Here and elsewhere there was a contrast between generalised perceptions and hard evidence specific to the firm itself. The managers believed that the law 'must' affect firms, and this level of perception was distinct from their views of their own firm and its workers.

Just how, then, do small firms relate to employment rights? An extreme view would be one of isolation: small-firm informal practice carries on unchanged, possibly punctuated by some specific issues such as an ET case. In terms of substantive rights, the small-as-harmony view would argue that rights are simply met, albeit not through the law. The small-as-autocracy view would equate isolation with the denial of rights. An image of isolation might have had some credibility when legislation was new. Surveys have, however, found growing awareness of legislation (Blackburn and Hart 2002), and more detailed studies showed that small firms took more care in their decisions in areas such as dismissal, in order to remain within the law (Evans et al 1985). As shown above, moreover, it is not the case that small firms are relentlessly informal in their approach or that they are opposed to regulation of any kind. We have also seen that workers' experience equates neither to harmony nor to autocracy.

A second view is the mirror image of isolation: small firms lack formal structures, and need to implement them. This ignores arguments for functional equivalence, and applies a large-firm standard in inappropriate ways.

Small firms are not islands. They are influenced by employment legislation and the rights attached to it. In terms of overall relationship to the law, the study discussed above, of 18 very small firms (size range, 2–50 employees), found the following (Edwards et al 2003; 2004):

— There was little principled opposition to legislation, and there was acceptance of it, in particular of laws which had been in existence for some time.
— There was broad awareness of legal rights, and the expectation that they would be pursued. As a production manager put it, 'workers know their rights' and he put in 'a lot of effort' to manage the workplace so that these rights were observed.
— There was no evidence of any impact in terms of the freedom of managers to take decisions in issues such as dismissal.

As for the specifics of the law, aspects such as the National Minimum Wage were implemented with few problems. As earlier research showed, a key mechanism allowing for the absorption of any costs was the flexibility of pay structures, meaning that there were few pressures to restore differentials (Gilman et al 2002).

Other aspects of the law clearly impinged, notably when a firm experienced an ET case and had to deal with the relevant costs. There was some evidence that a case could lead a firm to review its personnel procedures, possibly in ways that promoted fairness. However, there is little within small-firm practice to suggest a long-term dynamic towards more substantive fairness in handling dismissals (Earnshaw et al 2001). In any one firm, a lesson may be drawn but this lesson may decay if it is not formalised procedurally; and the growth of new firms will mean that the population of small firms is refreshed with firms that have not been exposed to such lessons.

As for administrative burdens, there was little evidence of specific costs. One key reason is that small firms do not typically estimate costs in any exact way: they themselves have little way of knowing what the costs might be. It is of course possible that the costs exist, but it is also true that surveys claiming to measure them will be imposing measures inappropriately. Administration in small firms tends to be handled by the owner, possibly with family members' help, and costs associated with employment laws will be absorbed within the general tasks of running the business.

Variations in Response

We have seen that small firms vary in character, and that they filter the law in terms of their own structure and experience. Some may wish to remain isolated from the law, others may try to follow basic legal requirements, and yet others may even use the law as a positive device to modernise their employment relations. We can grasp this variety by identifying four illustrative ideal types. These are presented in declining levels of likely positive engagement with the law.

The Modernising Firm

Research throws light on the issue of formalising employment relations—an approach often implicit in the idea of making rights effective. There are small firms in which formalisation has an affinity with the direction of the business. One such food manufacturing firm with about 45employees (analysed under different pseudonyms in Ram, Edwards et al 2001 and Edwards et al 2004, and visited also in 2010) has clearly modernised its operations along with increasingly moving its market from small local customers to large supermarkets. Personnel practice has also become more formal, with the employment of an HR manager and the development of procedures. As a manager memorably put it, some employment rights were a 'wake-up call', meaning that they encouraged the firm to do what it should be doing in any event.

Firms of this kind can be expected comfortably to meet minimum employment standards. A few such firms, such as the one just mentioned, may even take a proactive approach to rights. This is, however, very unusual, reflecting the self-consciously modernising and socially responsible ambitions of the owner. Most 'modern' small firms are likely to take a more passive approach. That said, they are likely to be able to incorporate rights much as larger firms will do.

The Owner-managed Firm

A variant on the modern firm is the firm in which the owner-manager retains an active and direct role in personnel questions. Research has found that such firms may formally embrace rules and procedures, but that in practice the owner will use discretion in terms of such things as pay awards (Cox 2005). These owners tend to see the firm as their own fiefdom, and they want to retain the personal touch. This can work effectively, albeit with a degree of uncertainty as to how pay is in fact set. But it clearly also has the potential for bias, and thus the neglect of rights to equal treatment: valuing people with characteristics such as one's own is a well-established tendency in performance appraisal systems. A solution may be to ensure that such firms are alive to their responsibilities—and it might be that they would benefit more widely from a degree of formalisation because this would reduce the dangers of ad hocmanagement. There none the less remains a tension between formality and informality, and this needs to be recognised in both analysis and prescription.

The Niche and the Family Business

Family firms are often taken as the archetype of the small firm: they are run in a highly personal style and are not necessarily growth orientated. It is such firms where the benefits of informality are most likely to be appreciated by employees (Storey et al 2010). They are unlikely to have formal systems, and may well recruit in a relatively closed way via family and kin. Employment rights may be hard to enforce. Equal opportunities in selection and promotion, for example, may be neglected.

Yet what do such rights mean in this context? Scholars of small firms commonly complain that small firms are measured against large-firm standards. They have a point, in that it may be hard to translate an abstract right meaningfully in the context of the family firm. If the firm is structured informally, with for example the succession of family members, rights in terms of promotion may have little meaning.

This does not, however, mean that all informality is good or that questions of rights are wholly inappropriate. A reasonable approach would be to encourage firms to think constructively of their options and how they may be unintentionally neglecting rights. An owner might, for example, assume that his son will take over the business. But have other options been considered and the potential claims of others been taken into account? Such a 'soft' and contextualised approach might in fact be more effective than an attempt to enforce rights through 'hard' measures.

The Sweatshop and the Informal Economy

None of the above denies that employment rights can be systematically repudiated but I argue that such practices cannot be explained by the size of the firm alone and that its specific contingencies need to be understood. It is then possible to consider remedies. As the sweatshop is the most extreme example of the denial of rights, some attention will be given to it.

The sweatshop is most likely to be found in the informal economy. The nature of the informal economy is heavily debated, but it can be taken to embrace the production of goods and services which are legal but with the returns from the process being hidden in relation to the payment of tax and wages (Williams 2004). This does not mean that the informal economy and the sweatshop are identical, for the former contains a range of own-account activities where there is no employment relationship. Sweatshops could also in principle operate legally, for the definition of sweating is often based on evaluations of fairness. In the nineteenth century, 'sweating became generally identified with excessive hours, an insanitary working environment and, above all, with the payment of exploitation wages' (Blackburn 2009: 214–15), with the whole point, of course, being to make the relevant practices illegal. Basic regulation of pay and working time through the National

Minimum Wage (NMW) and the Working Time Regulations (WTR) now means that 'exploitation wages' would be illegal and hence that any sweatshop in the UK will be in the informal economy; we may define it as a workplace with an employment relationship in which wages are clearly and systematically below the NMW level, or there is some other lasting breach of rights.

The informal economy is impossible to measure accurately. Estimates across developed economies put it at around seven per cent of GDP, with the UK at the lower end, about two per cent (Williams 2004). Similarly, the Low Pay Commission has been unable to estimate the extent of non-compliance with the NMW, though one former commissioner believed it to be increasing (Metcalf 2007: 25). The overall level must, however, be small; as Metcalf notes, most employers comply.

Metcalf himself reports non-compliance among Chinese-owned businesses in such sectors as restaurants and clothing. The standard mechanism was to under-state hours worked so that a true pay rate of £3 an hour would appear at that time to be compliant. A more detailed study looked at 17 low-wage firms in clothing and restaurants, of which four were compliant (Ram et al 2007). Results included the following:

— Pay rates as low as £2 per hour in 2003–04, compared to the NMW at the time of £4.50, were recorded. In the 13 non-complying firms average pay was below the NMW, in the range £2.75–4.00 per hour.
— Non-compliance with the law tended to involve several aspects together, such as paying below the NMW along with flouting the WTR.
— As in Metcalf's study, the under-recording of hours was a central device to hide under-payment.
— Some workers were illegal immigrants, while others lacked skills and education.
— There was some collusion, in that if hours and pay were under-reported, workers could gain increased state benefits. Other means of gaining consent included a regime which could allow breaks when work was light and implicit bargaining based on familial obligations. Some workers enjoyed the work, and 'exploitation' was moderated by a degree of give and take. Workers also expressed a resigned acceptance of the situation, and many did not feel that they were 'exploited' in the sense of being paid less than the market could currently bear.
— There was no evidence that worker grievances or indeed any other mechanism would be likely to lead to the assertion of employment rights.

There are two possible implications here. The first says that these firms can exist only by operating below the floor of rights and that the solution is to squeeze them out of existence. The average rights of *workers in employment* would thus rise through a batting average effect. In terms of *the working population* as a whole, the result would depend on whether people were absorbed into better firms or pushed out of the labour market altogether. Longitudinal monitoring of relevant groups would be needed to establish the nature of such effects.

The second implication is that at least some firms might be brought into compliance with employment laws, which is why the study included four compliant firms. Two of these were growth-orientated, and compliance was consistent with their business path, though not a route chosen voluntarily. Having taken it, however, the owners recognised some benefits in terms of the quality of workers that they could attract. A third firm had changed the location of its business dramatically, downsizing from 90 to eight workers in the process. The fourth mentioned fear of detection, an unusual response, as Metcalf (2007) demonstrates that inspections are extremely rare. Compliance reflected particular contingencies and was far from automatic. None the less, as argued below, there may be some routes towards it.

MECHANISMS TO STRENGTHEN RIGHTS AND THEIR UTILISATION IN SMALL FIRMS

The above analysis may be summarised as follows. There is a small number of small firms in the informal sector where employment rights are extensively denied. A substantial number of others comply with minimum standards but little more, and it is not the case that product market upgrading is a strong driver towards raising wages or improving training (Edwards et al 2009). Many others are above the minimum. It is not the case that the small firm as a category is uniquely prone to neglect rights.

The following comments focus on the problem cases. This includes the issue of how to move from minimal compliance to a more active effort to raise the enjoyment of substantive rights.

One potential way of promoting good employment practice in the small firm is through the supply chain. The extensive literature on global supply chains points to the role of large firms in pressuring their suppliers to eliminate practices such as child labour (Frenkel and Scott 2001; Khan et al 2010). However, it is not clear how this would work in the UK. The leading evidence relates to illegal or clearly exploitative conditions in the Third World. In the absence of such conditions, there is no particular focus for large firms in relation to small suppliers. The rarity of any kind of direct pressure in relation to employment terms from large customers is a notable feature of much of the research discussed above. There was also rather little specific pressure in relation to quality standards and the like: large firms in sectors such as food do not seem to have product process templates that they impose on small suppliers.

There may be some even more indirect pressure in that any small firm seeking to supply leading supermarkets will need to attain certain quality standards, which will in turn have some implications for training; and to the extent that the firm modernises and rationalises it may then offer better jobs and be more likely to recognise employment rights. An example is the 'modernising' food manufacturer discussed above, which consciously modernised its operations, entailing the employment of an HR manager and the development of a series of policies on good practice.

Yet the evidence suggests that such firms are unusual (Edwards et al 2009). Even within them, any tendency for a shift to higher value-added products to drive up pay and conditions was weak. The supply chain cannot be relied on as a general solution.

The same is true of membership of business associations. Such associations are notoriously weak in the UK (Crouch and Trigilia 2001). Among small firms, membership is patchy, and the focus tends to be on broad business development issues and not employment (Edwards et al 2010). There may again be some very indirect effects, but these will be limited. They will also relate to those firms that are trying to strengthen their business positions; the archetypical 'bad employer' will not be affected.

A more realistic approach starts from the fact that potential mechanisms are not automatic. Some proponents of minimum wages argue that such minima necessarily had effects on the efficiency of firms. Research in Denmark and New Zealand points to the need for a set of strong institutions to make the potential 'shock effect' of a NMW real (McLaughlin 2009). The evidence in the UK suggests that this effect is weak or absent (Arrowsmith et al 2003; Metcalf 2007). Non-compliant firms continue to exist, relatively insulated from labour laws; other firms may be driven towards the informal sector in the face of global competition and pressure on price, together with the availability of illegal migrant labour; and more established firms lack any particular driver to identify what the supposed efficiency effects are, let alone put them into effect. Research for one study illustrated how drivers are not automatic (Arrowsmith et al 2003): interviewing a manager, the researcher asked whether the NMW might not encourage improvement in the firm's payment system; the manager had not thought of this, though he claimed that he now might do so.[2] Talking through with firms how they might improve their employment practices could be a simple and desirable step—as was at least sometimes the case under the Trade Boards (see Sells 1939).

One specific lever is to require any small firm that takes a state investment loan or other form of support to undertake an employment relations health check with an Acas adviser. An alternative route is an inspection

---

[2] I am grateful to Mark Gilman for this recollection.

regime in which one inspector deals with all regulatory matters including tax, health and safety, and pay and conditions. Inspectors could work with firms to change the key practices that need addressing while, perhaps, tolerating minor infractions in other areas.

As explained above, compliance with labour laws does not come about automatically, and existing means to promote it are weak. It is also the case, however, that firms in the informal economy are not inherently dedicated to offering sweatshop conditions. They find themselves where they are because they have few options and the structure of labour and product markets creates space for them to survive. They may thus be open to suggestions as to how they can amend their business models, though a driver at the level of the firm alone may be very weak.

A less direct lever might encourage firms in sectors such as the restaurant trade to develop business associations to embrace employment conditions. Members could display a certificate confirming that they paid a certain level of wages and conformed to working time and other regulations. The relevant standards could be above the NMW. Several cities have argued for living wages above the NMW and, depending on local labour market and product market conditions, associations could require members to pay at or near to the relevant living wage standard. In these sectors, moreover, competition is primarily local. There is in principle the possibility of 'taking wages out of competition' (that is, setting common wages across a group of firms), or at least reducing the very intensive cut-throat competition that exists in some parts of the restaurant trade.

These two mechanisms, of working directly at the level of the firm and strengthening business associations, are complementary, but relatively weak. As Blackburn (2007) concludes on efforts to eliminate sweating in the early twentieth century, reformers hoped that the Trade Boards established in 1909 would modernise their industries and improve wages. Several reformers, notably RH Tawney, exaggerated the boards' effectiveness and played down the extent to which employers evaded their regulations. Reliance on the boards closed off more radical routes. The mechanisms suggested here are better than nothing, but would need support through a radically reformed inspection regime, with inspectors working as critical friends of firms, encouraging them to pursue good practice and having reserve powers if persuasion did not work. Whether such a regime is feasible or likely is a big question.

APPENDIX: ANALYSIS OF WERS 2004

This appendix details some further analyses of the WERS 2004 data. It follows Forth et al (2006: 5) in identifying three kinds of private sector workplace: those owned by small firms (5–49 employees), medium-sized firms (50–249 employees) andlarge firms. It differs in excluding workplaces owned by foreign companies, for these could in principle belong to massive organisations. It also focuses on making comparisons within sectors where there are reasonable numbers of small firms; the utilities for example are excluded.

The purpose is to consider the extent of variation between SME workplaces across sectors, and to look at similarity or difference in relation to large firms within a sector. In other words, are small firms in some sectors like large firms in the sector, while in other sectors size differences exist? This is a simple but informative exercise: 'no cross tabulation from WERS has ever been overturned by a regression analysis' (Metcalf 2007: 19).

I looked at three aspects of policy with an evident link to the exercise of employment rights: the presence of a grievance procedure, a discipline and dismissals procedure, and a written policy on equal opportunities or managing diversity. The existence of a joint consultation or similar committee (variable DJOINT in WERS) was also considered, as an indicator of formal systems to engage with employees that might affect the exercise of rights. I also looked at the following broader indicators of employment practice: the presence of an HR specialist; the use of performance appraisal; and the use of formal job evaluation. These measure aspects of formality and hence how far a workplace might be open to the formalisation of rights. Finally, the presence of trade union members, the reporting of a complaint to an ET, and the staff turnover rate were assessed.

Table 1 reports these items with the exception of the presence of disciplinary or disputes procedures and of equal opportunities procedures, where the patterns were identical to that for grievance procedures. The following facts stand out. First, grievance (and as just noted, other) procedures were virtually universal in large firms. However,small firms differed widely in their use. In the health and community services sectors, which embrace care homes and similar, procedures were very common whereas fewer than half the workplaces in the construction and hotels sectors had them. The same conclusion applies to the use of performance appraisals. As might be expected, an HR specialist was also relatively common among small firms in the health sector.

Second, sector effects were clear in the sense that there were similar variations among large and small firms. The presence of union members, for example, was very low throughout the hotel and restaurant sector. Small firms here were not very different from their large-firm counterparts, as was also the case with the use of joint consultation committees. In manufacturing, by contrast, there was a very wide divide. Staff turnover rates also varied sectorally, with SME workplaces on average, in fact, having a low rather than a high rate.

Table 1. Employment practices by firm size and sector

	Grievance proce.			Joint consult cttee			Pfm appraisal			Job eval.		
	S	M	L	S	M	L	S	M	L	S	M	L
Mfg	58	89	100	2	31	46	26	58	90	2	12	33
Constr	42	59	100	0	6	11	45	47	82	0	6	39
Trade	46	86	98	3	2	8	23	42	92	3	5	21
Hotels etc	43	100	94	0	0	6	49	75	94	0	0	19
Bus. Servs	74	80	99	2	11	9	63	96	95	6	13	17
Health	92	100	100	8	4	14	78	100	100	16	25	14
Other community servs	82	100	100	6	8	11	78	83	67	4	17	38
TOTAL	62	86	98	3	9	12	48	68	91	5	11	22

	HR specialist			TU members			ET complaint			Quit rate		
	S	M	L	S	M	L	S	M	L	S	M	L
Mfg	2	41	46	14	26	64	6	15	24	9.7	9.0	7.6
Constr	7	6	71	10	25	29	0	12	18	13.5	16.1	24.8
Trade	8	13	35	0	2	19	3	1	3	9.2	9.5	29.1
Hotels etc	6	25	23	0	11	10	0	0	4	27.7	22.5	36.5
Bus. Servs	8	18	44	5	25	21	2	16	15	15.6	14.8	13.9
Health	13	21	29	26	25	60	0	7	9	13.9	14.4	18.0
Other community servs	0	50	32	6	25	43	0	8	7	15.1	16.6.	14.8
TOTAL	7	21	36	8	14	26	2	9	8	14.1	12.6	24.0

Source: Calculated from WERS 2004 data set.

Notes:

Figures are cell percentages, ie % of workplaces with a characteristic, except for the quit rate, which is the mean quit rate per 100 workers.

S, M and L are workplaces owned by small, medium and large firms, as defined in the text.

Trade = wholesale and retail trade.

Hotels etc = hotels and restaurants.

Total is total for above sectors, omitting all other sectors.

HR specialist = cases where HR is identified as the respondent's main responsibility.

Forth et al (2006: 35) report no difference by size of firm on this measure. The present measure was the stated number of voluntary resignations (ZRESIGNED) divided by employment the year before the survey. Quite why this differs from the Forth et al result would need more investigation, but there is clearly agreement that leaving is not especially common in small firms.

Third, if we look at the figures for ET complaints, comparisons between sizes of firm are not accurate since large firms have more employees who may wish to make a complaint. But the figures across the small firm category are notable: very few such firms experience a complaint, and if we wish to understand the place of small firms in the ET system we should not seek the answer in the characteristics of all small firms.

BIBLIOGRAPHY

Arrowsmith, J, Gilman, M, Edwards, P and Ram, M (2003) 'The Impact of the National Minimum Wage in Small Firms' 41 *British Journal of Industrial Relations* 435.

Baines, S and Wheelock, J (1998) 'Working for Each Other: Gender, the Household and Micro-business Survival and Growth' 17 *International Small Business Journal* 16.

Better Regulation Task Force (2002) *Employment Regulation: Striking a Balance* (London, BRTF).

Bewley, H and Forth, J (2011) 'Vulnerability and Adverse Treatment in the Workplace', Paper to Capitalism and Work Conference, Centre for Global Labour Research, Cardiff University, January.

BIS (Department for Business, Innovation and Skills) (2010) 'Small Business Statistics 2010', www.stats.bis.gov.uk/ed/sme.

Blackburn, RA and Hart, M (2002) 'Small Firms' Awareness and Knowledge of Individual Employment Rights', Employment Relations Research Series 14 (London, DTI).

Blackburn, SC (2007) *A Fair Day's Wage for a Fair Day's Work? Sweated Labour and the Origins of Minimum Wage Legislation in Britain* (Aldershot, Ashgate).

—— (2009)'Curse or Cure? Why Was the Enactment of Britain's 1909 Trade Boards Act so Controversial?' 47 *British Journal of Industrial Relations* 214.

Blyton, P and Turnbull, P (2004)*The Dynamics of Employee Relations*, 3rd edn (Basingstoke, Palgrave).

Bolton (1971) 'Report on the Committee of Inquiry on Small Firms' Cmnd 4811 (London, HMSO).

Casebourne, J, Regan, J, Neathey, F and Tuohy, S (2006) 'Employment Rights at Work: Survey of Employees 2005', Employment Relations Research Series 51 (London, DTI).

Clifton, R and Tatton-Brown, C (1979) 'Impact of Employment Legislation on Small Firms', Department of Employment Research Paper 6 (London, HMSO).

Cox, A (2005) 'Managing Variable Pay in Smaller Workplaces' in S Marlow, D Patton and M Ram (eds), *Labour Management in Small Firms* (London, Routledge).

Crouch, C and Trigilia, C (2001) 'Conclusions' in C Crouch et al (eds), *Local Production Systems in Europe* (Oxford, OUP).

Curran, J and Stanworth, J (1981) 'A New Look at Job Satisfaction in the Small Firm' 34 *Human Relations* 343.

Dex, S and Scheibl, F (2001) 'Flexibility and Family-friendly Working Arrangements in UK-based SMEs' 39 *British Journal of Industrial Relations* 411.

Earnshaw, J, Marchington, M and Goodman, J (2001) 'Unfair to Whom? Discipline and Dismissal in Small Establishments' 31 *Industrial Relations Journal* 62.

Edwards, P (2010) 'Skills and the Small Firm: A Research and Policy Briefing', UK Commission on Employment and Skills, June,www.ukces.org.uk/research-and-publications.

Edwards, P, Ram, M and Black, J (2003) 'The Impact of Employment Legislation on Small Firms: A Case Study Analysis', Employment Relations Research Series 20 (London, DTI).

—— (2004) 'Why does Employment Legislation not Damage Small Firms?' 31 *Journal of Law and Society* 245.

Edwards, P, Sen-Gupta, S and Tsai, C-J (2009) 'Managing Low-skill Workers: A Study of Small UK Food Manufacturing Firms' 19 *Human Resource Management Journal* 40.

—— (2010) 'The Context-dependent Nature of Small Firms' Contact with Support Agencies' 28 *International Small Business Journal* 543.

Evans, S, Goodman, J and Hargreaves, L (1985) 'Unfair Dismissal Law and Employment Practice in the 1980s', Research Paper 53 (London, Department of Employment).

Fevre, R, Nicols, T, Prior, G and Rutherford, I (2009) *Fair Treatment at Work Report: Findings from the 2008 Survey*, Employment Relations Research Series 103 (London, BIS).

Forth, J, Bewley, H and Bryson, A (2006) *Small and Medium-sized Enterprises: Findings from the 2004 Workplace Employment Relations Survey* (London, DTI).

Frenkel, S and Scott, D (2002) 'Compliance, Collaboration and Codes of Practice' 45 *California Management Review* 29.

Gilman, M, Edwards, P, Ram, M and Arrowsmith, J (2002) 'Pay Determination in Small Firms in the UK: The Case of the Response to the National Minimum Wage' 33 *Industrial Relations Journal* 52.

Goss, D (1991) 'In Search of Small Firm Industrial Relations' in R Burrows (ed), *Deciphering the Enterprise Culture* (London, Routledge).

Harris, L and Foster, C (2005) 'Small, Flexible and Family-friendly: Work Practices in Service Sector Businesses', Employment Relations Research Series 47 (London, DTI).

Khan, FR, Westwood, R and Boje, DM (2010) '"I Feel Like a Foreign Agent": NGOs and Corporate Social Responsibility Interventions into Third World Child Labour' 63 *Human Relations* 1417.

Li, M and Edwards, P (2008) 'Work and Pay in Small Chinese Clothing Firms' 39 *Industrial Relations Journal* 296.

Marchington, M, Carroll, M and Boxall, P (2003) 'Labour Scarcity and the Survival of Small Firms: A Resource-based View of the Road Haulage Industry' 13 *Human Resource Management Journal* 5.

McLaughlin, C (2009) 'The Productivity-enhancing Impacts of the Minimum Wage: Lessons from Denmark and New Zealand' 47 *British Journal of Industrial Relations* 327.

Metcalf, D (2007) *Why Has the British National Minimum Wage Had Little or No Impact on Employment?* Centre for Economic Performance Discussion Paper 781 (London, London School of Economics).

Moule, C (1998) 'Regulation of Work in Small Firms' 12 *Work, Employment and Society* 635.

Peters, M, Seeds, K, Harding, C and Garnett, E (2010) *Findings from the Survey of Employment Tribunal Applications 2008*, Employment Relations Research Series, 107 (London, BIS).

Rainnie, A (1989) *Industrial Relations in Small Firms* (London, Routledge).

Ram, M (1994) *Managing to Survive* (Oxford, Blackwell).

Ram, M, Abbas, T, Sanghera, B, Barlow, G and Jones, T (2001) '"Apprentice Entrepreneurs?" Ethnic Minority Workers in the Independent Restaurant Sector' 15 *Work, Employment and Society* 353.

Ram, M and Edwards, P (2010) 'Industrial Relations in Small Firms' in T Colling and M Terry (eds), *Industrial Relations: Theory and Practice* (Oxford, Blackwell).

Ram, M, Edwards, P, Gilman, M and Arrowsmith, J (2001) 'The Dynamics of Informality: Employment Relations in Small Firms and the Effects of Regulatory Change' 15 *Work, Employment and Society* 845.

Ram, M, Edwards, P and Jones, T (2007) 'Staying Underground: Informal Work, Small Firms and Employment Regulation in the United Kingdom' 34 *Work and Occupations* 318.

Saridakis, G, Sen-Gupta, S, Edwards, P and Storey, DJ (2008) 'The Impact of Enterprise Size on Employment Tribunal Incidence and Outcomes' 46 *British Journal of Industrial Relations* 469.

Sells, D (1939) *British Wages Boards* (Washington, Brookings).

Storey, DJ, Saridakis, G, Sen-Gupta, S, Edwards, P and Blackburn, RA (2010) 'Linking HR Formality with Employee Job Quality: The Role of Firm and Workplace Size' 49 *Human Resource Management* 305.

Tsai, C-J, Sen-Gupta, S and Edwards, P (2007) 'When and Why Is Small Beautiful?' 60 *Human Relations* 1779.

Westrip, A (1982) 'Effects of Employment Legislation on Small Firms' in D Watkins, J Stanworth and A Westrip (eds), *Stimulating Small Firms* (Aldershot, Gower).

Williams, CC (2004) *Cash-in-hand Work* (Basingstoke, Palgrave).

9

Management and Employment Rights

JOHN PURCELL

EMPLOYERS' VIEWS OF EMPLOYMENT LEGISLATION

In January 2011 the Director of Policy at the Engineering Employers' Federation (EEF) commented[1] that:

> In recent years employers have become fearful of the impact of employment legislation ... The bigger picture remains how we sweep away the barriers to growth and make a difference to employers' ability to create the private sector jobs we need. This will require far more radical action.

The Prime Minister has echoed these sentiments concerning employers' views on legislation: '[b]ut speak to businesses and they say ... the balance of rights is tilted far too much in favour of employees over employers'.[2] These statements neatly capture the views of employers toward employment legislation in general. The need for some regulation is not disputed but its current range and influence is considered antithetical to business interests and seen to impede competitiveness and job creation.

The views of top managers toward statutory employment rights are best seen as ambivalent and can take a number of forms. Some resent the imposition of statutory rights preferring a focus on privileges to be granted while asserting the right to manage. Others place emphasis on the direct cost involved in monitoring and enforcing statutory rights in terms of the managerial time required to ensure compliance, that is, the 'red tape' argument. A wider objection is the effect on costs compared with overseas competitors not 'suffering' under the same burden of legislation. A different line of reasoning is the reliance on markets. If good management of labour is needed this will be reflected in the market performance, with 'bad'

[1] www.eef.org.uk/policy-media/releases/uk/2011/EEF-response-to-Employers-Charter-and-ETS-consultation.htm.
[2] www.number10.gov.uk/news/the-employers-charter-driving-growth-and-supporting-business.

employers penalised by low quality work, poor customer service and a flight of customers. Self-interest replaces the need for state regulation. This argument is frequently used to seek to persuade governments that there is no need for a particular legislative initiative. An extra twist is reference to the traditions of voluntarism within the UK which rest on the parties to the employment relationship finding their own forms of social and institutional regulation best suited to their circumstances.

The other side to this ambivalence is an acceptance that not all employers can be relied upon to abide by ethical standards and good practice models or see compliance to be in their best interests. Employment legislation can be welcomed if it has the effect of outlawing bad practice which allows the unscrupulous employer to undercut competitors. The National Minimum Wage is a good example, preventing under-cutting by providing a minimum floor for basic wages. This rationale can be seen in the support many temporary work agencies gave to the principle, but often not the detail, of the Agency Workers Directive because it would stop the 'cowboys' in an industry where the cost of entry is so low that anyone can establish a labour agency. Legislation may have a positive benefit for the majority of employers by creating a level playing field.

While some free market ideologues object to most, if not all, employment legislation, many managers look at legal requirements through the lens of 'fairness'. If a particular statute accords with their notion of 'fairness', and enforcement is not seen to be burdensome, it is more likely to be accepted. Perceptions of fairness are, of course, subjective. Legislation built on current perceptions of good practice, or social norms, is more likely to be seen as 'fair' and accepted since only rogue employers will be affected. Calls for 'fairness' broaden the scope of analysis to cover the social forces which impinge on managerial conduct, whether self-induced or reflecting social pressures. This is discussed later in the chapter.

The chapter first sets the issue of managing employment rights within the context of corporate and business strategy by showing that it is never a high priority. However, discussion of employers' or managers' application of employment rights has to allow for a wide diversity of approaches both structurally and behaviourally if an, even partially, accurate picture is to be developed. Once this is done, attention can turn to management style, the preferred way of managing employees, since this can vary between companies, over time and between different groups of managers in a firm. This allows for a deeper consideration of 'fairness' and the associated concept of 'justice'. Firms are not monolithic entities able to pursue their interests in an economically rational way. The political and behavioural dimensions of management decision making have to be addressed; in particular the question of who makes decisions on employment issues is rarely straightforward. The role of line managers, and the difficulties often associated with managing people, as opposed to 'things' and 'systems', needs to be examined since it is key to any appreciation of how, and how well (or badly), employment rights are implemented. The proliferation of statutory employment rights in the last 25 years and the widespread adoption of human resource (HR) management has led to much greater emphasis placed on line managers, especially front line managers, as the agents of the organisation applying, enforcing or ignoring employment rights. At a higher level in the firm it is usually assumed that the HR manager is the person with responsibility for ensuring compliance with employment rights. But is this as the 'custodian of rights' or as the 'gatekeeper'? The former champions employment rights and good management practice and increasingly places emphasis on alternative disputes procedures within the organisation. The latter minimises the exposure to legal processes, acting as a problem-solver, but often with little authority to change managerial behaviour. In conclusion some of the key factors shaping the way management interacts with employment rights are summarised.

EMPLOYMENT RIGHTS IN THE CONTEXT OF CORPORATE AND BUSINESS STRATEGIES

It is inevitable that firms give priority to the setting and achievement of their business goals. In doing so, few give much of a priority to labour standards and employment rights unless it is clearly in their interests for reasons of social legitimacy where publicised breaches affect reputations and trade. In part, this is because there are implicit assumptions made about fairness in managerial conduct. It is not that employers inevitably seek to get away with unlawful or unethical conduct and are kept to reasonable standards of behaviour only by constant monitoring by social organisations such as trade unions, campaigners and legal processes. However, competitive pressures, especially a pressure on costs, and often a belief that swift action precludes drawn-out consultation and communication, can lead to the process required to implement employment rights being overridden, and, at times, the labour standards being ignored. There are always exceptions often originating in the personal beliefs of top managers such as Howard Schultz, Chief Executive of Starbucks,[3] or traditions of ownership as, for example, in Quaker firms.

  HR management is a third order activity in business strategy attended to after corporate goals are set and the shape and size of the firm determined in order to achieve these goals. In the famous words of Alfred Chandler, 'structure follows strategy'. One of the classic distinctions between types of business is between those large, diversified, companies which emphasise central control—the strategic planning companies—and others which

---

[3] www.bbc.co.uk/bbcfour/documentaries/profile/howard_schultz.shtml.

place emphasis on forms of decentralisation in operational decision making while imposing tough financial controls—financial control companies (see Purcell 1989). The growth of private equity companies in recent years and the 'financialisation' of decision making (Sisson and Purcell 2010: 91–99) has placed further emphasis on forms of financial control and a 'nexus of contracts' which favours short-termism and shareholder value through commodification. Under modern forms of financial control, calls for the effective implementation of employment rights are given very little attention at corporate levels and can be a low priority at the unit or subsidiary company level, being treated as a cost.

There are usually four goals within strategic HR management although these are rarely made explicit (Boxall and Purcell 2011: 11–23). The first is the achievement of cost-effective labour. All firms face a requirement to be viable. Cost pressures on labour will always be present and any response to employment rights will be viewed through a cost lens. The problem is, of course, not simply one of cost but of unit labour cost, the combination of cost with productivity. All firms have to have the ability to hire the most appropriate people and provide the conditions, from training to technology, to enable them to perform effectively. Employment legislation can be seen as a source of additional costs. The, often unconvincing, attempts to quantify and assert the 'business case' for employment rights, found, for example in relation to the management of diversity, are an attempt to shift the case for employment rights to employers' self-interest. In times of economic uncertainty, when pressures on cost mount and the need to reduce costs becomes imperative, the requirement for viability and survival outweighs other considerations. Within some sectors, such as low skill intensive manufacturing, which is increasingly likely to be located in low-wage economies, and the discount retail sector, the pursuit of cost effectiveness is likely to lead to insecure jobs often with a large number of migrant and ethnic minority staff and workers on short-term contracts and variable hours, such as students, agency workers and part-time staff with uncertain hours (Standing 2011). Investment in HR, such as training, will be low and a high turnover of staff inevitable except when there are high levels of unemployment.

The second economic goal in HR is the achievement of organisation flexibility. The use of short-term contract staff is one manifestation of this. Restrictions on the ability of employers to dismiss staff, in terms of notice periods and the need to justify the selection process, can be resented. For example, the government promised in May 2011, after pressure from employers, to review the period of consultation required for large scale redundancies and have announced that the period of employment required before a claim for unfair dismissal can be made is to rise from 12 to 24 months. It is clear that this achievement of organisation flexibility is now a permanent aim and not just a response to hard times. It is a reflection of 'a neo-liberal agenda to allow market principles to permeate all aspects of life' (Standing 2011: 1). Employment risks are increasingly transferred to workers themselves with the creation of what Standing calls 'the precariat'. Here flexibility is focussed on making it easier to dispose of labour, or cut hours of work, when circumstances require it, rather than achieve flexibility in other ways such as functional task flexibility.

A third goal in strategic HR management is socio-political: the preservation of managerial power to act, sometimes referred to as the 'management prerogative'. This can be seen as a security objective alongside the profit motive (Gospel 1973). The goal is 'to maximise managerial control over an uncertain environment including threats to its power base from work groups and trade unions' (Boxall and Purcell 2011: 22–23). This can include resisting the application of employment rights if these are seen to interfere unduly with management freedom of action. This goal also helps to explain why so much effort can be placed on political lobbying to forestall, or weaken, legislative initiatives especially where these are seen to challenge the right to manage. A good example is the drafting of the Information and Consultation of Employees Regulations (ICE) in 2004, following the EU Directive of the same name in 2002, itself subject to intense lobbying from employers across Europe but especially from the UK and Ireland (Hall 2010). The ICE Regulations eventually gave employers significant freedom to choose how, if at all, to establish consultative bodies for information and consultation purposes.

Given a choice, once fundamental business reasons for investment location have been met, multinational companies tend to favour investment in countries with less demanding employment legislation (Cooke 2007: 493). The ability to shift production from one country to another is a form of 'regime shopping' which places constraints on nation states in the enactment of statutory employment rights. Government ministers in the UK have often pointed to the UK's relatively 'flexible labour markets' as an attraction for foreign direct investment. What this euphemism really means is that, compared with continental Europe, it is easier to dismiss workers in the UK. Multinational corporations (MNCs) in the UK use agency workers more than domestic firms and have done so for many years (Edwards and Walsh 2009: 298). In effect, the costs of exiting the business in the UK are significantly lower than in, say, France or Germany, a matter of bitter complaint from trade union leaders (Boxall and Purcell 2011: 292).

The fourth, and final strategic HRM, goal, that of a requirement to achieve social legitimacy, can be seen as a counter weight to the preservation of managerial power and need for cost effectiveness and flexibility. Social legitimacy is the need for employers to be seen to be 'good citizens' and to be concerned that accusations of poor conduct can have a deleterious impact on consumer choice, including gaining government contracts, and the ability to recruit and retain the most effective employees. At its basic level it leads to an acceptance of the need to comply with minimum standards.

The need to achieve social legitimacy is not merely about compliance with labour standards enshrined in legislation but includes meeting the social standards expected of employers. The 'institutional perspective' pioneered by DiMaggio and Powell (1983; 1991) places emphasis on the origins of strategic decisions by looking at institutional, or societal, pressures leading to conformity. Scott (2008: 50–59), in a major review of this perspective, identifies three forms of institutional pressure: 'regulative', 'normative' and 'cultural-cognitive'. The first relates directly to employment rights established in legislation but often these are themselves no more than reflections of normative patterns. One example often given is the growing movement to foster equal rights in employment through the elimination of discrimination on grounds of gender, race, sexual orientation and age. The largest companies increasingly invest in practices which foster diversity and social inclusion (Kossek and Picher 2007). Lining up to support diversity employment campaigns can gain useful publicity. Normative pressures affect, and are influenced by, the way members of a society think and behave. Managers are no different from others in being citizens, consumers and parents save, perhaps, that in larger companies with graduate recruitment programmes they can be expected to have a higher level of education and greater awareness of societal issues. Social legitimacy can be seen in a wider context as part of the movement to emphasise corporate social responsibility (CSR) with the notion of the 'triple bottom line' (financial, environmental and social) (Elkington 1997).

The social legitimacy agenda is encouraged by the use of awards, audits and accreditation requirements such as Investors in People (IiP) and industry standards such as those developed by the Retail Consortium. Suppliers to major supermarkets have to reach certain minimum standards, for example in training. However, it is rare for these to specify employment standards in much detail beyond statutory requirements. As discussed by McCrudden (ch 6, this volume) the use of procurement pressure may be one route to encouraging the adoption of employment rights in, often small, supplying companies. The Best Workplaces Programme organised by The Great Place to Work Institute covers more than 5,500 workplaces worldwide and provides annual awards to the best companies. A great workplace is defined as an organisation where employees trust the people they work for, have pride in what they do and enjoy working with their colleagues (Guardian supplement 31 May 2011). To the extent that organisations want to achieve recognition as a 'good employer' such awards can be helpful but they downplay employment rights and emphasise effective leadership.

Some pressure groups and international bodies which monitor labour standards use audits to test for compliance. For example, Social Accountability International has developed an international standard called SA 8000 based on key conventions drawn from the International Labour Organization, the Universal Declaration of Human Rights and the UN Convention on the Rights of the Child. Companies seeking this standard must be audited and certified by an accredited audit agency (similar to IiP accreditation). Auditors must consult with workers and their unions and the audit includes a mechanism for workers to bring complaints about non-compliance. Some MNCs, especially in clothing and footwear, are particularly sensitive to accusations of labour exploitation in developing countries. The use of social media by campaign groups to report on infringements of labour standards can be very damaging to the reputation of major retailers and producers.

STRUCTURAL AND ORGANISATIONAL FACTORS INFLUENCING THE ADOPTION OF EMPLOYMENT RIGHTS

The capacity, and willingness, of firms to apply employment rights varies, and certain structural and organisational factors make it harder for some to build these into their employment regimes. The size of the firm is a strong influence. For example, there is clear evidence that medium-sized firms experience a disproportionate number of claims to employment tribunals (ETs) accounting for 21 per cent of applications while only employing four per cent of the aggregate workforce (Dix, Sisson and Forth 2009: 187). One explanation for this is that medium-sized firms have lost the intimacy and informality sometimes associated with certain small firms (see Edwards in this volume) but have not developed the resources to build more formal employment systems most often found in large firms. As for larger companies, formality can be seen in the adoption of procedures that seek to regulate aspects of the working relationship. This is often associated with the presence of a professionally qualified HR manager or department (Guest and Bryson 2009: 125). Large companies often have other advantages leading to fewer employment problems. They tend to pay higher wages and have a greater capacity to deal with absence and flexible working arrangements in ways which make smaller firms vulnerable in cost terms. The campaign to 'roll back' employment legislation is generated particularly by small firms.

A second organisational factor is the recognition of trade unions which can lead to higher levels of adoption of a wide range of employment rights. The presence of unions is associated with lower levels of ET claims, and the reduction in union recognition in the last 30 years, especially in the private sector, has been associated with a rise in ET applications. Union recognition is associated with the adoption of formal procedures for dealing with disputes and handling disciplinary and grievance matters. What is important is the presence of means for dealing with employment conflicts within the workplace, including worker representation in grievance and disciplinary hearings. Paradoxically, this can mean that there is a higher level of individual disputes in the unionised firm, compared with the non-union company, but fewer of these end up in an ET. This is particularly the case where there is an on-site union representative. This direct representation 'engenders greater critical awareness on the part of workers and perhaps increases voice-induced complaining' (Bryson 2004: 235). The evidence supports the idea that workplace representation encourages the internal resolution of disputes (Burgess et al 2000; Dix et al 2009: 197–98).

Casebourne et al (2006) report that only a quarter (24 per cent) of those who experienced a problem at work put their concern in writing to their employer, and just three per cent brought a tribunal case as a result of their complaints. This suggests that the enforcement of employment rights depends on the aggrieved individual being prepared to complain. In so doing management may take action to attend to the problem but may not have done so had pressure not been applied. Unionised procedures allow the issue to escalate to a more senior level if there is no immediate resolution. Where unions work effectively with management, especially where they are strong, the number of problems can reduce (Bryson and Freeman 2007: 85).

All this can be uncomfortable for management since unionisation and employee voice appear to increase the number of complaints that they have to deal with although the number that end up in an ET will be lower than elsewhere. In addition, management perceptions of the employment-relations climate have always been worse in union workplaces than in non-union ones according to the long-run WERS data (Blanchflower and Bryson 2009: 69) and union members are often more negative in their views toward their employer than non-members (ibid: 71). In these circumstances traditional pluralist acceptance of trade unions (Fox 1966) can come to be strained. It is profoundly out of fashion with most, but not all, top managers in the private sector, including many of those in HR where the current, unitarist rhetoric is 'engagement' (MacLeod and Clarke 2009) and the shades of paternalism it implies.

A third structural factor is damage caused by labour turnover. Where there are no effective mechanisms allowing employees to express conflicts it is likely that labour turnover will be higher (Dix et al 2009: 199). Labour turnover can be more of a problem for some firms than others and in different periods of the economic cycle. All employers find hiring and training costs increase when labour is in short supply. This then places greater emphasis on retention strategies to keep existing employees. This may well lead to higher pay but it is the social factors in employment which are of greater benefit such as job satisfaction, relationships with managers and higher levels of autonomy and 'voice' typified in the 'high involvement work systems' (Boxall and Purcell 2011: 134–40). The adoption of these forms of management was evident in the buoyant labour market around the turn of the century when labour retention was a pressing issue for many employers. This was before the impact of the recession but we do not yet have a clear view on how employee attitudes have changed in the current climate. The expectation, partly confirmed by the 2011 Chartered Institute of Personnel and Development (CIPD 2011) survey, is that there will be a worsening of relations and lower levels of trust in senior managers.

Aside from these cyclical trends there are grounds to suggest that an increasing number of employers are conscious of the need to keep labour turnover down and manage retention. The growth in knowledge work, and emphasis on standards of customer service, tend to increase employers' dependence on the quality of work provided by their staff. This type of work, whether emotional labour, or the use of cognitive skills, is classically discretionary. That is, it is up to the employee to deliver the level of service required and it is not something that can be enforced by dictatorial management or automated technology. This explains why so much attention has been given to the connection between HRM and business performance with emphasis placed on the need to ensure positive psychological contracts, organisational commitment and employee engagement (see Purcell and Kinnie 2007). This, in turn, makes the achievement of being 'an employer of choice' an imperative especially for firms where the quality of labour is a source of sustained competitive advantage. The effective management of employment rights is part of such an approach since this is associated with lower labour turnover. It is instructive to find that of the 50 top organisations in the 2011 awards for 'UK's best workplaces'[4] only six were in manufacturing while the great majority were professional services, IT, financial and retail firms. Even among those in the manufacturing sector it is clear that, in some cases, the majority of employees were professionals rather than manual workers.

The final structural issue is the shape of the organisation and the use of outsourcing and off-shoring. This has become one the biggest issues in business strategies in recent years. One of the most influential approaches to the analysis of strategy has been the 'resource based view' which places emphasis on internal firm resources, as opposed to external market factors, as the source of sustained competitive advantage in successful firms (see Boxall and Purcell 2011: 97–124). Here a distinction is often made between the different contributions that groups of employees make. Some are more important than others. Leonard (1998) distinguishes between types of capabilities required by the firm. Some are 'core capabilities' which are firm-specific, superior and cannot easily be imitated (financial market analysts, for example), others are 'enabling' and have to be present if the firm is to compete in its chosen market (banking staff in the high street) but which all firms in the sector must have. The third category of capabilities is 'supplemental'. These staff help those with core capabilities to perform but are easily copied (call centre staff). Lepak and Snell (2007) distinguish

---

[4] www.greatplacetowork.co.uk/publications/52-uks-2010-best-workplaces-publication.

between employees with core knowledge about the firm and its operations, which has to be developed internally and managed especially well through commitment-based HR, and others who have less unique skill and may be of less importance. Such roles may be externalised to contract workers or managed internally but with more transactional types of HR such as productivity-based or compliance-based practices. Labour turnover among the core staff is especially damaging while the more peripheral workers can be easily replaced, need less training and become fully competent more quickly than core workers. The challenge is to decide which employees fit into each of the categories. The trend in the private sector, and now in the public sector, has been to reduce the core and increase the periphery as seen in outsourcing, sub-contracting and the growing use of contract labour. The extensive application of employment rights and good practice is focussed on the valuable core while responsibility for others is increasingly passed to the contracted external provider (see Rubery, Earnshaw and Marchington 2005).

A good example of core and periphery strategies comes from the motor industry. In many ways the industry has been more sophisticated in its response to the recession in 2008–09 than in the slowdowns in the early 1980s and 1990s. Great efforts were made, in association with the trade unions, to keep assembly and track workers in employment.[5] Honda, for example, had a four-month shutdown between February and May in 2008 while extended Christmas holiday shutdowns were common. Redundancies were kept to a minimum and a full redundancy consultation was entered into. The established view was that these workers were now more skilled and flexible than their predecessors and the cost of replacing them higher. Labour retention, even if it meant paying some wages to laid-off workers, was economically more sensible than using a blunt redundancy dismissal approach. This was the approach of BMW Oxford, the home of the Mini, with a reduction in shift patterns and the closure of the night shift. The factory had won a number of awards for the quality of its HR. Controversy erupted, however, when 850 agency workers were dismissed on one hour's notice on 17 February 2009 with the various temporary work agencies being given one day's notice. One agency worker told the BBC that 'I've been here for four years and I've never been sick, I've never missed work and they tell me one hour before that I've been sacked. That's not on'.[6] Unfortunately it was 'on' and while the union called it a 'disgrace' (but were shouted at by agency staff) and a government spokesman promised a review on how to implement the Agency Workers' Directive, agency workers lacked employment rights in these circumstances, and still do. The advantage for employers in using agency and temporary or fixed term

---

[5] news.sky.com/home/business/article/15238980.
[6] news.bbc.co.uk/1/hi/business/7891913.stm.

contract staff is that the exit costs are low while for permanent staff they are much higher, not just in the period of notice and redundancy payments but in hard to replace competency losses.

MANAGEMENT STYLE, FAIRNESS AND ORGANISATIONAL JUSTICE

The preferred approaches taken in managing people at work are commonly referred to as management style. This has two linked meanings. The style of individual managers in leading and managing their team or department is of growing importance. But individual styles are strongly influenced by the overall style, related to corporate culture, adopted by the organisation since this can delineate acceptable from unacceptable conduct. This comes from senior management as part of their conscious, or unconscious, approach to labour questions. This is usually seen as the combination of the way each employee is managed and the collective relationship with trade unions or other representative bodies such as consultative committees.

The choice in the direct management of employees is crudely between relational and transactional approaches, sometimes called 'commitment and involvement' compared with 'command and control'. This was reflected in the previous discussion of the core and periphery. A commitment based, or relational style places emphasis on longer term employment relationships with an expectation of a reciprocal relationship between management and employees based on trust. Reciprocation is at the heart of socio-psychological approaches to the psychological contract and organisational commitment. Positive employee perceptions of the support the organisation provides, such as training, job autonomy and security, are associated with reciprocity through positive discretionary behaviour, or 'organisational citizenship behaviour' and thus better performance (see Coyle-Shapiro et al 2004). Perceptions of organisational support come from the way the organisation 'delivers on the deal' (Guest 2007) in terms of meeting employee needs and expectations: broadly defined employment rights, best summarised as 'fairness'. To the extent that the organisation places emphasis on a high trust relational style, whether for reasons of ethics or economic self-interest, it can be expected to ensure that 'fair' employment rights are effective. As we have noted above, this is more likely where employees have high discretion jobs and firm performance is dependent on employee commitment and engagement.

Command and control HR, sometimes called 'administrative HR', sees labour management as transactional, short-term and directional. It is more often found where skills are relatively low and labour replacement relatively easy and cheap. It rests on an assumption that jobs have relatively low levels of discretion and employee choice is minimal in the way the job is performed.

A good illustration comes from some types of call centre work where contact with customers is of short duration and transactional. Interactions with the customer service advisers (CSA) will typically be of around one minute or less, such as checking a bank balance or a train enquiry. These CSAs will rarely use more than one computer programme on screen and will be closely monitored for time on-call and for performance in keeping to the script. At the other end of the scale, business to business CSAs typically have to navigate between five or more computer programs, spend 20 minutes or more on a call with one customer and are expected to use relational skills to sell the product. This is particularly where calls are 'out-bound', initiated by the CSA. The amount of surveillance is minimal. They are better educated and receive much higher compensation than their counterparts in transactional call centres (Batt 2002). Again echoing the earlier discussion on core and periphery work patterns, some transactional call centres can have between half and three-quarters of their staff supplied by temporary work agencies (Kinnie, Purcell and Adams 2008). The management of most employment rights is assumed, sometimes wrongly, to be the responsibility of the agency and the mix of agency staff with 'normal' employees can cause problems (Purcell, Purcell and Tailby 2004). In the case of the BMW agency workers it was the responsibility of the agencies to tell these workers that they were to be dismissed since they were employed by the agency even though the work they performed was managed by BMW.

The second dimension to management style is the approach to collectivism whether via trade union recognition or the creation of information and consultation bodies such as staff councils or works councils. A growing number of employers seek to avoid any form of recognition of collectives and deal directly with their employees. This is the case both among those firms with a commitment and involvement approach to employees and those with employers adopting a command and control system. The difference between them is the way they avoid collectivism. A commitment based style places emphasis on extensive direct communication and involvement practices with frequent employee engagement surveys seeking to engender employee loyalty and engagement. Command and control companies tend to opt for forceful opposition, a long-running employer approach to avoid unionisation (Bain 1967).

Employers who recognise trade unions for some employees, and may also have a consultative forum for all, may be caught in an adversarial relationship as would appear to be the case for London Underground and British Airways. Others have more cooperative relationships sometimes amounting to a partnership approach (Samuel and Bacon 2010). The interconnection with ways of managing individual employees influences the overall style. Cooperative relationships with trade unions and/or consultative bodies linked to commitment based approaches to employees are a form of what was termed a 'sophisticated modern' approach placing emphasis on wide ranging consultation over management strategies and decisions (Purcell and Sisson 1983: 115). Walton, Cutcher-Gerschenfeld and McKersie (1994) suggest that, in managing change, such firms give priority to 'the improvement of the social contract' in employment by emphasising fostering, rather than forcing, strategies. This involves consultation on business strategies and extensive communication and involvement with individual employees. There is evidence that some employers with consultative bodies, both union and non-union based, do operate in this way, approaching consultation 'with a view to reaching agreement' as specified in the standard provisions of the ICE Regulations (Hall and Purcell 2012).

These types of employers tend to place emphasis on organisational justice in the management of employment rights. Organisational justice concerns the way employees evaluate the fairness of a decision. It is seen to have three components: procedural justice, distributive justice and interactional justice (Folger and Cropanzano 1998). The successful management of organisational justice requires embedded procedures, the adoption of fairness and equity in decision making and of good behavioural standards by line managers in communicating with employees. An example can be taken from decisions concerning redundancy. Procedural justice is the way the decision to make staff redundant was taken and the extent to which the employees and their representatives were consulted in time for the decision to be reviewed and alternatives explored. This involves the provision of information and explanations and debate over the scale, timing and compensation provided. Procedural justice requires that employees, both those directly affected, and those indirectly involved, feel that every effort was made to avoid the situation and that their concerns had had a fair hearing. Distributive justice requires that the final choice of who is to lose their job is seen to be fair and unbiased. It also concerns the allocation of redundancy payments and other support arrangements such as access to job searching and training. Any perceived violation of procedural justice can have a greater impact on feelings of fairness than the justice, or injustice, of the final outcome (McFarlin and Sweeny 1992). Both procedural and distributive justice in redundancies are strongly supported by legal provisions.

Interactional justice is more personal, and beyond the scope of legal regulation, since it relates to the way in which employees are told that they are to be made redundant. A few years ago a major management consultancy company told employees by email that they were dismissed in a redundancy exercise. This was widely seen as a breach of interactional justice and a dereliction of the line manager's duty to speak directly with each member of staff. It was a form of moral panic. The canons of organisational justice can be applied to the implementation of virtually all employment rights whether covered by employment law or relating to personal conduct and decision making.

The evidence we have of consultation in redundancies shows that three-quarters of employers did consult especially where unions were present or there was a joint union and non-union representative body (Kersley et al 2006: 203–04). It would appear from the same WERS survey that most employers did consult with trade unions when a large scale redundancy of 20 or more employees was planned. In terms of the topics of consultation the vast majority (86 per cent) covered the criteria for selection, over half (59 per cent) were concerned with redundancy payments and in two-thirds of cases options for reducing the number of redundancies were discussed (ibid: 203). These data reflect the need for organisational justice in dealing with the emotive issue of redundancy.

While the need for organisational justice in managing difficult change may influence senior managers, a further conclusion could be that the collective redundancy law is seen by employers as 'hugely expensive if they get it wrong ... It may be that in times of recession the sanction of a protective award may be more effective in acting as an incentive to follow the legal requirements' (Ranieri 2010: 5). What such a 'hard' law does is to increase the pressure on employers to ensure that forms of organisational justice are in place and understood, especially by senior and line managers.

THE VEXED ROLE OF LINE MANAGERS IN THE APPLICATION OF EMPLOYMENT RIGHTS

Line managers are now much more involved in the management of HR, and thus in making employment rights effective, or not, at the workplace. There are a number of linked aspects to this role. In the 1990s the trend was 'to return HRM to the line' (McGovern et al 1997). This movement, which continues, involved making line managers more responsible than they previously had been for the enactment of HR policies and practices. It is a misnomer to refer to this as 'returning HR to the line' since what it really entails is the spreading of practices such as appraisal and performance management, previously limited to higher echelons, to all or most of the workforce. At the same time, partly in response to the growing volume of individual rights enshrined in legislation, line managers took on more responsibility for the application of policies on discrimination, flexibility and grievance and disciplinary matters. This was inevitable since it is only the manager with direct responsibility for a team of employees who is able to make the micro-level decisions in these matters and deal with the conflicts that can arise in their application. It may be that decisions can be escalated up the chain of command but, from the employees' perspective, it is the line manager who embodies the organisation. If perceived organisational support is crucial for reciprocation through effort and good work then this is triggered by line managers in what is known as 'leader-membership exchange' (Uhl-Bien et al 2000: 138).

There are a number of problems associated with this greater line management responsibility for the application and management of employment issues. First, there is clear evidence that this growth in the line manager's role was achieved by adding responsibilities to an already complex set of duties (Hales 2005) leading to role overload. Second, one consequence of this overload is that it is often the case that what ought to happen does not take place, such as performance appraisals, team briefings and dealing effectively with grievances. There is often a clear difference 'between espoused and enacted HR practices with the gap often explained by ... lack of training, lack of interest, work overload, conflicting priorities and self-serving behaviour' (Purcell and Hutchinson 2007: 5). What this means is that there is often 'a strong disconnect between the "rhetoric" of human resource management as expressed by the HR department and the reality as experienced by employees' (Truss 2001: 1143). Third, line managers may give a low priority to dealing with employment issues. One study (McGovern et al 1997: 21) asked line managers to 'rank in order what motivates you to be involved in personnel activities'. The first ranked answer was 'personal motivation' as opposed to targets, company values, career advancement and other possible reasons. In other words, the attention line managers give to HR issues is discretionary and for some is something best avoided. Fourth, line managers often complain of a lack of support from senior managers making the role harder still (Hutchinson and Purcell 2010). This reluctance was magnified when issues involved legal complexities where they lacked both specialist knowledge and time to devote to issues seen as 'too hot to handle' (Harris: 2005: 81).

Part of the difficulty for line managers is to know the limits of their authority. When should a matter be referred to senior managers? Sometimes an enthusiastic manager can make a decision on how to handle a particular issue only to find the approach taken was not supported, or was even undermined by the HR or senior line manager. This ambiguity in the line manager's role is confirmed by WERS research which shows that 'three-quarters of line managers could not make final decisions' on any of the 15 potential 'job duties' in employment (Kersley et al 2006: 54). For example, in handling their equal opportunities job duties line managers in branch sites were supposed to follow policy in three-quarters of cases and/or consult others before making a decision in two-thirds of such workplaces (ibid: 55). This may seem sensible but, as noted, there is often a big gap between espoused and enacted practices.

Part of the problem, as recent research (Teague and Roche: 2012) in Ireland has shown, is that line managers commonly receive no training in 'people management', nor do these duties form part of any assessment of their competence as line managers. Not surprisingly, many were seen by their managers as lacking in confidence when handling workplace conflict.

The exception to this general trend was found in those firms which had explicitly adopted commitment-orientated HR policies. Here it was more likely that line managers had been supported by training, were monitored and their people management duties were included, and rewarded, in recurrent performance assessment. These firms were more likely 'to assign line managers and supervisors a developed and well-supported role in conflict management'.

Acas (2010: 8) notes that it is line managers who bring the employment policies, designed by professional HR departments, 'to life' in daily application. 'Unfortunately it is also line managers who are most often implicated in areas of poor employment practice which come to Acas' attention through individual conciliation linked to applications to employment tribunals'. Weaknesses in the effective application of employment rights can most often be traced back to line manager neglect or confusion abetted by senior managers setting performance targets while failing to give support to the people management part of the front-line manager's job. It is rare to find employers deliberately flouting recognised practice in employment rights leading to the conclusion that managerial problems are the product of neglect. One element of this is that most line managers are appointed to their jobs because of their technical or professional skills related to the commercial objectives of the firm rather than for their people management skills. Teague and Roche concluded that 'putting in place appropriate organisational support structures is the most likely way to ensure that line managers perform a positive role'. This could be expected to be the responsibility of the HR department but there are doubts about whether they are willing and able to do this. This is discussed in the next section.

HR PROFESSIONALS: CUSTODIANS OR GATEKEEPERS?

Unlike most other management specialisms, the HR function has always been beset with ambiguities and tensions. This, in large part, derives from the fact that the delivery of employment practices rests on other members of management. This raises questions about how HR professionals at the workplace undertake their work in association with senior and line managers. One route is to seek to be the custodian of best practice, innovating new ways of handling employment and HR practices, and through training and the exercise of organisational political skills, encouraging and supporting line managers to deal effectively with conflicts. This would be seen in the adoption of commitment-orientated HR policies backed by support structures for line managers. The evidence for this innovative, custodian role is limited. In a detailed analysis of WERS survey data from 1980 to 2004, Guest and Bryson (2009: 149) find that 'personnel specialists have been bringing up the rear, holding on to the well-established industrial relations practices, rather than championing the introduction of human resource management'. The alternative approach, associated with these well-established industrial relations practices, is to adopt a 'gatekeeper' role 'where the prime function is to keep threats at bay' (Purcell 1995: 78). This is generally reactive, dealing with problems as they arise, seeking to minimise organisational and financial damage, intervening especially where there is a danger of an issue or a conflict escalating to an ET or involving external trade union officers.

Harris's study of the effect of increasing external regulation of employment rights (Harris 2005) suggested six organisational responses. First, there may well be a growth in procedures which aim to ensure that line managers adopt a consistent approach in dealing with employment problems. This can become a form of system control at odds with the need for flexibility and a developmental role in handling cases. As Dickens (2000) has noted in the context of employment equality, it can have negative consequences by reinforcing a compliance and penalty avoidance approach to employment relations rather than the development of a proactive diversity policy. This is associated with the second response to external regulation: increasing centralised control. Here more decisions concerning the application and interpretation of employment rights are handled at the centre in the HR department. This trend was identified by WERS with 'the employment relations function ... characterised by centralised decision-making and relatively under-developed monitoring systems' (Kersley et al 2006: 70). This is at odds with the intention of making line managers responsible for such matters and it increases the risk of excessive formalisation. It is also expensive. In recent years there has been a growth in efforts to pare down HR departments, most recently seen in government plans to reduce expenditure in the civil service.[7] Outsourcing in HR has grown significantly as has the use of shared service arrangements where similar organisations combine resources, often with a greater reliance on the interactive web and call centres for line managers to use. The friendly HR manager down the corridor is replaced by a remote advice line and a distant HR manager with no intimate knowledge of people, processes or precedents in the organisation.

A third response, typical when the gatekeeping role takes precedent, is for legal minima to become the norm. Here 'the avoidance of litigation can provide a very tangible form of measurement' (Harris 2005: 82–83). This tends to minimise a proper understanding of the purposes of regulation and the supporting managerial behaviours. This avoidance approach shows little understanding of cultures and behaviour, especially managerial behaviour in people management.

---

[7] www.pcs.org.uk/en/campaigns/next-generation-human-resources-hr/what-is-next-generationcivil-service-hr.cfm.

One route out of this is training to develop line managers' awareness and capabilities in dealing with employment issues. Where HR adopts a custodian role such training and development activities are given greater emphasis and can include the modification of performance targets to include aspects of employment management. Some firms provide mentoring or buddying for newly appointed line managers or special monthly meetings for line managers where employment issues can be discussed, as well as technical matters. This allows for knowledge transfer from more experienced staff, and from the HR professionals. Some organisations see this as a reflection of a 'blame-free' culture often with a deliberate effort to learn from 'near misses'. Behavioural competency is seen to be the most effective way to ensure the effective application of employment rights in the context of business needs and organisational performance. The two are not seen to be in conflict.

The final two responses to external regulation identified by Harris relate to the role of HR providing internal advice to line managers and taking on a role of third-party referee. This can include facilitating third-party involvement when it is seen to be appropriate, and when those directly involved concur. Much of this takes on attributes of alternative dispute resolution (ADR). Among the innovative solutions being attempted are those which give HR a greater role in conciliating and occasionally mediating in disputes and the use of mediation (Acas/CIPD 2009). Some large organisations such as the West Midlands Police Force train middle-ranking officers as mediators while some organisations also train employee representatives in mediation (ibid: 13). An alternative is to appoint an external mediator. This is best termed 'relational' mediation since it focuses on interpersonal problems between workers or between the manager and an employee. In Ireland it is quite common among multinational companies for an ombudsman to be appointed to hear complaints rather than using union officers or applications to tribunals (Purcell 2010). The most common form of ADR is the use of disciplinary and grievance procedures which allow for a fair hearing and for appeals. This is where the expert role of HR can play an important part in ensuring that standards of fairness and justice are maintained. However, Teague and Roche (2012) were unable to find that the adoption of ADR practices enhanced the role of line managers in dealing with conflicts at work and suggest that the role of ADR 'may be overplayed'.

The custodian role means developing appropriate policies around core principles and gaining their acceptance at senior management level, building line management competence to deal with employment matters and ensuring that ADR processes are applied effectively. To be credible, these need to relate to business strategies and be seen to contribute to business success. Some organisations use the 'balanced score card' approach showing the interconnections between customer satisfaction, employee satisfaction and financial results as a new form of management accounting (see Boxall and

Purcell 2011: 324–26). These are the best run organisations, most often found in large customer service firms emphasising market differentiation or in advanced manufacturing. They tend to adopt commitment and involvement management styles and some have collective relationships usually with a partnership approach. HR is seen as strategically important. Fairness and organisational justice tend to be embedded. Elsewhere there is a wide range of practices with some companies taking a minimalist approach to employment rights. Here the HR manager, if there is one, takes the role of 'gatekeeper' to prevent difficulties escalating, especially externally. This manager often does not have the authority or status to gain the adoption of better standards of management behaviour, necessary to make employment rights effective, either in the boardroom or on the shop floor.

CONCLUSION

A narrow definition of employment rights, meaning those employer obligations enshrined in legislation, may cause resentment in management circles since it implies the need for external regulation over otherwise untrustworthy employers. Taking this line, it is easy to complain of the current volume of legislation. But to do so also requires a belief that managers can be relied on to be good employers, who know best how to ensure that good standards of employment are applied. The evidence for self-regulation is not persuasive. A better line, both in practice and theory, is to suggest that forms of social regulation can be effective. This broadens the analysis of employment rights to include a wide variety of 'forces' which tend to have an impact on employers' choices on how to manage labour. Labour law, especially if it is 'hard' law with effective sanctions, can spur compliance, as we have seen with redundancy legislation. Other agencies, such as trade unions and campaign and pressure groups, especially in the age of social media, can be influential in particular circumstances, such as the exploitation of migrant labour or child employment. Institutional pressures play a part both in leading to a form of 'forced comparisons' allowing the spread of good practices, for example on diversity, or articulated by powerful agencies such as accreditation bodies, major customers or public opinion. There is a widespread form of copying within management from one firm to another especially if the practice under the spotlight is associated with performance improvements. A further dimension is that firms which rely on their employees to achieve a high level of performance are usually more concerned to ensure that good standards of labour management apply. They want to be 'employers of choice' and ensure that talented members of staff do not leave. There is a strong self-interest, in these firms, in ensuring that employment rights are applied effectively.

Even in the best run firms the application of high standards of HR through competent line managers is not enough to ensure that problems do not arise. It would be foolish to assume otherwise. All the evidence suggests that access to, and the proper operation of, procedures for complaint and access to representation are vital. This is why unionised firms tend to have fewer ET cases. Even although union members are more aware of their rights than others, it is not unionisation per se which leads to a lower number of cases but the existence of procedures giving employees a relatively risk-free avenue of redress and access to representation. This is where procedural justice is so important as a feature of ensuring that employment rights are made effective. Having a voice, having access to representation and having an opportunity to use them are important prerequisites which some employers clearly recognise. These, too, are the sort of firms where the canons of social legitimacy are important for their reputation and to meet their own standards. Others, with a more negative perspective, see them as troublesome and, at heart, a challenge to the right to manage since the procedures require them to justify their actions. Labour law becomes especially important in such circumstances.

This broader social definition of employment rights recognises the reality of working life. What it implies is that statutory regulation is more likely to influence managerial conduct in employment when it reflects accepted standards of good practice, and when enforcement processes are effective. In the end, however, it is the social players, and in some cases the social partners, who have the most influence over making employment rights effective. Only a small proportion of employees ever find themselves in an ET. For the large majority it is the way employment rights, or more generally HR policies and practices, are applied by their line manager which is of greatest influence. Making employment rights effective means finding ways to increase the importance attached to them within employing organisations and improving the quality of line management rather than relying on external enforcement procedures.

BIBLIOGRAPHY

Acas (2010) *Building Employee Engagement*, Policy discussion paper (London, Acas).

Acas/CIPD (2009) *Mediation: An Employer's Guide* (London, CIPD).

Bain, G (1967) *Trade Union Growth and Recognition*, Research Paper 6, Royal Commission on Trade Unions and Employers' Associations (London, HMSO).

Batt, R (2002) 'Managing Customer Services: Human Resource Practices, Quit Rates, and Sales Growth' 45 *Academy of Management Journal* 587–97.

Blanchflower, D and Bryson, A (2009) 'Trade Union Decline and the Economics of the Workplace' in W Brown, A Bryson, J Forth and K Whitfield (eds), *The Evolution of the Modern Workplace* (Cambridge, Cambridge University Press).

Boxall, P and Purcell, J (2011) *Strategy and Human Resource Management 3rd Edition* (Basingstoke, Palgrave Macmillan).

Bryson, A (2004) 'Managerial Responsiveness to Union and Nonunion Worker Voice in Britain' 43 *Industrial Relations* 213–41.

Bryson, A and Freeman, R (2007) 'What Voice do British Workers Want?' in R Freeman, P Boxall and P Haynes (eds), *What Workers Say: Employee Voice in the Anglo-American World* (Ithaca, NY, Cornell University Press).

Burgess, S, Propper, C and Wilson, D (2000) *Explaining the Growth in the Number of Applications to Industrial Tribunals 1972–1997*, Employment Relations Research Series No 10 (London, Department of Trade and Industry).

Casebourne, J, Regan, J, Neathey, F And Tuohy, S (2006) *Employment Rights at Work: Survey of Employees 2005*, Employment Relations Research Series No 51 (London, Department of Trade and Industry).

CIPD (2011) *Employee Outlook*, Autumn 2011 (London, CIPD).

Cooke, WN (2007) 'Multinational Companies and Global Human Resource Strategy' in P Boxall, J Purcell and P Wright (eds), *The Oxford Handbook of Human Resource Management* (Oxford, Oxford University Press).

Coyle-Shapiro, J, Shore, M, Taylor, S and Tetrick, L (eds) (2004) *The Employment Relationship: Examining Psychological and Contextual Perspectives* (Oxford, Oxford University Press).

Dickens, L (2000) 'Still Wasting Resources? Equality in Employment' in S Bach and K Sisson (eds), *Personnel Management – A Comprehensive Guide to Theory and Practice*, 3rd edn (Oxford, Blackwell).

DiMaggio, P and Powell, W (1983) 'The Iron Cage Revisited: Institutional Isomorphism and Collective Rationality in Organizational Fields' 48 *American Sociological Review* 147–60.

——(1991) *The New Institutionalism in Organizational Analysis* (Chicago, University of Chicago Press).

Dix, G, Sisson, K and Forth, A (2009) 'Conflict at Work: The Changing Patterns of Disputes' in W Brown, A Bryson, J Forth and K Whitfield (eds), *The Evolution of the Modern Workplace* (Cambridge, Cambridge University Press).

Edwards, T and Walsh, J (2009) 'Foreign Ownership and Industrial Relations' in W Brown, A Bryson, J Forth and K Whitfield (eds), *The Evolution of the Modern Workplace* (Cambridge, Cambridge University Press).

Elkington, J (1997) *Cannibals with Forks: The Triple Bottom Line of 21st Century Business* (Oxford, Capstone).

Folger, R and Cropanzano, R (1998) *Organizational Justice and Human Resource Management* (Thousand Oaks, CA, Sage).

Fox, A (1966) *Industrial Sociology and Industrial Relations*, Research Paper 3, Royal Commission on Trade Unions and Employers' Associations (London, HMSO).

Gospel, H (1973) 'An Approach to a Theory of the Firm in Industrial Relations' 11 *British Journal of Industrial Relations* 211–28.

Guest, D (2007) 'Human Resource Management and the Worker: Towards a New Psychological Contract?' in P Boxall, J Purcell and P Wright (eds), *The Oxford Handbook of Human Resource Management* (Oxford, Oxford University Press).

Guest, D and Bryson, A (2009) 'From Industrial Relations to Human Resource Management: The Changing Role of the Personnel Function' in W Brown,

A Bryson, J Forth and K Whitfield (eds), *The Evolution of the Modern Workplace* (Cambridge, Cambridge University Press).

Hales, C (2005) 'Rooted in Supervision, Branching into Management: Continuity and Change in the Role of the Front-line Manager' 42 *Journal of Management Studies* 471–506.

Hall, M (2010) 'EU Regulation and the UK Employee Consultation Framework' 31 *Economic and Industrial Democracy* 55–69.

Hall, M and Purcell, J (2012) *Consultation at Work: Regulation and Practice* (Oxford, Oxford University Press).

Harris, L (2005) 'Employment Law and Human Resourcing Strategies' in J Leopold, L Harris and T Watson (eds), *The Strategic Management of Human Resources* (Harlow, Finiancial Times Prentice Hall).

Hutchinson, S and Purcell, J (2010) 'Managing Ward Managers for Roles in HRM in the NHS: Overworked and Under-resourced' 20 *Human Resource Management Journal* 339–76.

Kersley, B, Alpin, C, Forth, J, Bryson, A, Bewley, H, Dix, G and Oxenbridge, S t(2006) *Inside the Workplace: Findings from the 2004 Workplace Employment Relations Survey* (London, Routledge).

Kinnie, N, Purcell, J and Adams, M (2008) 'Explaining Employees' Experience of Work in Outsourced Call Centres: The Influence of Clients, Owners and Temporary Work Agencies' 50 *Journal of Industrial Relations* 209–28.

Kossek, E and Pichler, S (2007) 'EEO and the Management of Diversity' in P Boxall, J Purcell and P Wright (eds), *The Oxford Handbook of Human Resource Management* (Oxford, Oxford University Press).

Leonard, D (1998) *Wellsprings of Knowledge: Building and Sustaining the Sources of Innovation* (Boston, MA, Harvard Business School Press).

Lepak, D and Snell, S (2007) 'Employment Sub-systems and the "HR Architecture"' in P Boxall, J Purcell and P Wright (eds), *The Oxford Handbook of Human Resource Management* (Oxford, Oxford University Press).

MacLeod, D and Clarke, N (2009) *Engaging for Success: Enhancing Performance through Employee Engagement. A Report to Government* (London, Department for Business, Innovation and Skills).

McFarlin, D and Sweeney, P (2001) 'Distributive and Procedural Justice as Predictors of Satisfaction with Personal and Organizational Outcomes' 35 *Academy of Management Journal* 626–37.

McGovern, F, Gratton, L, Hope-Hailey, V, Stiles, P and Truss, K (1997) 'Human Resource Management on the Line?' 7 *Human Resource Management Journal* 12–29.

Purcell, J (1989) 'The Impact of Corporate Strategy on Human Resource Management' in J Storey (ed), *New Perspectives on Human Resource Management* (London, Routledge).

—— (1995) 'Corporate Strategy and its Link with Human Resource Strategy' in J Storey (ed), *Human Resource Management: A Critical Text* (London, Routledge).

—— (2010) *Individual Disputes at the Workplace: Alternative Disputes Resolution* (Dublin, European Foundation for the Improvement of Living and Working Conditions).

Purcell, J and Hutchinson, S (2007) 'Front-line Managers as Agents in the HRM-performance Causal Chain: Theory, Analysis and Evidence' 17 *Human Resource Management Journal* 3–20.

Purcell, J and Kinnie, N (2007) 'HRM and Business Performance' in P Boxall, J Purcell and P Wright (eds), *The Oxford Handbook of Human Resource Management* (Oxford, Oxford University Press).

Purcell, J, Purcell, K and Tailby, S (2004) 'Temporary Work Agencies: Here Today, Gone Tomorrow? 42 *British Journal of Industrial Relations* 705–25.

Purcell, J and Sisson, K (1983) 'Strategies and Practice in the Management of Industrial Relations' in G Bain (ed), *Industrial Relations in Britain* (Oxford, Blackwell).

Ranieri, N (2010) *Collective Consultation on Redundancies*, Acas Policy Discussion Paper (London, Acas).

Rubery, J, Earnshaw, J and Marchington, M (2005) 'Blurring the Boundaries of the Employment Relationship: From Single to Multi-employer Relationships' in M Marchington, D Grimshaw, J Rubery and H Willmott (eds), *Fragmenting Work: Blurring Organizational Boundaries and Disordering Hierarchies* (Oxford, Oxford University Press).

Samuel, P and Bacon, N (2010) 'The Contents of Partnership Agreements in Britain 1990–2007' 24 *Work, Employment and Society* 430–48.

Scott, W (2008) *Institutions and Organizations: Ideas and Interests*, 3rd edn (Los Angeles, Sage).

Sisson, K and Purcell, J (2010) 'Management: Caught Between Competing Views' in T Colling and M Terry (eds), *Industrial Relations: Theory and Practice*, 3rd edn (Chichester, Wiley).

Standing, G (2011) *The Precariat: The New Dangerous Class* (London, Bloomsbury).

Teague, P and Roche, W (2012) 'Line Managers and the Management of Workplace Conflict: Evidence from Ireland' 22 *Human Resource Management Journal*.

Truss, K (2001) 'Complexities and Controversies in Linking HRM with Organisational Outcomes' 38 *Journal of Management Studies* 1121–49.

Uhl-Bien, M, Graen, G and Scandura, T (2000) 'Indicators of Leader–member Exchange (LMX) for Strategic Human Resource Management Systems' 18 *Research in Personnel and Human Resources Management* 137–85.

Walton, R, Cutcher-Gershenfeld, J and McKersie, R (1994) *Strategic Negotiations: A Theory of Change in Labor–Management Relations* (Boston MA, Harvard Business School Press).

10

Trade Union Roles in Making Employment Rights Effective

TREVOR COLLING*

INTRODUCTION

PROPOSALS AIMED AT making employment rights effective must be informed by an understanding of changing union roles. This is particularly the case in the British context, given its history of collective laissez-faire (a principal reliance upon collective bargaining through trade unions as the preferred method of standard setting). Almost half a century ago, Fox and Flanders (1969: 180) reflected on the strains emerging in the system of British industrial relations, the prospect even then of increased statutory intervention, and concluded: 'the law has a part to play, but it cannot enforce a regulative order where none exists'. This is because legal process lacks those adaptive characteristics which are particularly necessary in the realm of employment, where the nature of rights is subject inherently to dispute and to change. Under collective bargaining, employers, workforces, and unions as their representatives, are able to adapt and develop measures and are more likely therefore to feel bound by them. This representative mechanism is less direct in statutory processes provided by parliament rather than by unions, and enforcement falls principally to individuals' use of the tribunal and court system. These institutions are incapable on their own of developing the necessary 'normative regulation' to underpin and vitalise statutory principles. Wherever effective normative regulation is weakened, 'disorder becomes manifest in unpatterned behaviour leading to an undermining of integration and predictability in social action and events' (Fox and Flanders 1969: 180).

This is demonstrably the case at the present time. For large parts of the British economy, the development of statutory employment rights has now displaced regulation through collective bargaining. Regular reviews of the

* I am grateful for comments on earlier drafts provided by Linda Dickens and Edmund Heery.

employment tribunal (ET) system have acknowledged that, 'most employees experience problems in the workplace at one time or another' (Gibbons 2007: 7) and that the tribunal system is struggling to deal with the consequences (see Morris, this volume). Belying the individualised expression of statutory rights, single claims from single claimants are now the minority. Multiple jurisdictional claims have been increasing for some time, often requiring tribunals to disentangle complex dimensions of the same grievance, and grouped claims involving several applicants affected by the same grievance are now common too. In critical respects, the current crisis in dispute resolution stems from an individualised system of rights straining to deal with collective problems in terms anticipated by Fox and Flanders (1969: 158): 'disorder emerges as dislocation, disruption and a variety of other symptoms associated with frustrated expectations'.

Yet these two systems of regulation, based on statutory individual rights and collective bargaining, have never been entirely separate and are not so now. Following the work of Colin Crouch, Heery (2010) has proposed a 'recombination thesis'. Institutions do not follow social and political trends mechanistically; rather they continue to pursue distinct objectives using whatever resources the changing framework of governance affords them. Institutional change thereby fosters hybrid forms of governance and regulation. Specifically, Heery observes that unions currently use legal standards to reinforce their bargaining and organising strategies: 'substantive law has not displaced collective bargaining but has been incorporated within it as a precedent, sanction and standard. In combination, they point to British trade unions developing a post-voluntarist system of interest representation' (ibid: 89).

This chapter explores these issues further, focusing on the changing roles of trade unions and their use of statutory employment rights. It is necessary first to discuss the processes through which employment standards were developed under collective laissez-faire and what has happened following the demise of that system from the 1970s onwards. Union legal strategies are then located within that context. Heery's recombination thesis has force: talk of one system displacing the other entirely is inappropriate historically and premature in the current context. Just as unions were capable of demanding and using legal process under collective laissez-faire when it suited their purposes, so it is possible to see organising strategies now underpinned by statutory mechanisms. But development and qualifications are also necessary. Union roles in the statutory process have to be disentangled, to distinguish between the development of standards and their application within workplaces. In practice, opportunities to influence the former have not developed to a degree that might compensate for the loss of authority through collective bargaining. As a consequence, the law is rendered often in ways that unions find costly and counter-productive to use. In this weakened position, while union representation amplifies the spirit of legislation in the workplace in important ways, risks and partial rewards lead to formal engagement with the law that is more intermittent and selective than it might be. Making employment rights effective may depend to a significant degree on the ability to revitalise and reinstate their diffusion through representative structures.

STATE, TRADE UNIONS AND THE LAW:
CHANGING RELATIONS

Public policy reform over the past 30 years has left the union movement differently placed in the process of standard setting. Powers devolved to them through most of the twentieth century afforded them principal positions in the governance of industry, alongside employers. Gradually, that direct regulatory role has been diminished and dismantled, so that unions often now enforce the standards set by government. The next two sections outline the key policy developments facilitating this changed role.

Collective Laissez-faire, Unions and the Law

Famously the apparent separation of law from industrial relations became a defining feature of Britain's voluntarist system. Collective laissez-faire, as Kahn-Freund termed it, ensured, 'the retreat of the law from industrial relations and of industrial relations from the law' (Kahn-Freund quoted in Dukes 2009: 221). In the governance of industrial relations anyway, the law came to provide a regulatory role that was secondary to unions and collective bargaining. As Flanders (1970: 27) put it, 'whenever and wherever trade unions have gained enough strength to regulate wages and conditions of work by direct negotiation with employers they have dispensed with government assistance'. Left unelaborated, this is a caricature—in order to provide the conditions for effective governance, the law and public policy continued to play important roles in supporting the functions assumed by trade unions.

By promoting the interests of individual parties to the employment contract over collective rights, Britain's common law system was intrinsically hostile to developing structured representation in the workplace. Contract law recognised the individual contract of employment as the principal conduit of rights and responsibilities in the employment relationship. Collective terms were valid only to the extent that they were incorporated into individual contracts of employment but this process was very far from automatic and could be construed by judges in ways that did not inevitably support the claimant's case (see Wedderburn and Davies 1969: 45). This structural feature of the law complemented an ideology of individualism amongst judges that was not consistent with the development of collective rights.

Since enforcing collective rights implies to some extent restrictions on individual freedom of choice, 'the distrust of the unions against the courts and the lawyers is well grounded in the hostility which the courts have often shown to the union movement and sometimes still show' (Kahn-Freund 1970: 267). This presented tactical dilemmas to those crafting a system of industrial regulation: how to integrate a largely individualised legal system with the developing system of collective rights? Positive rights to union representation and bargaining protections would always be subject to interpretation and challenge by judges. Best perhaps to remove their jurisdiction altogether by creating immunities from the law, a terrain on which unions might pursue their regulatory objectives with employers, provided broad conditions are met: 'on the whole their main purpose is to remove obstacles which the courts have erected and which threatened to impede the operation of industrial relations. The law has not created rights, but immunities from disabilities' (Kahn-Freund 1970: 303).

For some political scientists, this amounted to the anointment of unions and collective bargaining as *governance structures* in their own right, an autonomous system of regulation assuming from government some of its functions and sanctions. Elaborating Commons' perspective on the governance function of trade unions Kaufman (2000: 195) argued that:

> The highest form of government in society is the political government that claims sovereignty over the land and people and the right to use the sanction of physical violence to enforce the working rules and defend the state against enemies. Below the nation state are a host of other organizations, including corporations, unions, churches, and political parties, forming a diffuse network of jurisdictions and power centers. From an analytical point of view, all such organizations can be viewed as a pluralistic set of governments for each is the product of collective action, is governed by working rules that specify authority relations and the distribution of rights, liberties, duties, and exposures and employs sanctions to enforce the working rules.

Unions are well suited to governance roles of this kind due to their 'bridging capacity', the ability to identify, accommodate, and articulate the interests of their constituencies at all levels, from the workplace to government (Fick 2009). From this characteristic stems the capacity of unions to generate and maintain the normative regulation identified by Fox and Flanders (1969). Union leadership emerges from grassroots constituencies in workplaces and is accountable to them. Members are dependent upon their leaders to articulate their interests but leaders are dependent upon members and their potential for collective mobilisation to underpin their bargaining power. Employers and government rely on union leaders for that connection to feelings in the workplace but may also insist that union leaders act to ensure compliance with agreements reached. In this sense unions, 'have the capacity for both horizontal and vertical interaction' (Fick 2009: 259).

For Flanders, these features of collective bargaining were superior to other forms of regulation (expressly including legal regulation):

> It would be impossible for industry to operate with a sensitive regard for the varied human interests of all the equally varied categories of workers by means of regulations imposed by an outside authority. Industrial processes are constantly changing and with them the conditions of employment. In every workshop there is a host of detailed problems which affect and interest the workers and can only be settled satisfactorily by organizations intimately connected with them. (Flanders 1968: 78)

In Britain, the unique development of industrialisation and of the state meant that unions tended to assume direct governance functions, and trade union members were eager that they should do so. Relatively early industrialisation and the rise of organised labour meant that working people assumed through their unions rights that were unobtainable through political means (Kahn-Freund 1969: 302). Writing about the first faltering steps of collective laissez-faire, Middlemas (1979: 21) suggested that unions and employers' organisations, 'behaved ... in some degree as *estates of the realm*' (emphasis added): 'what had simply been *interest groups* crossed the political threshold and became part of the extended state; a position from which other groups, even if they too held political power, were still excluded' (ibid 1979: 373).

However, three factors relevant to considerations later in this chapter must be noted here. First, union capacity depended upon their ability potentially to enforce sanctions; that is upon the acceptance and institutionalisation of their *power*. This has both external (power to discipline employers) and internal (power to discipline members) dimensions and, according to Fox and Flanders (1969: 155), they develop in conjunction: '[a] union that is internally weak is normally one that is externally weak; equally the unions cannot be deprived of their external strength without weakening them internally as well'. Second, it is necessary also to acknowledge that this settlement was not simply bequeathed to industry by an insightful state but was secured by 'the real struggles of workers and trade unions to have a variety of legal rights recognised by Parliament' (Dukes 2009: 222). Landmark statutes in the edifice of collective laissez-faire were extracted in part by unions themselves, following their active engagement with both legal and political channels (Lewis 1976). Third, however negotiated, the active support of the state was critical to the operation of collective laissez-faire to a greater degree than is often appreciated from the vantage point of the twenty-first century.

Kahn-Freund identified three functions for labour law (1970: 302). *Regulatory* functions are apparent where the state establishes detailed codes governing employment standards and their enforcement. Clearly, this was not a central feature of industrial relations for much of the nineteenth and twentieth centuries. *Restrictive* functions, however, govern the nature and extent of the powers devolved to the parties and the reciprocal responsibilities owed by them to government, to the public, and to each other. Active and evolving roles in this sense certainly were evident throughout the life of collective laissez-faire, and inevitably so. Famously, however, Kahn-Freund also identified a third necessary function which was *auxiliary* to collective bargaining: 'by providing norms and sanctions to stimulate the bargaining process itself, and to strengthen the operation, that is *promoting the observance of concluded agreements*' (ibid, emphasis added).

Arguably this aspect of collective laissez-faire has been under-emphasised in more recent treatments but it is centrally relevant to the concerns of this volume. Probably the most important mechanisms for enforcing and extending collective terms were deployed by the parties themselves. Quoting McCarthy, Kahn-Freund (1970: 243) observed that in 1970,

> about two-fifths of all members of unions and about one-sixth of the total labour force work in a 'closed shop' of some sort; that is, in order to have access to the labour market, they must be or become members of a union or of a particular union.

The effect was to bind employers, workers, and unions to the institutions of collective bargaining but the state did not leave this function solely to the parties themselves. It undertook an important *auxiliary* role, one referred to by Kahn-Freund as 'organized persuasion' and which he considered, 'a very fundamental social institution in this country' (Kahn-Freund 1969: 304). This captures the *administrative* mechanisms through which collective bargaining was encouraged or compliance with it required. Wage setting in industries without collective bargaining was intended to encourage its development:

> [A]part from being a substitute for collective bargaining machinery the minimum wage law also serves as a training ground or education towards collective bargaining. The two sides, ie, employers and trade unions, meet within the statutory wages councils and get an opportunity of acquiring the habit of negotiating. (Kahn-Freund 1965: 37)

Where bargaining was established, mechanisms were available to encourage the diffusion of terms across workforces. The Fair Wages Resolution 1946 and the Terms and Conditions Act 1959 (which was to become Schedule 11 of the Employment Protection Act 1975) provided for the extension of prevailing terms to workers engaged in work in the public sector and private industry respectively (Baker 1976; Bercusson 1975).

Discussion so far has provided some historical backdrop to the development and enforcement of rights today. In important respects, unions assumed governance roles under the period of collective laissez-faire, enabling them to establish employment norms directly. This provides a template against which to evaluate the altered position of unions today, a task begun below.

It is not accurate, however, to say or to presume that law in the sense established by the state did not influence such processes in the past. While it did not establish rights directly for the most part, or prescribe the form or content of collective bargaining, it did define the perimeters within which the parties could define employment terms and support their broader diffusion once agreed. In recent years, the influence of law has become much more prominent and direct and it is to that process that we turn now.

Neo-Liberalism, Unions and the Law

The roles afforded to unions today have altered substantially, with important implications for opportunities for 'recombination.' Conservative governments of the 1980s and 1990s were explicitly hostile to collective bargaining as a regulatory mechanism, viewing it as inherently coercive over individual freedoms and pursued irresponsibly in practice by trade unions (see Smith 2009). Subsequent policy innovation dismantled much of the framework supporting collective laissez-faire. Labour governments from 1997 modified this approach, supporting collective representation where it facilitated partnership working, but much of the framework of collective labour law established by the preceding governments remained in place and the body of individual employment law continued to expand. Collective bargaining has diminished substantially, in terms both of its scope (the range of workers covered) and its depth (the range of topics open to negotiation) (Brown 2010). Legislative change is not responsible by itself for such trends, but it has done little to prevent them and much to facilitate them. As Howell (2005: 134) has noted,

> the legacy of industrial relations policy over the last two decades has been to change the way in which trade unions think about their relationship with the state: this ideological shift may be the most profound implication of the British state's role during this period.

This is not the place for a comprehensive or detailed review of these developments (for which see Dickens and Hall 2010; Smith and Morton 2009). The analytical purpose here is selective, to highlight the terrain on which recombination takes place, and Kahn-Freund's typology of the function of labour law is helpful for this purpose.

The most obvious changes in policy relate to the *regulatory* function, in which the direct role of the state is now much more prominent. Key rights once delegated entirely to unions and employers through collective bargaining are now influenced by the state, most notably working time and minimum pay. This 'juridification' of industrial relations was underway for some time but accelerated markedly under recent Labour governments. It is not simply the expanded role of the state that is of significance; so too is the individualised form in which rights have been rendered. Where once unions were permitted direct roles in the development and enforcement of employment standards, rights are now accorded to individuals and it is for them to enforce them in discussions with their employers and the ET system thereafter. It may be too trite to argue that the expansion of individual employment rights has led directly to the weakening of collective rights (many of them after all have been demanded by unions themselves), but it is closely implicated in two senses. First, if rights are available to individuals through the law, why should they combine with others to assert and defend them? Second, growing exposure to statutory rights prompts particular responses from management. Brown (1992: 302) long ago detected a connection between employment law and the decline of sector level collective bargaining, for example: 'there can be little doubt that increased legislative intervention, by forcing companies individually to get a tighter grip over potentially litigious aspects of employment, also furthered their attempts to get a tighter grip on collective bargaining'.

Such developments were augmented by changes in the 'restrictive' function of labour law, which had a direct impact on the roles available to unions. Critical here have been changes to both the external and internal dimensions of union power referred to above. Externally, and critically, the ability of unions to impose sanctions on employers using their own organisational resources has been severely eroded. Definitions of legitimate industrial action have been narrowed to those connected to terms and conditions of employment and action can be taken only against the immediate employer. Strikes in support of policy or political objectives are unlawful as are those aimed at ensuring collective rights amongst associated employers. Unions can exhort employers to defend and extend jointly agreed terms across industries but bargaining power available to them in such efforts has been constrained. Internal power resources and the ability to ensure coherence and compliance amongst diverse memberships have also been undermined by changes imposed upon previously autonomous rule-making. For example, unions cannot discipline members who refuse to comply with calls to observe collective industrial action, even where such action has been supported by a majority of union members in the requisite ballot.

Finally, and most easily overlooked, are changes to those functions of labour law auxiliary to collective bargaining. Most of these were dismantled during the 1980s, consistent with the hostility to collective bargaining within the Conservative administrations of the day. The closed shop was effectively abolished, as were the wages councils, and extension mechanisms such as the Fair Wages Resolution and Schedule 11 were removed. These seem minor adjustments when set beside those reforms outlined above, but by removing those powers of 'organized persuasion' their ramifications are significant (Simpson 1986). At the point when employer engagement with collective bargaining was in decline, the state removed any element of encouragement or compulsion thus facilitating the further atrophy of this governance mechanism. The Labour government subsequently enacted a right to trade union recognition where there was an evident demand for it amongst workforces, but voluntary approaches were preferred and the public policy stance remained firmly agnostic. Opportunities to reinstate auxiliary mechanisms have been firmly eschewed. The Posting of Workers Directive (96/71/EC) permits host member states to designate collective agreements as a source of minimum standards to be observed by companies from other countries deploying their workers within their boundaries. In Britain, this would effectively require the reinstatement of those extension mechanisms previously abolished, or the creation of analogous provisions. Governments have consistently refused to do this, preferring simply to extend to posted workers national minima established in statute (Novitz 2010).

The effect of the changes outlined here has been to relegate unions to minor and subsidiary roles in the definition and enforcement of employment standards. From a system in which they exercised principal and direct influence across industry through collective rights, they now mediate, in workplaces, individual rights that have been established by statute. Such processes are far from complete; the institutions of collective laissez-faire remain important in the public sector and in some isolated parts of private industry. But the trends are longstanding: as Simpson noted (1986: 809), 'what has happened is that trade unions, the collective representatives of workers' interests, have become incorporated in a system which institutionalises conflicts into individual, justiciable disputes'. More recently, Ewing (2005) outlined five functions of trade unions, from lower level activities involving the provision of services and representation to members to higher level ones involving regulation via collective bargaining and participation in public administration and government. Broadly, the pattern of public policy has been to emphasise the service and representation functions while reshaping those higher level roles:

> [T]o the extent that unions have a regulatory role it is one which is changing and which is being diluted. As such it is now partly indirect and vicarious in the sense that the trade union regulatory function has become political as much as industrial, with regulatory ambitions secured by political campaigning and by legislation rather than by collective bargaining. (ibid: 15)

This is the terrain upon which unions develop their legal strategies and it is to that effort that we now turn.

UNION LEGAL STRATEGIES IN A CHANGED CONTEXT

Certainly, the consequence of changing policy pressures has been to push unions further towards the law, ensuring 'recombination' to some degree. The critical issue determining union revitalisation has been unions' ability to regenerate bargaining power. Many unions have turned to the philosophy of 'organising' (Simms and Holgate 2010) with the intention of galvanising collective identities amongst workforces and encouraging willingness to act. But in circumstances where this cannot be guaranteed, unions have looked to statutory rights to augment their leverage in bargaining contexts (Hickey et al 2010): 'British trade unions have effectively abandoned voluntarism. By the early 1990s, recognising their vulnerability to both a hostile state and a hostile employer class, the trade union movement had adopted a position calling for extensive juridification of industrial relations' (Howell 2005: 170). But the weakened position from which unions attempt recombination carries important consequences. The following sections review trade union legal strategies across the two dimensions of 'legal enactment' specified by the Webbs (1898), the *getting* and *enforcement* of legal protections.

Recombination and Statutory Development

As the Webbs pointed out at the turn of the nineteenth century (1898: 247), 'we do not need to remind the student of the *History of Trade Unionism* that an Act of Parliament has, at all times, formed one of the means by which British Trade Unionists have sought to attain their ends'. For reasons set out above, connected to the ideology of collective laissez-faire, such reminders have in fact become necessary today. Though British unions have preferred first and foremost opportunities to bargain directly with employers, the preference was pragmatic. Wherever bargaining was not available or insufficient, unions have always turned without any qualms to the law (see Davies and Freedland 1993: 64).

As the reach of collective bargaining and the regulatory role of trade unions have diminished, unions have fallen back on such instincts more and more. Heery (1998) notes preparedness within the TUC to develop political and policy influence from the mid-1990s onwards. Significantly, this went beyond traditional reliance upon the Labour Party to involve alliance building across a spectrum of organised interests (including employer and community groups) in support of broad regulation. Individual unions faced by challenging labour market developments affecting their constituencies have sought statutory protections. Unions representing freelance workers, for example, cannot rely upon traditional workplace-based organisation and traditionally enforced minimum standards through the pre-entry closed shop and the threat of secondary action against non-compliant employers. When these resources were rendered unlawful, unions moved towards 'political and legal action ... designed to reduce competition within, and promote the regulation of, freelance labour markets' (Heery et al 2004: 31).

Developments of this kind have been encouraged by the evolution of 'multi-level governance' (Marginson and Sisson 2006). From the 1990s, British unions turned increasingly to the European Union, over the heads of national policy makers, to stimulate community wide legislation that might influence domestic policy and practice through the necessary transposition of Directives (Monks 1992). The return of three successive Labour governments from 1997 promised 'partnership' that had been unavailable under preceding Conservative administrations but also deepened and extended the influence of quasi-federal institutions. The European Social Charter (1989) providing fundamental employment rights was signed, finally, by a UK government, ending several years of solitary refusal to do so. The creation of a Scottish Parliament and Assemblies in Wales and Northern Ireland instituted some measure of devolution, with further opportunities for union roles in policy making (see Pike et al 2006). To some extent, this context afforded opportunities for unions to engage with 'reflexive law making'. Such processes are intended to involve subsidiary bodies in the development of legislation by which they will be bound, with the intention of maximising their compliance with it thereafter. In the context of the European Union it applies to national governments (Deakin 2006) but it has been applied also to sub-national actors, including employers and trade unions. Attempts to extend employee participation and representation have involved active input of this kind (Gold 2010) and reform of equality legislation has increasingly used this approach, in part to meet 'the aims of reflexive governance in enhancing communication between the legal and industrial relations systems' (Hobbs and Njoya 2005: 304).

However, the constraints facing British unions have limited severely the fruitfulness of approaches such as these. Over a century ago, the Webbs were very well aware of 'certain grave disadvantages' for unions engaged in the process: 'its chief drawback is the prolonged and uncertain struggle that each new regulation involves' (Webbs 1898: 253). In order to secure the necessary political support, unions must demonstrate not only that the grievance in need of remedy affects their specific membership but that it has ramifications for broader constituencies. Ensuing debate about the extent and cause of such harm usually results in legislation that falls short of the needs claimed by unions: 'some kind of clause is inserted to effect, usually not what the Trade Union has been asking for, but the minimum which, in the light of all the evidence, seems indispensable to avert the grossest of evil' (ibid: 254).

Despite the developments described above, political engagement on offer to unions more recently has done little to improve the likelihood of legislation adequate to meet their objectives. There have been some limited and partial successes but the external and internal dimensions of union power remain highly circumscribed. Reflecting on the final Warwick agreement reached between Labour ministers and union leaders in 2004, Ewing (2005: 2) asked,

> [H]ow is it that trade unions can proclaim so loudly the contents of a document which does not include a commitment to union autonomy? How is it that unions can proclaim so loudly the commitments of a document that does not include a commitment to core labour standards?

Likewise, time and again individual employment rights have been criticised for being timid in ambition and complex in application and enforcement (for overviews see Dickens and Hall 2010; Smith 2009; Smith and Morton 2009). Examples include limitations on the scope and level of regulations governing the National Minimum Wage (Simpson 2004); working time (Barnard 2000); parental leave (McColgan 2000); part-time workers (McKay 2001); and agency workers (Countouris and Horton 2009).

Explanations lie partly in the substantially weakened position of unions in the policy making process. Limited standing in policy circles (see Crouch 1999; Ludlum and Taylor 2003) has diluted opportunities to mobilise rationales for legislation that go beyond the 'business case'. While Labour ministers recognised a role for regulation in providing 'fairness', famously this has always had to be balanced against 'flexibility.' Improvements to employment standards could be conceded but only to the extent that they contributed to partnership and competitiveness at the level of the firm. Qualifications were justified wherever regulation risked jeopardising such conditions and new proposals were subjected systematically to 'Impact Assessments' conducted using these criteria. As a consequence, Labour governments were receptive to arguments from employers about the need to trim regulations (see Heyes and Nolan 2010). Coalition ministers since 2010 have gone much further, instituting a full scale review of employment regulation and exhorting employers to get involved and articulate the case for deregulation (see, for example, Colling 2011).

Recombination and Statutory Enforcement

Limitations on the impact of unions on statutory frameworks do not by themselves eradicate their involvement in standard setting through (quasi-) legal process. Unions have long played critical roles in interpreting and amplifying the practical effect of law within workplaces, a role that fell centrally to unions by virtue of their 'bridging capacity', the ability to link institutional developments at national or industry level to the workplace. Two dimensions to this role might be identified. *Formal litigation* is the most obvious, since it involves explicit union engagement with legal institutions and process. Prior to that, however, is the active role of unions in communicating and interpreting statutory rights within the workplace.

Such processes might be dubbed *organic enforcement*, because they develop within employment relationships at the workplace independent initially of formal legal institutions. Critical to both, and a unique feature of union organisation, is the network of workplace representation that connects specific workplaces to higher level regulation (whether through collective bargaining at regional or industry level or legal process).

The outcomes of organic enforcement may be substantive or procedural and remain significant. Substantively, for example, it is now very well established that unionised workplaces are more likely to have written statements of terms and conditions of work (Latreille 2009; Peters et al 2010). Taking statutory provision as minima to be improved upon through negotiation is almost instinctive to union organisers (see Latta and Lewis 1974: 66). Thus, unions routinely lift minimum statutory entitlements to sick pay, pensions, and holidays and provide the strongest workplace protection in relation to health and safety (Brown et al 2000: 623–26; see also McKay 2001). In this sense, the originating rationale for legislative intervention is extended and developed in workplaces, and adapted to their specific circumstances.

The procedural benefits of organic enforcement are more easily overlooked but are, arguably, of even greater significance. Awareness of statutory rights is highest amongst union members: 'it may be that being a trade union/staff association member is likely to make an employee more aware of their employment rights as they have access to information and advice from their union on rights at work' (Casebourne et al 2005: 23). Union members are also more likely to report dissatisfaction with their workplace and to pursue grievances. These findings appear to be linked—employer actions falling short of statutory standards are more likely to be highlighted where knowledge of those rights is greatest. But, knowledge of rights is not the only or most important factor—indeed, some studies find awareness is only marginally higher among union members. It is the effectiveness of procedures to resolve disputes arising from them that matters most and union presence plays a critical role here. Formal disciplinary and grievance procedures are more likely to be found in unionised workplaces (Peters et al 2010: 30) and union members are more likely than non-members to report that procedures in place have actually been followed (ibid: 32). Consequently, disciplinary problems in unionised workplaces result less often in dismissal (Antcliff and Saundry 2009) and union members are less likely than other workers to complain that grievances were ignored by their employer (Latreille 2009). They are more likely to have discussed problems with their employer before and to have met face to face (rather than by telephone, etc) (ibid). The availability of advice within the workplace is significant too; union members are substantially more likely to seek advice on employment problems (73 per cent as against 45 per cent of non-union members) (Casebourne et al 2005: 107). They are also more likely to be happy with the advice they receive from union representatives than non-members reliant principally upon advice from HR managers, other managers, or colleagues at work (ibid: 113). As a consequence, in some non-union workplaces, even where workers are aware that their rights have been breached, they are unable to secure effective redress within the organisation. Pollert and Charlwood (2009: 352) found that more than half of their sample of non-union workers pursuing a grievance was unable to secure *any outcome at all*; fewer than one in five reached a conclusion they found satisfactory. Overall, union members are almost seven times more likely to report that their grievances are addressed effectively within the workplace (Casebourne et al 2005: 190). It is hardly surprising then that non-members are more likely to seek external redress through applications to ETs (Latreille 2009: 7). We have here something of a double-edged sword: as Purcell notes (this volume) unions encourage a preparedness to challenge employers and strengthen the institutions at workplace level through which disputes can be pursued. Arguably, however, this is the necessary price for an effective system of employment rights.

To ensure effectiveness, however, organic enforcement must be augmented by a realistic threat of sanctions: 'most legislation operates not by the lesson it teaches or the sermon it preaches but by the promise of rewards or the threat of deprivations attached to its observance or breach, that is, by the expectation of its enforcement' (Kahn-Freund 1970: 241). For unions, traditionally this involved the mobilisation of collective sanctions, including industrial action. In current contexts where the law makes this more difficult, if not actually impossible, sanctions turn increasingly on the threat of formal litigation. In fact, this has always been a feature of union activity (see Latta and Lewis 1974; Roberts 1956). This work was costly in terms of time and resources but its value came from cementing connections between members and their union and strengthening bargaining leverage with employers. As Benson and Sykes (1997: 48) observed of the mineworkers' unions,

> whilst direct experience of legal action seems to have been limited to a small minority, one can only guess at the effect on wider confidence and morale that resulted from the initiation of, and successful conclusion to, a legal claim for damages.

It is difficult to establish precisely the extent of formal engagement with the law by trade unions (see later discussion) but two factors might suggest that the pressure towards it has intensified. First, the extension of a greater range of individual protections can be expected to have increased *demand* for representation from union members. Second, and as important, the *supply* of legal services might have increased as a mechanism to regenerate bargaining power. Legal advice is now one of the most prominent of the union services offered to members and may be one manifestation of the shifting axis of employment regulation in Britain, and unions' changed role within it. Deakin and Wilkinson (2004: 43) argued that revival in the fortunes of organised labour is unlikely to be secured by 'an exclusive focus on the method of collective bargaining'. Arguably, statutory rights expand the range of mechanisms through which unions can reinforce their influence with employers (Howell 2005). Armour et al (2003) provide a detailed and vivid account of recombinant strategies of this kind (though they do not use the term themselves), in which organisational strength provided by members' willingness to act was supplemented by legal challenge. In 1999, BMW announced plans to sell its stake in Rover Group, underpinned by the prospect of the business being liquidated if no buyer materialised. Discussions with one buyer, Alchemy Partners, proceeded initially without the knowledge of the recognised trade unions. They quickly voiced opposition to that sale when negotiations were made public subsequently, on the ground that production at the Birmingham plants would be substantially reduced. BMW refused to enter into negotiations with an alternative buyer, the Phoenix Consortium, until unions began a concerted and complex programme of action. This included litigation to protect the unions' collective rights to consultation but also action on behalf of individual members on the ground of breach of contract: 'altogether, the potential value of these claims exceeded £300million' (ibid: 544). Subsequently, Alchemy Partners withdrew from negotiations and the business was sold instead to Phoenix. In the view of Armour et al, use of the law provided unions with an indispensable mechanism:

> [C]learly, the law did not operate here in isolation; Rover was a strongly unionised company, and local communities were active in their support. But without the intervention of the law, it is doubtful that these factors alone would have saved the company. (ibid: 545)

Critically, of course, these two dimensions are intimately connected. *Formal litigation* is launched often with the hope of securing the kind of negotiated settlement characteristic of *organic enforcement*. Unions are willing to pursue judgments for their intrinsic value, where precedent might establish authoritative statements of the law for use more broadly. But case authority by itself rarely provides a secure basis for that broader application; it is usually highly qualified (subject to the facts of the instant case) and it is likely to be contested by employers where it is not. Unions have always preferred negotiated settlements, for the direct influence they afford to negotiators; for the application beyond the immediate case they ensure; and for the acceptance they generally command from all parties. A significant proportion of the multiple cases currently working through the ET system arise from equal pay claims in the public sector. Many have been taken recently by 'no win, no fee' solicitors but litigation-based initiatives by unions outnumber and predate them and have been undertaken with a view to strengthening bargaining positions (Moorhead 2010: 765; Thornley 2006: 353). Litigation arising from the Rover case discussed above was also settled eventually through negotiation. In such contexts, there is important scope for unions to combine organising, negotiating and legal strategies in novel ways.

The Limits of Recombination

There are signs though that union engagement with the law may not be limitless, indeed it may even be in retreat. If the benefits of legal engagement are to be maximised, outcomes need to provide either *inspirational* or *radiating* effects that can be diffused from individual cases to wider organising strategies (Colling 2009). Inspirational effects are those which might validate a sense of injustice amongst (potential) members and galvanise support for action. Radiating effects are those that can extend from the specific case to change behaviour among other employers or membership constituencies. The prospects for each are diminished by weakened 'bridging capacity' and the formal features of legal process. In this context, recombination is likely to be contingent upon the jurisdiction in question and the organising context to which the proposed action is connected.

Those connections between workplaces and higher levels of regulation have been severely weakened by the changes outlined above. Collective bargaining coverage has narrowed, leaving smaller proportions of the workforce covered by agreements and, as important for these themes, without access to *connected* representation. The number of union representatives fell by about two thirds over the 20 year period to 2004 (Stuart et al 2009: 18). At that point, only 23 per cent of workplaces with 25 or more employees had a union representative, compared to 55 per cent in 1984. Non-union representation has developed to some degree but tends to be much more introspective and workplace centred. Research by Moore et al (2008: 12) found that union representatives were more than twice as likely to have been on a training course in the last 12 months and more than three times as likely to have sought advice from an external body. This weakened representational capacity is apparent even in unionised workplaces. The majority of these had a representative but this proportion declined from 83 per cent to 62 per cent (Terry 2010: 277). As important, whereas the majority of union representatives were once trained and fully accredited stewards, today many have only limited spheres of influence. There are now nine statutory areas where union representatives have rights to paid time off and facilities and seven areas affecting non-union representatives (Wynn and Pitt 2010). The strain on this reduced and fragmented representative structure has been increased by the proliferation of individualised statutory employment standards:

> [O]ne reason for the increased complexity of the representational role, especially for trade unions, is the growth of the individual rights framework. Whereas

twenty years ago shop stewards would have been involved predominantly in a negotiating role at a collective level, they are now increasingly being drawn into the role of individual representation and associated case work. (Acas 2008: 5)

This context carries important implications for the depth of organic enforcement and potential connections with formal process. Even in the minority of workplaces that are unionised currently, there is clear potential for grievances to go undetected and for representation through to formal litigation to be rationed by scarce resources. This potential limit to recombination is exacerbated by the institutional context and formal features of legal process. Here we come up against the lack of diffusion mechanisms in the British system: just as mechanisms extending collective agreements are generally absent so it is difficult to broaden the impact of individual tribunal and court decisions. There is no basis in Britain's employment law for representative or class actions, for example. The potential for outcomes that might support broader organising strategies are contingent therefore upon the jurisdiction in question and the organising context to which litigation is connected. It may be noteworthy, for example, that legal action in the Rover case (discussed above) included union claims against collective rights alongside support for individual contractual claims. Conversely, where process and outcomes are likely to be limited closely to the individual case, union representatives are much less likely than representatives of other kinds to anticipate positive outcomes from the tribunal system and much less satisfied with the operation of the system (Latreille et al 2004: 22).

This is not a novel finding but there are grounds to argue that the potential costs to unions of formal engagement have increased and proliferated at a time when the resources available to them are contracting. Empirical investigation into the early use of unfair dismissal provisions found union officers reluctant to take individual claims where this might undermine local bargaining relationships or future credibility with tribunal panels (Evans et al 1985: 98–100). While financial considerations were not pivotal in the decision-making they observed, greater demand for legal advice from members has subsequently increased their prominence in the current context. Colling (2006: 152) reported pressure on officials to limit commitments to 'exit stuff', tribunal casework arising from dismissal: 'there is no growth in that ... so the union could say, "you have been spending your time losing us members"'. Moorhead and Cumming (2009) found unions using merits tests before agreeing to support cases and Latreille et al (2004) found union representatives were more likely than other representatives to secure settlements ahead of full tribunal hearings.

It seems plausible that union dissatisfaction with the system may stem from the previously discussed trend towards individualisation of the employment relation and the associated trend towards individual (cf. collective) prosecution of employment rights. This may therefore involve unions in more individual casework, which is, by its nature more time-consuming and expensive than collective activities, while typically being lower profile. (ibid: 46–47)

Certainly, proactive litigation in some jurisdictions continues to be much lower than expected. Unions have shown very little interest in the Information and Consultation of Employees Regulations, for example, confounding prior expectations that it might support drives to organise workforces (Hall 2006). Provision of advice on ET claims is a very common union function but it is difficult to quantify exactly (Colling 2006), as noted above, and appears to be in decline. The Survey of Employment Tribunal Applications provides some insights based on a sample of claims. According to the most recent survey (Peters et al 2010: 45), around one in six claimants were advised by a union or a Citizens' Advice Bureau. Those data suggest that the use of formal representation by claimants has fallen (from 40 to 32 per cent since 2003) and union engagement in litigation has decreased accordingly: 'overall, nine per cent of claimants were represented or received advice from a trade union after submission of the ET1. This is a fall from 2003, where thirteen per cent had received such representation or advice' (Peters et al 2010: 54). Moreover, though trade union members comprised one quarter of claimants overall, 'less than a third (31 per cent) of these received advice or representation from their union. This is significantly less than the proportion that had done so in 2003 (49 per cent)' (ibid).

Such trends may fluctuate, of course, but, at a point when the scope of individual rights was increasing, a finding that unions appear to be using litigation more selectively suggests some limits to the extent and durability of *recombinant strategies*.

CONCLUSION

The terrain available to unions has altered substantially and prompted changed orientations to the law. To a considerable extent, their central role in the establishment of employment standards has been displaced by a focus on the development and enforcement of individual statutory rights. Unions have become engaged actively in those processes, and to that extent social and legal regulation have been recombined in imaginative ways. However any expanded role for unions depends on the potential to regenerate bargaining power. Where unions anticipate significant benefits from engagement with the law recombination can be expected but weakened bridging capacity (manifest in increasingly skeletal workplace representation) and difficulties in diffusing positive outcomes from legal process means that this is likely to be highly selective.

It is plausible to argue that unions' historic preference for collective bargaining left them with an incomplete appreciation of the potential benefits of a legal framework. Equally, however, those expecting unions to extend their use of the law should acknowledge the potential costs to them in doing so. Engagement with the law was partial and selective in the past, principally because the institutional framework provided other opportunities to unions to meet their needs. Simply because those opportunities have evaporated does not mean that union engagement with the law will now become more complete. For those interested in making employment rights effective, any such gaps in the potential for recombination should be pressing concerns.

BIBLIOGRAPHY

Acas (Advisory Conciliation and Arbitration Service) (2008) *Employee Representatives: Challenges and Changes in the Workplace*, Acas Policy Discussion Papers (London, Acas).

Antcliff, V and Saundry, R (2009) 'Accompaniment, Workplace Representation, and Outcomes in British Workplaces' 47 *British Journal of Industrial Relations* 100–21.

Armour, J, Deakin, S and Konzelman, S (2003) 'Shareholder Primacy and the Trajectory of UK Corporate Governance' 41 *British Journal of Industrial Relations* 531–55.

Baker, C (1976) 'Employment Protection: Individual Rights' 5 *Industrial Law Journal* 65–79.

Barnard, C (2000) 'The Working Time Regulations 1999' 29 *Industrial Law Journal* 167–71.

Benson, J and Sykes, R (1997) 'Trade Unionism and the Use of the Law: English Coalminers' Unions and Legal Redress for Industrial Accidents, 1860–1897' 3 *Historical Studies in Industrial Relations* 27–48.

Bercusson, B (1976) 'The New Fair Wages Policy: Schedule 11 to the Employment Protection Act' 5 *Industrial Law Journal* 129–47.

Brown, W (1992) 'Bargaining Structure and the Impact of the Law' in W McCarthy (ed), *Legal Intervention in Industrial Relations: Gains and Losses* (Oxford, Blackwell).

—— (2010) 'Negotiation and Collective Bargaining' in T Colling and M Terry (eds), *Industrial Relations: Theory and Practice* (Oxford, Wiley).

Brown, W, Deakin, S, Nash, D and Oxenbridge, S (2000) 'The Employment Contract: From Collective Procedures to Individual Rights' 38 *British Journal of Industrial Relations* 611–29.

Casebourne, J, Regan, J, Neathey, F and Tuohy, S (2006) *Employment Rights at Work: Survey of Employees 2005*, Employment Relations Research Series (London, Department of Trade and Industry).

Colling, T (2006) 'What Space for Unions on the Floor of Rights? Trade Unions and the Enforcement of Statutory Individual Employment Rights' 35 *Industrial Law Journal* 40–160.

—— (2009) *Court in a Trap? Legal Mobilisation by Trade Unions in the United Kingdom*, Warwick Papers in Industrial Relations (Coventry, Industrial Relations Research Unit).

—— (2011) 'Changes to the Regulation of Outsourcing and Employment Transfers' *European Industrial Relations Observatory Online* (EIRO), www.eurofound. europa.eu/eiro/2011/07/articles/uk1107039i.htm.

Countouris, N and Horton, R (2009) 'The Temporary Agency Work Directive: Another Broken Promise?'38 *Industrial Law Journal* 329–38.

Crouch, C (1999) 'Employment, Industrial Relations and Social Policy: New Life in an Old Connection' 33 *Social Policy and Administration* 437–57.

Davies, P and Freedland, M (1993) *Labour Legislation and Public Policy* (Oxford, Oxford University Press).

Deakin, S (2006) 'Legal Diversity and Regulatory Competition: Which Model for Europe?' 12 *European Law Journal* 440–54.

Deakin, S and Wilkinson, F (2004) 'The Evolution of Collective Laissez-Faire' 17 *Historical Studies in Industrial Relations* 1–43.

Dickens, L and Hall, M (2010) 'The Changing Legal Framework of Employment Relations' in Colling, T and Terry, M (eds), *Industrial Relations: Theory and Practice* (Oxford, Wiley).

Dukes, R (2009) 'Otto Kahn-Freund and Collective Laissez-Faire: An Edifice Without a Keystone?' 72 *Modern Law Review* 220–46.

Evans, S, Goodman, J and Hargreaves, L (1985) 'Unfair Dismissal Law and Changes in the Role of Trade Unions and Employers' Associations' 14 *Industrial Law Journal* 91–108.

Ewing, K (2005) 'The Function of Trade Unions' 34 *Industrial Law Journal* 1–22.

Fick, B (2009) 'Not Just Collective Bargaining. The Role of Unions in Creating and Maintaining a Democratic Society' 12 *Working USA* 249–64.

Flanders, A (1968) *Trade Unions* (London, Hutchinson University Press).

—— (1970) *Management and Unions: The Theory and Reform of Industrial Relations* (London, Faber).

Fox, A and Flanders, A (1969) 'The Reform of Collective Bargaining: From Donovan to Durkheim' 7 *British Journal of Industrial Relations* 151–80.

Gibbons, M (2007) *Better Dispute Resolution: A Review of Employment Dispute Resolution in Great Britain* (London, Department of Trade and Industry).

Gold, M (2010) 'Employee Participation in the EU: The Long and Winding Road to Legislation' 31 *Economic and Industrial Democracy* 9–23.

Hall, M (2006) 'A Cool Response to the ICE Regulations? Employer and Trade Union Approaches to the New Legal Framework for Information and Consultation' 37 *Industrial Relations Journal* 456–72.

Heery, E (1998) 'The Relaunch of the Trades Union Congress' 36 *British Journal of Industrial Relations* 339–60.

—— (2010) 'Debating Employment Law: Responses to Juridification' in Blyton, P, Heery, E, and Turnbull, P (eds), *Reassessing the Employment Relationship* (Basingstoke, Palgrave).

Heery, E, Conley, H, Delbridge, R and Stewart, P (2004) 'Beyond the Enterprise: Trade Union Representation of Freelances in the UK' 14 *Human Resource Management Journal* 20–35.

Heyes, J and Nolan, P (2010) 'State, Capital and Labour Relations in Crisis' in Colling, T and Terry, M (eds), *Industrial Relations: Theory and Practice* (Oxford, Wiley).

Hickey, R, Kuruvilla, S and Lakhani, T (2010) 'No Panacea for Success: Member Activism, Organizing, and Union Renewal' 48 *British Journal of Industrial Relations* 53–83.

Hobbs, R and Njoya, W (2005) 'Regulating the European Labour Market: Prospects and Limitations of a Reflexive Approach' 43 *British Journal of Industrial Relations* 297–319.

Howell, C (2005) *Trade Unions and the State: The Construction of Industrial Relations Institutions in Britain, 1890–2000* (Princeton, NJ, Princeton University Press).

Kahn-Freund, O(1965) 'Report on the Legal Status of Collective Bargaining and Collective Agreements in Great Britain' in Kahn-Freund, O (ed), *Labour Relations and Law* (London, Stevens and Sons).

—— (1969) 'Industrial Relations – Retrospect and Prospect' 7 *British Journal of Industrial Relations* 301–16.

—— (1970) 'Trade Unions, the Law and Society' 33 *Modern Law Review* 241–67.

Kaufman, G (2000) 'The Early Institutionalists on Industrial Democracy and Union Democracy' XXI *Journal of Labor Research* 189–209.

Latta, G and Lewis, R (1974) 'Trade Union Legal Services' 12 *British Journal of Industrial Relations* 56–70.

Latreille, P (2009) *Characteristics of Rejected Employment Tribunal Claims*, Employment Relations Research Series (London, Department for Business Innovation and Skills).

Latreille, P, Latreille, J and Knight, K (2004) *Findings from the 1998 Survey of Representatives in Employment Tribunal Cases*, Employment Relations Research Series (London, Department of Trade and Industry).

Lewis, R (1976) 'The Historical Development of Labour Law' 14 *British Journal of Industrial Relations* 1–17.

Ludlum, S and Taylor, A (2003) 'The Political Representation of the Labour Interest in Britain' 41 *British Journal of Industrial Relations* 727–49.

Marginson, P and Sisson, K (2006) *European Integration and Industrial Relations: Multi-level Governance in the Making* (Basingstoke, Palgrave Macmillan).

McColgan, A (2000) 'Family Friendly Frolics? The Maternity and Parental Leave Regulations 1999' 29 *Industrial Law Journal* 260–67.

McKay, S (2001) 'Between Flexibility and Regulation: Rights, Equality and Protection at Work' 39 *British Journal of Industrial Relations* 285–303.

Middlemas, K (1979) *Politics in Industrial Society: The Experience of the British System Since 1911* (London, Andre Deutsch).

Monks, J (1992) 'Gains and Losses after Twenty Years of Legal Intervention' in W McCarthy (ed), *Legal Intervention in Industrial Relations* (Oxford, Blackwell).

Moore, S, Tasiran, A and Jefferys, S (2008) *The Impact of Employee Representation Upon Workplace Industrial Relations Outcomes*, Employment Relations Research Series (London, Department for Business, Enterprise and Regulatory Reform).

Moorhead, R (2010) 'An American Future? Contingency Fees, Claims Explosions, and Evidence from Employment Tribunals' 73 *Modern Law Review* 752–84.

Moorhead, R and Cumming, R (2009) *Something for Nothing? Employment Tribunal Claimants' Perspectives on Legal Funding*, Employment Relations Research Series (London, Department for Business Innovation and Skills).

Novitz, T (2010) *UK Implementation of the Posted Workers Directive*, Formula Working Paper (Department of Private Law, University of Oslo).

Peters, M, Seeds, K, Harding, C and Garnett, E (2010) *Findings from the Survey of Employment Tribunal Applications 2008*, Employment Relations Research Series (London, Department for Business, Innovation and Skills).

Pike, A, O'Brien, P and Tomaney, J (2006) 'Devolution and the Trades Union Congress in North East England and Wales' 16 *Regional and Federal Studies* 157–78.

Pollert, A and Charlwood, A (2009) 'The Vulnerable Worker in Britain and Problems at Work' 23 *Work Employment and Society* 343–62.

Roberts, B (1956) *Trade Union Government and Administration in Great Britain* (Cambridge, Mass, Harvard University Press).

Simms, M and Holgate, J (2010) 'Organising for What? Where is the Debate on the Politics of Organising?' 24 *Work Employment and Society* 157–68.

Simpson, B (1986) 'British Labour Relations in the 1980s: Learning to Live with the Law' 49 *Modern Law Review* 769–818.

—— (2004) 'The National Minimum Wage Five Years On: Reflections on Some General Issues' 33 *Industrial Law Journal* 22–41.

Smith, P (2009) 'New Labour and the Commonsense of Neoliberalism: Trade Unionism, Collective Bargaining and Workers'40 *Industrial Relations Journal* 337–55.

Smith, P and Morton, G (2009) 'Employment Legislation: New Labour's Neoliberal Legal Project to Subordinate Trade Unions' in G Daniels and J McIlroy (eds), *Trade Unions in Neoliberal World: British Trade Unions Under New Labour* (London, Routledge).

Stuart, M, Martinez-Lucio, M and Charlwood, A (2009) *The Union Modernisation Fund – Round One: Final Evaluation Report*, Employment Relations Research Series (London, Department for Business Innovation and Skills).

Terry, M (2010) 'Employee Representation' in T Colling and M Terry (eds), *Industrial Relations: Theory and Practice* (Oxford, Wiley).

Thornley, C (2006) 'Unequal and Low Pay in the Public Sector' 37 *Industrial Relations Journal* 344–58.

Webb, S and Webb, B (1898) *Industrial Democracy* (London, the Authors).

Wedderburn, K and Davies, P (1969) *Employment Grievances and Disputes Procedures in Britain* (Berkeley, Cal, University of California Press).

Wynn, M and Pitt, G (2010) 'The Revised Code of Practice 2010 on Time Off for Trade Union Duties and Activities: Another Missed Opportunity?' 39 *Industrial Law Journal* 209–17.

11

Fairer Workplaces: Making Employment Rights Effective

LINDA DICKENS[*]

INTRODUCTION

THIS VOLUME ILLUMINATES issues of enforcement and compliance which are important in terms of making employment rights effective, by which is meant reducing the likelihood of adverse treatment being experienced at the workplace, helping translate formal statutory rights into substantive rights and thereby helping to achieve 'fairer' workplaces. In focusing on issues around rights enforcement and compliance with a view to the effectiveness of rights in terms of delivering fairer workplaces, it has to be acknowledged that the law (employment rights) is only one, incomplete, mechanism for promoting fairer workplaces. Indeed the part played by the law may appear minor when compared to other macro factors shaping employment relations and workplace practice (Dickens 2007). Clearly it is not possible simply to legislate for fairness, but the law can have efficacy and legislation can be part of a multi-pronged approach involving regulatory and non-regulatory measures and actors (eg Edwards 2007; Coats 2005; Dickens 1999). As is made clear in the three chapters in this volume which consider regulation and small firms, the management of employment rights, and the role of trade unions, the impact of law is affected by its interaction with other structural and contextual factors. Nonetheless legal employment rights can play an important role and the nature and effectiveness of enforcement does matter.

The focus of current policy concern in this area is reform of employment tribunals (ETs) (BIS 2011a). Although aspects of this reform agenda are engaged with, the main concern of this volume is alternative (additional) approaches to enforcement and to securing compliance and with illuminating the varying employment contexts within which rights fall to be exercised and which help shape their practical impacts. This final chapter discusses

[*] I am grateful to Michael Terry and Trevor Colling for comments on a draft of this chapter.

the perception of employment rights which underpins the reluctance of successive governments to pay appropriate attention to the enforcement of employment rights; critically examines the limitations of current approaches, which require little pro-activity on the part of employers and have limited ability to bring about change; and draws on the contributions to this volume to discuss alternative, additional enforcement approaches as ways of making employment rights effective.

FLAWED ENFORCEMENT APPROACH AND PERCEPTION OF EMPLOYMENT RIGHTS

Chapter one indicated how the development of a more comprehensive role for legislation in setting minimum standards and providing protections for workers, which has taken place in Britain over the past 40 or so years, has not been accompanied by any strategic overview and consideration of the mechanisms, institutions and processes for rights enforcement. The current system of enforcement, described in chapter two, reflects this lack of attention. In the words of a former President of Tribunals in England and Wales the ETs have been used as a convenient 'dustbin' for handling the increasing number of statutory rights (Meeran 2006: 131). The ETs constitute the predominant mechanism for employment rights enforcement. There is some state enforcement but the emergence and scope of other bodies has reflected ad hoc, one-off solutions to immediate problems (for example the response to abuses in the shellfish industry leading to the setting up of the Gangmasters' Licensing Authority), adding to an incomplete and uneven patchwork of enforcement agencies. When key individual statutory employment rights began to emerge in Britain in the 1960s and 1970s they were minor players in a voluntarist system resting on social regulation through collective bargaining. Statute law was seen largely as 'gap filling'— extending protection to those falling outside the protections offered by collective bargaining and organised workplaces. Enforcement was given to the Industrial Tribunals (now ETs). The balance between social regulation and legal regulation has shifted considerably, with protection at work now resting largely on the latter, and there has been a considerable growth in sectors and workers falling outside the scope of social regulation—but ETs remain the centerpiece of employment rights enforcement.

There is widely acknowledged discontent with the current arrangements but, in terms of action taken, the problem has tended to be defined as one of a flawed (and expensive) *system*—namely the ETs—rather than as (also) a flawed approach to enforcement. The approach to enforcement in Britain is flawed in that too much reliance is placed on individuals having to assert and pursue their statutory employment rights, which generally require only passive compliance from employers, and too little weight is placed on state agency inspection, monitoring and enforcement, and on other levers which would require or encourage proactive employer action to deliver fairer workplaces by addressing structural, systemic and organisational issues, going beyond individual cases of rights infringement. Further, opportunities to enhance the regulatory and enforcement capacity of the state through engaging non-state actors as co-regulators, monitors and enforcers are not being taken. This flawed logic of enforcement and lack of attention to it reflect a particular perception of employment rights.

Piecemeal measures have been introduced at various times but there has been reluctance on the part of governments of all political shades to address the issue of rights enforcement strategically, and to embrace reform suggestions likely to enhance delivery of fairer workplaces. An explanation for this reluctance rests at least in part on government ambivalence about the extent to which worker protection and 'fairer workplaces' should be objectives of labour legislation, as opposed to regulation in the interests of a free market economy (on which see generally Davies and Freedland 2007) and the view that workers' rights constitute burdens on employers which need to be minimised. This view characterised the deregulation ideology of Conservative governments in the 1980s and 1990s, the legacy of which was reflected in the contingent nature of New Labour's pursuit of fairness at work between 1997 and 2010. As Dickens and Hall describe, the declared attempt at that time was a synthesis and mutual reinforcement of social (fairness) and economic (market) goals but in practice there was a hierarchy (Dickens and Hall 2006; see also Fredman 2004). Fairness was not pursued as an end in itself and the UK government's willingness to promote social justice and ensure fairer workplaces was contingent on the extent to which it could be argued to promote and support business interests and to underpin (employers' views of) economic efficiency. The Conservative-led coalition government elected in 2010 has also used the language of fairness but the ideology of deregulation is back in the ascendancy. Protections for workers are portrayed as hampering labour market flexibility and efficiency and as a barrier to growth (eg BIS 2011a). The government has acknowledged the need for workers to be 'provided with a strong foundation of employment protection', but considers this should be 'limited to the minimum necessary' (BIS 2011b: 4). Furthermore, as Bewley and Forth (2010) argue, the current unfavourable economic context is being used to undermine workers' rights and fair treatment rather than the law being seen as a source of protection for those whose position is weakened by these economic conditions.

Successive governments' positioning of 'fairness' in opposition to 'efficiency' (rather than seeing that the former might serve the interests of the latter), and the prioritisation of 'efficiency', narrowly defined as reflecting the interests articulated by some employer lobby groups, has affected governments' willingness to legislate, with, for example, opposition to, weakening of, and then minimal implementation of EC Directives (see for example Barnard et al 2003; McKay 2001; McColgan 2000). Increasingly governments have required social rights to be legitimised in terms of their contribution to business (Dickens and Hall 2009). It has also influenced the nature of legislation, with a preference for 'soft' law (such as codes of practice, guidance and good practice exemplars), and for 'better' and 'light touch' regulation. Kilpatrick and Freedland (2004: 334, cited in Bell 2011: 265) note for example how in implementing aspects of the Part-Time Work Directive the government 'drifted from hard to soft and even softer law', opting for guidance rather than issuing a statutory code of practice, having decided legislative intervention was not necessary. At times 'light touch' regulation has edged into 'no regulation'. The government is proud of the fact that the OECD ranks the UK as one of the most lightly regulated labour markets amongst developed countries (BIS 2011b: 3). The ideology has carried through also to employment rights enforcement. In chapter five Tombs and Whyte demonstrate, for example, how enforcement in the area of health and safety has been affected by the 'better regulation' agenda, and chapter three indicates how the concern to reduce perceived 'burdens' on employers has helped shape the ET reform agenda.

Statutory employment rights are more likely to have purchase at the workplace and to deliver substantive outcomes where there is employer acceptance of them and their objectives (discussed by Purcell in chapter nine; Colling 2010: 327–28; Dickens and Hall 2006: 348). There appears to be little in current policy discourse likely to generate such acceptance. Social justice and moral arguments for employment rights tend to be muted currently and there is little emphasis on the responsibilities of business. Although 'fairness' is still presented as an aim there is less emphasis on its potential contribution to efficiency than was found in earlier policy and consultation documents (eg DTI 1998). Ways in which business interests may be served through introducing or enhancing particular employment rights, as demonstrated by research, have been articulated at various times in policy discourse (eg DTI 2002, 2006a). These include, for example, providing a level playing field, preventing undercutting by unscrupulous employers and a 'race to the bottom'; facilitating employee resourcing and skills retention; and promoting employee commitment and engagement as an aid to productive, high performance workplaces. Currently, however, it is more common for employers' beliefs about potential harmful effects of employment rights to be highlighted, even though they are not necessarily supported by robust evidence (discussed by Edwards in chapter eight). Surveys of employer opinion need to be interpreted carefully. Blackburn and Hart (2002: 73), for example, found in their survey of small firms that most employers were vague in their knowledge of employment rights. Only one-fifth felt confident or very confident of their knowledge of employment rights legislation, and that confidence waned when the depth of knowledge was investigated. Nonetheless employers in the survey were prepared to be critical of the effects of such legislation on their enterprise, suggesting 'that results of surveys of this kind are influenced by a negative predisposition on the effects of Government intervention'. Furthermore, experience shows that survey predictions of adverse impacts of increased rights for workers—for example protection from unfair dismissal making employers reluctant to hire, or the job-destroying impact of the NMW—do not necessarily materialise (Dickens and Hall 2006: 347; Metcalf 2008).

Deregulation ideology poses rights against competitiveness although detailed analysis of available evidence does not support the free market contention that employment protection is inevitably inimical to job creation, growth and competitiveness (see Reed 2010 for a review of the theoretical and empirical evidence in this area). This has been recognised by the OECD which has distanced itself from the free-market position, concluding on the evidence that countries with quite different levels of employment protection can experience equal levels of success in generating employment and that there is no single combination of policies for good labour market performance (OECD 2006). As indicated above, it is possible to make a case for social justice as an aid to economic efficiency (Deakin and Wilkinson 1994), and to argue for strong and effective employment rights in order to produce 'beneficial constraints' on employers which are likely to foster longer term productive efficiency (Streeck 1977). Some employers recognise such positive benefits. In a Confederation of Business and Industry (CBI) survey of its members on the impact of employment legislation, for example, half of the respondents reported that employment rights can have the positive effect of stimulating organisations to consider more innovative working arrangements (CBI, 2000).

Positive arguments are not being made as part of public policy which instead emphasises rights as 'burdens' on employers. At the time of writing, employers and others are being invited to identify rights which should be removed as part of the government's 'Red Tape Challenge', which aims to 'reduce the overall burden of regulation by reducing the stock of regulations' (BIS 2011b: 2) and its 'one in one out' initiative (where no new rights should be introduced unless an existing one is removed). Potentially, the enactment of employment rights, embodying notions of fairness, can help effect attitudinal change, shape the climate of employment relations and provide levers, legitimacy and impetus for those within organisations wishing to act, and so affect positively managerial attitudes and practice over time. However the predominant state rhetoric of rights as imposing 'burdens' on employers which need to be minimised, and as hampering competitiveness, is unlikely to foster employer acceptance of them. It helps generate a climate within which statutory employment rights are less likely to be effective in substantive terms, reducing the likelihood of those employers who lack other drivers developing employment policies to embrace the fairness objectives of the legislation.

It is of course the case that administrative costs may be incurred in order to comply with legal requirements, and some rights may impose costs at the level of the firm while benefits accrue at the level of society (as with some aspects of equality legislation). The government's 'employment law administrative burden survey' in 2008 explored the estimated costs to employers of complying with information obligations imposed by various employment rights—the need to keep records on pay for the NMW and on working time and leave; issuing employees with written statements of particulars of the employment contract etc (Lambourne et al 2008). These administrative costs were found to have decreased considerably since the previous survey in 2005 and were not particularly high—especially if seen as part of improving management information systems and human resource management practice, and not simply a legal compliance cost.

Some of the costs incurred which were reported in the administrative burden survey arose from a perceived need to pay for external advice as the law was seen as a 'grey' area, one of change and uncertainty. As this and other surveys indicate, some employer concerns arise not from the substance and impact of employment rights per se, but relate to their complexity; the frequency and piecemeal nature of change; and the administrative consequences of having to deal with this (Patel 2011; Better Regulation Taskforce 2002; CBI 2000, 2005 cited in Dickens and Hall 2006: 346). There are also problems for employers, as well as for workers, arising from the complexity of the enforcement landscape and the fragmentation and (in)appropriateness of enforcement mechanisms for certain rights, as discussed in this volume. Aspects of these concerns have been recognised to a limited extent, for example in steps taken to harmonise the timing of legislative changes and improvements in the extent and sources of advice and guidance for employers, including on-line. Some progress has also been made on cross-agency working and information sharing (BERR 2008). As this discussion indicates, reduction of 'red tape' and administrative costs may be achieved by addressing complexity and fragmentation, while 'solutions' involving reducing employment rights or making their enforcement more difficult may fail to match the nature of concerns being expressed by employers.

Ironically, some of the complexity, frequent changes and other problems for employers arise through what have purported to be 'business friendly' legislative actions of successive governments. A number of examples may be given. Making extensive use of derogations and exemptions in implementing European law to meet employer objections can lead to greater complexity and also give rise to the need for further legislation in order to get into compliance (as has occurred in a number of areas). It can also undermine the potential of such legislation to bring about organisational changes with longer term business benefits. Research undertaken by Barnard and colleagues, for example, shows how the 'business friendly' individual opt-out provisions within the Working Time Regulations hamper potentially positive impacts in terms of innovative and modernised working arrangements (Barnard et al 2003).

Another example is misplaced reform attempts, such as the ill-advised and short lived mandatory three-step discipline and grievance procedure, introduced despite warnings of adverse consequences from a range of expert commentators (Hepple and Morris 2002; Sanders 2009). Also, opportunities to encourage self-enforcement of rights through ensuring awareness have been undermined by the desire to minimise immediate costs—as seen, for example, in the dropping of a proposal for workers to be given a right to a minimum wage statement when being paid (Simpson 1999: 171). Repeated tinkering with the qualification requirements for various rights not surprisingly leaves employers (and workers) uncertain as to who is covered by which protections and imposes some administrative costs on employers in taking account of the frequent changes. At its introduction, protection under the unfair dismissal legislation required employees to have two years' continuous service with their employer before they could bring a claim—a period chosen for administrative convenience to allow time to gauge demand (Weekes et al 1975: 26). The service qualification was soon reduced to one year and then to six months' service, but was increased again in 1979 to a year's service. Then followed a short period where service length required depended on employer size, with less protection for those in firms of 20 workers or fewer and in the mid-1980s the requirement was changed again to two years' service regardless of employer size. The service qualification was reduced subsequently to one year's service, but from April 2012 it reverts to two years' service, and consideration is being given to introducing special arrangements for employers with fewer than 10 employees (BIS 2011a). No service qualification applies where dismissal is on certain prohibited grounds and certain other rights apply from 'day one'. The final example concerns uncertainties for employers which arise through the legislature choosing to leave key aspects of the coverage of rights to judicial interpretation—notably whether or not someone has 'employee' status. As discussed in chapter two, this defines the boundary of protection for access to some—but not all—rights and is characterised currently by lack of a coherent approach.

THE NATURE OF COMPLIANCE REQUIRED

Obviously the precise nature and content of rights, and their interpretation by the courts, are important issues, but generally discussion of this falls without the scope of this book. Some relevant issues (for example the scope and coverage of various employment rights) are touched upon by Gillian Morris in chapter two. Here I want to note that the impact of statute law can be expected to vary according to what the legislation requires of employers, or other actors—that is, what 'compliance with the law' amounts to. In considering this I distinguish requirements for passive/reactive compliance as opposed to active/proactive compliance in the formulation of employment rights, and distinguish individualised from structural/organisational approaches and outcomes.

Compliance may require action from employers only on request or when challenged by someone claiming an infringement of rights (passive/reactive). Alternatively, compliance may require employers to take proactive steps to achieve specified objectives. The approach may be individualised or collective/structural. That is to say, compliance may involve adjustments relating to an individual employee, or simply compensation for individual loss, or—in contrast—may require (also or instead) redress, adaptation and adjustment relating to categories of workers or social groups, and/or changes to organisational policies, practices and structures. Greater impacts are to be expected from the proactive, collective, structural approaches yet currently the approach taken in Britain is predominantly passive and individualised. The introduction of positive equality duties (on race, disability and gender) is a rare example of a proactive, structural approach in Britain (Dickens 2007). However the single equality duty enacted in the Equality Act 2010 (replacing the previous separate duties) applies only in the public sector (as did the earlier duties) and as Hepple describes in chapter four, is more limited than originally proposed. He argues further that the potential for it to be an effective component of 'responsive' or 'reflexive' regulation, whereby formal legal devices are integrated with self-regulation on the part of social actors, is being undermined (see also chapter seven for a discussion of reflexive law). While seeing reflexive regulation as holding the key to more effective enforcement of workplace equality, Hepple demonstrates that currently there are weaknesses or omissions relating to all three of the interlocking mechanisms he identifies as necessary for responsive regulation: strong incentives for organisations to engage in self-scrutiny; engagement with stakeholders; and an effective independent enforcement agency with access to deterrent sanctions should voluntary measures fail.

Currently, compliance with many of the employment rights does not require much of employers. The common passive/reactive individualised approach is not only a weak lever for bringing about change, as discussed below, but in fact may be counterproductive for employers since it means they are only likely to realise, or at least confront the fact, that they are 'not complying' when challenged and facing a potential ET claim. At that stage the focus get narrowed down to the individual legal claim, suggesting recourse to a lawyer (a common but costly response), rather than exploring and addressing underlying workplace practice issues of which the claim may be symptomatic, and which might give rise to future ET claims or other expressions of discontent, such as absenteeism (Dix et al 2009). In contrast, as discussed further later in this chapter, proactive approaches through imposing positive duties allow monitoring and permit enforcement agencies to provide assistance through education and advice, and not just focus on enforcement. However, as argued by Hepple in chapter four, and by Tombs and Whyte in chapter five, the availability of appropriate enforcement powers and sanctions and a credible threat of enforcement action are essential to ensure such advice is heeded.

Potentially, the enactment of employment rights embodying public policy can help effect attitudinal change, shape the climate of employment relations and provide levers, legitimacy and impetus for those within organisations wishing to act. The individualised, private law model of rights enforcement which characterises the British system, however, is a weak lever; it has limited ability to effect social change. Although employment rights enforced through ETs can provide legal redress for those individuals who are unfairly treated, they often fail to have a broader impact on employer behaviour and workplace relations—even among those employers who are taken to tribunals (Blackburn and Hart 2002; Dickens chapter three, this volume). Reporting on data from the representative 2004 Workplace Employee Relations Survey (WERS), Kersley et al (2006: 228) note that the majority of companies who experienced an ET claim made no changes to their procedures; of those who did, the majority acted only to try to ensure that existing procedures were followed in future. Less than a third of the minority of employers who had changed their procedures following the ET case introduced any new policies.

The limitations of the individualised, complaints-led model are particularly pertinent in considering how to tackle employment discrimination and gender pay inequality since its ability to address structural causes is limited (see Hepple, chapter four in this volume; Dickens 2007). As Fredman (2011: 408) observes, 'the focus of proof on breach by a named perpetrator means that structural and institutional inequalities which cannot be traced to a named perpetrator are outside the scope of enforcement … If there is no appropriate complainant discrimination goes unremedied'. As noted elsewhere in this volume, even where there is an appropriate complainant prepared and able to bring a case, the remedies where a tribunal case is pursued successfully are focused on the individual rather than requiring the employer to address the organisational structure and practices which gave rise to the discrimination. As Hepple notes in chapter four, the sanctions available in discrimination cases have been widened by the Equality Act 2010, so the ET can make an action recommendation affecting persons other than just the individual complainant but there is no power to compel compliance with such a recommendation and his assessment is that it is unlikely to be used frequently.

In other jurisdictions, including unfair dismissal, there are no sanctions directly aimed at requiring employers who are found to have breached employment rights to take action to address underlying issues. A provision could be introduced to enable the ETs to require such employers to take a 'health check', conducted by Acas for example, with a requirement to act on any deficiencies revealed, for example remedying a lack of procedural justice. This, I suggest, would be more likely to address inadequate processes and poor practice giving rise to successful ET claims than the current proposal that employers found by an ET to have breached an individual's rights should incur a financial penalty payable to the exchequer in addition to any remedy for the complainant. It was suggested that such a fine would encourage employers to comply with legislation (BIS 2011a: 53) although an important motive appears to be to help offset or transfer the costs of the ET system—a particular concern of the current reform agenda, as discussed in chapter three.

The impact on practice of employment rights enforced through the ETs will be affected, among other factors, by the perceived risk of individual claims being made and the consequences of non-compliance. Currently the risk is low. As chapter one discussed, recourse to an ET is a minority response of those experiencing adverse treatment at work. WERS 2004 found on average 2.2 claims to ETs per 1,000 employees across all workplaces, affecting eight per cent of employers. In a small follow-up survey of people consulting Citizens' Advice Bureaux who were assessed to have had their rights breached, 54 per cent reported that their employer knew they were breaching their rights and over three quarters of these reported that they thought their employer did not expect to be challenged, and in most cases nor were they (Mitchell 2009). As described in chapter two, where recourse is made to the ETs the consequences in terms of outcomes and remedies are not likely to produce a strong deterrent/compliance effect.

Employment rights as currently enforced can and do have indirect effects, apart from their actual use, which may help to achieve adherence to minimum standards. This may occur through a 'shadow of law' impact of the existence of a right encouraging some change at the workplace. For example, it is clear that there has been widespread formalisation and development of dismissal rules and disciplinary procedures stimulated by the unfair dismissal legislation, and guided by the relevant code of practice. Statutory rights can be seen to have encouraged the development and spread of equal opportunity polices, and have shaped their nature and content (Kersley et al 2006; Dickens 2006). It is easier, however, to establish a more direct link between legal regulation and changes in *procedures* and *espoused* policies to comply with legislative requirements, than it is to demonstrate a consequential change in employment *practice* (Dickens and Hall 2009: 348–49). This indicates relatively shallow impact in terms of delivering fairer workplaces. It remains the case that there is often a gap between the existence of policies and their use (eg Hoque and Noon 2004). Part of the explanation for this is what Purcell, in chapter nine, calls the 'vexed role of line managers in the application of employment rights', highlighted also by other research (eg Creegan et al 2003; Cunningham and James 2001).

Some of the points above can be illustrated by reference to data relating to workplace equality. WERS 2004 data show 73 per cent of workplaces say they have a written formal policy on equality or diversity (Kersley et al 2006). Although lack of formal policy does not necessarily mean a lack of equality practice, WERS data reveal that practices associated with fair treatment are more likely to exist where there is a formal policy (ibid). However, only a small minority of those workplaces with a formal policy were found to undertake action which might be expected to flow from having a policy, including quite basic action such as monitoring recruitment, selection and promotion procedures to check for indirect discrimination, and reviewing relative pay rates. Under a quarter of workplaces undertake monitoring for race, sex, disability or age discrimination (only three per cent monitor across all four of these characteristics). Where monitoring occurs it is generally of recruitment and selection procedures rather than other areas. The WERS data show that pay remains a neglected aspect of equality policies: overall only seven per cent of workplaces in the 2004 survey said they review relative pay rates as between men and women; even less review by other characteristics (ibid). The lack of attention to pay revealed in the research—where the aggregate data shows continuing gender and racial pay gaps—has to be seen in the context of the lack of any general legislative requirement for employers to undertake equality pay audits. As demonstrated in the research reported by Deakin, McLaughlin and Chai in chapter seven, when left to take voluntary action, few employers act. They conclude that in the absence of a general requirement for mandatory pay audits, disclosure in the private sector is limited and information flows restricted. The existence and nature of equality and diversity *policies* provide evidence of some positive impact of equality legislation; the lack of equality and diversity *practice* also demonstrates impact—but negatively in that workplace practice reflects the limitations of the current legal framework.

PROACTIVE ENFORCEMENT APPROACHES

Some of the problems just indicated of reliance upon a passive compliance, complaint-driven approach could be avoided through administrative/ agency inspection and enforcement. This represents an alternative to the individualised, private law model characteristic of the British system which leaves individuals to enforce their rights. The focus of effective agency enforcement goes beyond simply providing *individual* redress for breaches of rights once they occur, to helping produce the kind of workplaces where breaches are less likely to occur in the first place. It requires employers to be proactive rather than reactive and is more likely to have a structural, organisational impact compared to rights enforcement through ETs. Agency enforcement has a number of positive features. It allows unfairness to be tackled where no individual may be in a position to bring a complaint.

It overcomes problems arising from individuals' lack of knowledge of, or ability or willingness to pursue and maintain, rights. Agencies can perform an educative role and assist proactive improvement through monitoring and inspection. They can build upon employers' acceptance of the basic principle of fairness involved in providing workers with protection, helping remedy and prevent non-compliance occasioned by lack of detailed awareness of the legal obligations—a role welcomed by employers, as shown for example in a study of the National Minimum Wage (NMW) and small employers (Patel 2011). Unlike the ET system, agency monitoring and enforcement of positive requirements imposed on employers do not rest on adversarialism, thus facilitating fairer workplaces being seen as a common goal to be achieved cooperatively—a point made by Fredman (2011: 408) in the context of the public sector equality duty. Furthermore, 'government enforcement' of rights serves to highlight the importance accorded by the state to the fair treatment of workers, emphasising this is in the wider public interest, rather than punishment of, or redress for, individuals.

There is no general labour standards inspectorate in Britain although in recent years various commentators have advocated a single comprehensive enforcement agency—a Fair Employment Commission—as a means of tackling unfairness at work and avoiding the problems experienced by individuals in relation to the ETs (eg Brown 2006; CAB 2001, 2004). It is clear, however, that the UK government has little appetite for wider or more comprehensive agency enforcement of the kind advocated. The previous Labour government stated that it was unwilling to 'risk unbalancing the UK model for dispute resolution where the emphasis is on individuals taking action to assert their rights and tilt the system towards more intrusive labour-inspectorate models common in other EU states' (BERR 2008: 41). In 2008 a TUC-led investigation and a government-initiated forum considered the state enforcement framework, specifically as it affected 'vulnerable' workers, and documented continuing weaknesses (TUC 2008; BERR 2008). Subsequently the government introduced limited measures designed to address some issues—for example to improve awareness of rights; providing a single shared Pay and Work Rights helpline for areas of the NMW, health and safety, Gangmasters' Licensing Authority and Employment Agency Standards; facilitating some information sharing between different inspectorates and agencies, and improving guidance to business—and some additional powers were given to some of the bodies.

This still leaves an incomplete and fragmented patchwork of bodies, described in chapter two, with various agencies and inspectorates enforcing different employment rights, with rights falling under the responsibility of various different government departments, and not adding up to a coherent system of enforcement. Even in combination, the remit of these enforcement bodies is far from comprehensive in terms of rights and the areas of activity, and there remain barriers to co-ordination and information sharing between them, even though firms found to be non-compliant in one area are likely to be non-compliant in others. The agencies vary in matters such as resource allocation, inspection rates and philosophy of enforcement, both as between each other and over time (as discussed, for example, in chapter four in relation to the equality commissions, and in chapter five regarding the Health and Safety Executive). Enforcement agencies and inspectorates offer advantages in rights enforcement with a view to delivering fairer workplaces but certain conditions need to be in place. These include the need for the body to have adequate resources; high visibility and credibility; a willingness and ability to operate proactively; sufficient appropriate powers; effective sanctions likely to deter non-compliance, and a will to resort to them if other forms of intervention (advice, education, persuasion) fail. These conditions have often been lacking in the case of agencies operating in Britain and, as chapters four and five discuss, current developments are undermining them further.

The current government has acknowledged the fragmented nature of the current enforcement landscape, which reflects historical accident rather than a set of principles (BIS 2011b), but it is highly unlikely to move towards a comprehensive labour inspectorate model. Budgets of existing bodies are being cut and agencies are asked to adhere to the 'better regulation' strategy which is a 'light touch' risk-based, targeted approach, concerned to reduce burdens on employers (discussed in detail in chapter five in relation to health and safety regulation). It encourages agencies to shift to 'educative' as opposed to 'purposive' approaches to enforcement (Colling 2010: 335–36). Tombs and Whyte argue in chapter five that these developments reduce the likelihood of inspections and undermine effective enforcement, while being over-reliant on employer goodwill, self-regulation and notions of corporate social responsibility (CSR), even though evidence of what drives compliance points to the need for legislation backed by credible enforcement. As Deakin and his colleagues show in chapter seven, CSR currently provides, at best, a very weak source of pressure for action in the area of employment rights (see also for example Hart 2010).

Rather than extend the reach of agency enforcement, a recent government document suggests that it might be restricted to 'the most vulnerable workers, those most likely to be exploited by unscrupulous employers', leaving others to take individual complaints to ETs (BIS 2011b: 7). There are some 'rogue' employers who persistently breach workers' rights—as indicated for example in Citizens Advice Bureaux client based research (Mitchell 2009). It is clear, however, as discussed by Paul Edwards in chapter eight, that a division of employers into 'good' and 'bad' (or 'scrupulous' and 'unscrupulous') is both difficult and simplistic. Edwards, in considering small firms, and Purcell in considering medium and large enterprises (in chapter nine), both point to a range of potentially interlocking external and internal factors which affect the likelihood of employer interest in, acceptance of, and adherence to legal standards, leading to divergence and difference within categories. This thwarts easy categorisation and the ready identification of 'good' or 'bad' employers.

Similarly, using 'vulnerability' to determine the boundaries to state enforcement neglects the complex nature of the concept. Narrowing down definitions of vulnerability to characteristics of employees in order to target enforcement action at 'bad' employers who exploit that vulnerability (eg DTI 2006b) may help to address problems of particular groups (for example, migrant workers, unorganised workers, young workers, those working in low paid sectors, ethnic minority workers), but it risks underestimating the extent to which workers experience problems at work and over-simplifies the concept (Pollert and Charlwood 2009). On the basis of their analysis of the 2008 Fair Treatment at Work survey, Bewley and Forth (2010) concluded that vulnerability cannot be defined by reference only to a small number of characteristics. They found that 'vulnerability is both complex in its make-up and also continuous in its nature' (ibid: x). They argue that it is 'an over-simplification to seek to categorise one group of workers who are vulnerable to adverse treatment (implying that the remainder are not). Vulnerability is instead a matter of degree' (ibid). Their analysis identified a varied range of factors related to the external labour market, the product market, the employing organisation and the job, as well as characteristics of the employee, which make an employee more (or less) vulnerable. These internal and external factors influence the balance of power in the employment relationship. It is this relative power which shapes worker vulnerability and so affects the likelihood of adverse treatment at work.

Trade unions have long been recognised as a source of countervailing power in the employment relationship and some consider that the evidence indicates that union organisation and collectively agreed terms and conditions are 'the only long term solutions to eliminate vulnerability' (Pollert 2007: 4). The context within which the number of ET cases has risen is a decline in trade union membership and collective bargaining and thus of social regulation as a form of protection. This underpins some commentators' calls for a general labour inspectorate, mentioned above. Any move towards a more comprehensive coherent role for proactive agency enforcement, however, need not be seen as an alternative to seeking to re-establish a collective representative dimension to fairness at work and rights enforcement as discussed in the next section.

SUPPORTING AND HARNESSING THE REGULATORY CAPACITY OF NON-STATE ACTORS

The proactive approach to enforcement of employment rights through inspectorates and agencies discussed above provides scope to engage other stakeholders in ensuring organisations fulfill their statutory duties and in achieving desired organisational and structural outcomes. Using the regulatory tools of non-state actors can enhance the regulatory capacity of the state. Non-state actors include trade unions, considered in this section. A potential role for employers is considered in the next section.

Social regulation through collective bargaining can make legal regulation based on statutory individual rights less necessary, and/or can assist in making it more effective. In chapter ten in this volume, Trevor Colling provides detailed consideration of the changing relationship and interaction between these two systems of regulation. He describes how the central regulatory role once played by unions in the establishment of employment standards has declined and been displaced by a focus on enforcement of individual statutory rights, the nature, content and form of which they may consider unsatisfactory. Research shows that workplace employee representation arrangements encourage internal solutions to individual employment disputes and that 'collective procedures are the custodians of individual rights' (Brown et al 2000: 627). As such they can and do play a role in reducing recourse to legal action (Dickens and Hall 2006). Trade unions are potentially effective mechanisms for helping translate formal employment rights into substantive change at the workplace. The decline in union membership and unionised workplaces, however, obviously affects this role in practice: that only 14 per cent of workplaces in Britain now have a lay union representative (Kersley et al 2006) limits the extent to which unions can help embed, monitor and enforce legal standards in workplace practice. Colling explores the critical roles of trade unions in interpreting and amplifying the practical effect of law within workplaces, and reviews evidence demonstrating the positive impacts—both substantive and procedural—of what he labels 'organic enforcement'. Purcell's consideration of the management of employment rights, in chapter nine, also points to the importance of trade unions as an organisational factor which can lead to higher levels of adoption of a wide range of employment rights in medium and large enterprises. The necessity of collective bargaining or other employee-based representative mechanisms as 'bridging institutions' between the legal system and the organisational field is highlighted by Deakin and his colleagues in chapter seven. Further, unions can provide sources of advice, support and representation where legal claims are made. However, as discussed by Colling, there are risks and costs for unions in engaging in formal litigation, especially as outcomes in individual cases may not contribute to their wider strategies. He notes among other points the lack of provision for representative or class action. Positive synergy and mutual reinforcement between legal regulation and social regulation is called for, yet the pay equality area discussed by Deakin, McLaughlin and Chai in chapter seven, for example, provides evidence that the individualisation of rights can lead to dissonance and conflict between these two routes to delivering fairness at the workplace (Dickens 2007).

Representation and voice arrangements at the workplace facilitate the exercise and maintenance of rights and encourage employers to comply with them and build upon them. However the implications of the connection between the collective and individual areas of labour law indicated by evidence of the kind reported by Colling in chapter ten have not been followed through. The state has not sought to forge a link between, on the one hand, legal support for trade unions and collective bargaining, and on the other, individual worker protection, fairer workplaces and reduction in claims to ETs (Dickens 2002). The decline of trade unions and their bargaining power has weakened representative voice at the workplace and Colling argues that 'making employment rights effective may depend to a significant degree on the ability to revitalise and reinstate their diffusion through representative structures'.

There is limited legislative support in Britain for either union or non-union voice mechanisms. The 1997–2010 Labour government supported a role for unions as employment-rights-awareness raisers and as providers of advice to 'vulnerable' workers, for example by providing funding under its 'union modernisation' scheme for such activity. However, although it acknowledged that unionised workplaces are 'better at managing individual employment disputes' (DTI 2001: para 3.4), there was a reluctance to privilege collective bargaining, or even collective voice, over more individualised methods of conducting employment relations. A statutory procedure for seeking union recognition was enacted but there was no return to the position before 1979 whereby public policy sought to encourage and support collective bargaining as the best method of conducting industrial relations—the 'auxiliary' function of labour law described by Kahn-Freund (1970: 302), discussed by Colling in chapter ten—and many of the legal restrictions imposed on trade union action by previous Conservative administrations were retained (Dickens and Hall 2009). Prompted by EC legislation, there is now statutory support in Britain for information and consultation of employees. Where, however, the UK government has had to address the 'representation gap' in non-union workplaces in order to implement European legal requirements for employer consultation with worker representatives over a growing range of issues, such as redundancy and health and safety, it has shown a preference for ad hoc, one-off solutions rather than institution building (ibid: 341). The reluctance to privilege collective voice also carried through to the Regulations implementing the Information and Consultation Directive, which—as noted by Purcell in chapter nine—give employers significant freedom to choose how, if at all, to establish consultative bodies for information and consultation purposes.

As noted above, proactive enforcement of employment rights through inspectorates and agencies provides scope to engage other stakeholders including trade unions. Issues of capacity, access to information and necessary authority would need to be addressed, but the state could harness the ability, knowledge and expertise of unions to enhance its own regulatory capacity and to make employment rights more effective. This approach is absent currently. For example trade unions could be 'written in' to the enforcement or implementation of employment rights but this has not been done, as Simpson notes in respect of the NMW (Simpson 1999). They could play an inspection and monitoring role in conjunction with state agencies. Hepple, in chapter four discussing the new single equality duty brought in by the Equality Act 2010, notes that, in contrast to previous separate equality duties,

> not only is there no duty in the new regulations to publish details of 'engagement' with interest groups, but it is also significant that no duty is imposed on employers to 'engage' with any specific class of representatives, such as recognised trade unions, or equality representatives.

Evidence demonstrates that statutory underpinning for workplace health and safety representatives has been positive in terms of giving substance to statutory rights (eg James and Walters 2002). The model it provides of requiring employers to consult with elected representatives (union or non-union), to ensure they receive training and permit them paid time off in order to perform their functions, could be adopted in other areas, but it has not been (Podro 2008) and, as Hepple notes, was resisted by the current government in respect of equality representatives.

There are other non-state actors such as community groups, voluntary sector advice bodies and social movement organisations which may have relevant expertise in particular areas and contacts with workers which state agencies often find hard to reach. In theory they might be harnessed as co-enforcers and monitors of compliance. Appropriate civil society organisations are not common in Britain, however, and those which exist currently are not well developed for such roles. McCrudden stresses the importance of 'a well informed and truculent civil society' to the operation of regulation equality in Northern Ireland and notes the absence of organisations representing ethnic minority groups from day to day engagement with public bodies in Britain in respect of the equality duty (McCrudden 2007: 266). Some bodies, such as Citizens Advice Bureaux, do play an important role in advising workers as to their legal rights and representing them and may help direct state enforcement activity (Abbott 1998; Tailby et al 2011). However, unlike unions, they lack presence at the workplace which constrains their role and effectiveness. The focus of activity of many bodies which fall under the general description of 'civil society organisations' tends to be on lobbying government and campaigning, although a minority seek to represent interests of workers through engaging positively with employers, disseminating information about best employment practice and using business case arguments to encourage organisations to adopt it (Williams et al 2011).

OTHER MEANS OF ENCOURAGING EMPLOYER
ACTION FOR FAIRNESS

Procurement and use of power within supply chains are potential levers whereby lead employing organisations might be encouraged or required to take action to ensure the other employing organisations with which they deal commercially comply with employment standards and take steps to make employment rights effective. They provide opportunities for the market power of some organisations to be used to drive substantive outcomes in other organisations in a way which individual litigation struggles to achieve. Potentially it also provides a way of overcoming some of the practical difficulties of proactive agency inspection and enforcement arising from changes in the organisation of work and industry structures, including growth in non-traditional forms of employment, subcontracting, outsourcing, and decentralisation of production and service provision to diffuse webs and networks of organisations (Weil 2009; Marchington et al 2005).

Public procurement has increased considerably through contracting out of public services and public-private partnerships. But national and local state bodies, as purchasers of goods and services, remain an underused tool for persuading and assisting organisations in Britain to comply with statutory standards and deliver fairer workplaces. In chapter six Chris McCrudden critically examines the potential and use of public procurement in the UK, providing evidence of the ability of this approach to deliver on social objectives, but also highlighting a range of factors which appear necessary for its effectiveness. He demonstrates that it is technically feasible to use public procurement to improve workplace fairness and that there is sufficient evidence that it can be effective, given certain conditions, in integrating workplace fairness issues into the organisation in ways which are not achieved through individual litigation. McCrudden points out that there is a particular rationale for procurement power to be used in the public sector, apart from the scale of the spending power it represents which directly contributes to the fulfilment of social priorities and objectives, namely that it 'also gives a signal to the market and to the general public in favour of social responsibility, and therefore influences and contributes to shaping choices and behaviours of suppliers and consumers' (chapter six). Edwards, in chapter eight, suggests that the linking of public money to desired social objectives, such as adherence to employment standards, could extend beyond public procurement to include, for example, a requirement that any small firm which takes a state investment loan, or other form of government support, undergoes an employment relations health check with an Acas adviser. However marketisation and cost cutting in the public sector, coupled with the deregulation perspective on employment rights discussed earlier in this chapter, suggest such developments are most unlikely currently.

Procurement power as a lever for promoting fairness at work through supply chains need not be confined to public sector purchasing. In some areas a private sector lead organisation will use its market power to seek to ensure that the large set of smaller companies with which it deals adheres to certain standards. This can be seen, for example, in respect of quality standards in manufacturing where companies can gain 'preferred supplier' status by meeting set standards. The imposer of standards in such cases generally provides assistance in equipping suppliers to be able to meet them. There are also examples of large companies in Britain leveraging the use of their supply chain to pursue environmental goals. This includes, for example, Marks and Spencer which launched its 'Plan A' in 2007 in a drive towards sustainability. As well as taking action in its own stores to apply Plan A principles and improve energy efficiency etc, Marks and Spencer suppliers who provide and make their products are expected to do the same—the ultimate consequence of not doing so being risk to their continued supplier status (*People Management* 2011). In this example, however, there were clear financial gains to be secured both for the lead organisation and its suppliers from taking the action required. Gains of this kind are likely to be less obvious or absent in the case of promoting fairer workplaces and competitive forces may exert strong pressure in the other direction. Supply chains and inter-firm linkages in fact may be part of the problem of adverse treatment at work with larger organisations (in practice if not through overt intention) exerting downward pressure on wages and conditions of employees in their supplier organisations through their desire to be price competitive in their product markets. Such effects have been well documented in relation to global supply chains in the food industry for example (Robinson 2010).

Concerns about reputational risk, damage to brand, consumer pressure for ethical products, and other 'business case' rationales may lead to some voluntary use of supply chain pressure to promote fairer workplaces. But business cases arguments are highly contingent, variable, selective and partial (Dickens 1999). In his consideration of small firms in chapter eight Edwards notes that research reveals the rarity of any kind of direct pressure in relation to employment terms coming from the large organisations with which the small firms interact, while Purcell, in chapter nine, indicates the limited attention to employment standards in business strategy of medium and large organisations. Furthermore, research suggests that, even where they are taken, the impact of business case or CSR-driven initiatives may not run very deep, for example leading to 'window dressing' policy statements rather than substantive implementation, as Deakin, McLaughlin and Chai show in chapter seven. Use of procurement power and supply chain pressure may appear as alternatives to legal regulation but the evidence suggests that 'hard law' is required to drive such employer action and to ensure substantive outcomes (McCrudden chapter six; Deakin et al chapter seven in this volume). Identifying and leveraging market power to regulate standards through using supply chains in particular sectors, however, potentially does offer another way in which the state might complement and extend its own regulatory activity, forming what Weil and Mallo (2007) call 'public/private enforcement partnerships' with non-state actors and it suggests one way in which scarce regulatory resources might be used with, for example, state agency enforcement focussed on major players in the supply chain (ibid; James et al 2007).

WHERE THERE'S A WILL ...

There has been considerable expansion in statutory employment rights; the ET system remains the main enforcement mechanism, with limited enforcement by state agencies. Public policy sees this *system* as flawed—mainly in terms of its costs and operation. The argument in this chapter is that the *enforcement approach* is flawed—in terms of reducing the likelihood of adverse treatment at work. I have argued that passive/reactive and individualised approaches to compliance offer less in terms of making employment rights effective in promoting fairness than those approaches which require and encourage employers to be proactive and to address structural and organisational issues. Yet in Britain, as discussed in this final chapter, most weight is placed on individuals having to assert and pursue their rights, and too little weight is placed on agency enforcement and inspection, and on other measures which could encourage proactive, structural employer action to deliver fairer workplaces. Furthermore, opportunities to complement and strengthen the regulatory capacity of the state through encouraging representative voice and forging partnerships with non-state actors in enforcement and co-regulation are not being taken. The reform agenda is being driven not by the evidence of the limited impact of individual rights in tackling continuing 'unfairness' experienced at work, but rather by concerns to save public expenditure and to lessen 'burdens' on employers which employment rights are seen to impose when viewed through a free-market lens.

The contributions to this volume, in exploring alternative additional approaches to that of individual rights enforcement through the ETs make clear that there are no 'magic bullets'—indeed existing alternative approaches as currently found are often inadequate to the task and themselves need improvement in ways indicated. The different contributions demonstrate also that in any consideration of how to progress fairness, there is a need to be sensitive to the varied contexts within which employment rights fall to be implemented, and to the differing orientations of key actors. It is clear that there are no easy, universal answers. Nonetheless the chapters in this collection help identify what does and does not 'work', and they illuminate steps which might be taken—were there sufficient political will to do so—to encourage and promote adherence to statutory employment standards; to help translate formal rights on the statute book into real, substantive rights at the workplace; to reduce the likelihood of adverse treatment and so make employment rights effective in promoting fairer workplaces.

BIBLIOGRAPHY

Abbott, B (1988) 'The Emergence of a New Industrial Relations Actor—the Role of the Citizens Advice Bureau' 29 *Industrial Relations Journal* 257–69.

Barnard, C, Deakin, S and Hobbs, R (2003) 'Opting Out Of the 48-Hour Week: Employer Necessity or Individual Choice?' 32 *Industrial Law Journal* 223.

Bell, M (2011) 'Achieving the Objectives of the Part-Time Work Directive? Revisiting the Part-Time Work Regulations' 40 *Industrial Law Journal* 254–79.

Better Regulation Taskforce (2002) *Employment Regulation: Striking a Balance* (London, Cabinet Office).

Bewley H, and Forth J (2010) *Vulnerability and Adverse Treatment in the Workplace* (London, BIS).

BERR (2008) *Vulnerable Worker Enforcement Forum Final Report and Government Conclusions* (London, Department for Business Enterprise and Regulatory Reform).

BIS (2011a) *Resolving Workplace Disputes: A Consultation* (London, Department for Business Innovation and Skills).

—— (2011b) *Flexible, Effective, Fair: Promoting Economic Growth Through a Strong and Efficient Labour Market* (London, Department for Business Innovation and Skills).

Blackburn R, and Hart, M (2002) *Small Firms' Awareness and Knowledge of Individual Employment Rights*, Employment Relations Research Series 14 (London, DTI).

Brown, W (2006) 'The Low Pay Commission' in L Dickens and A Neal (eds), *The Changing Institutional Face of British Employment Relations* (The Hague: Kluwer).

Brown, W, Deakin, S, Nash, D and Oxenbridge, S (2000) 'The Employment Contract: From Collective Procedures to Individual Rights' 38 *British Journal of Industrial Relations* 611–29.

CAB (Citizens Advice Bureau) (2001) *Fairness & Enterprise: The CAB Service's Case for a Fair Employment Commission* (London, Citizens Advice Bureaux).

—— (2004) *Somewhere to Turn: The Case for a Fair Employment Commission* (London, Citizens Advice Bureaux).

CBI (2000) *Cutting Through Red Tape* (London, CBI).

—— (2005) *Employment Trends Survey* (London, CBI).

Coats, D (2005) *Speaking up! Voice, Industrial Democracy and Organisational Performance* (London, The Work Foundation).

Colling, T (2010) 'Legal Institutions and the Regulation of Workplaces' in T Colling and M Terry (eds), *Industrial Relations Theory and Practice* (Chichester, Wiley).

Creegan, C, Colgan, F, Charlesworth, R and Robinson, G (2003) 'Race Equality Policies at Work' 17 *Work Employment and Society* 617–40.

Cunningham, I and James, P (2001) 'Managing Diversity and Disability Legislation: Catalysts for Eradicating Discrimination in the Workplace?' in M Noon and E Ogbonna, *Equality Diversity and Disadvantage in Employment* (Basingstoke, Palgrave).

Davies, P and Freedland, M (2007) *Towards a Flexible Labour Market: Labour Legislation and Regulation Since the 1990s* (Oxford, Oxford University Press).

Deakin, S and Wilkinson, F (1994) 'Rights vs Efficiency? The Economic Case for Transnational Labour Standards' 23 *Industrial Law Journal* 289–310.

Dickens, L (1999) 'Beyond the Business Case: A Three-pronged Approach to Equality Action' 9 *Human Resource Management Journal* 9–20.

—— (2002) 'Individual Statutory Employment Rights Since 1997: Constrained Expansion' 24 *Employee Relations* 619–37.

—— (2006) 'Equality and Work Life Balance: What's Happening at the Workplace?' 35 *Industrial Law Journal* 463–49.

—— (2007) 'The Road is Long. Thirty Years of Equality Legislation in Britain' 45 *British Journal of Industrial Relations* 463.

Dickens, L and Hall, M (2006) 'Fairness—Up to a Point. Assessing the Impact of New Labour's Employment Legislation' 16 *Human Resource Management Journal* 338.

—— (2009) 'Legal Regulation and the Changing Workplace' in W Brown, A Bryson, J Forth and K Whitfield (eds), *Evolution of the Modern Workplace* (Cambridge, Cambridge University Press).

Dix, G, Sisson, K and Forth, J (2009) 'Conflict at Work The Changing Pattern of Disputes' in Brown, W, Bryson, A, Forth, J and Whitfield, K (eds) *The Evolution of the Modern Workplace* (Cambridge, Cambridge University Press).

DTI (Department of Trade and Industry) (1998) *Fairness at Work*, CM 2968 (London, HMSO).

—— (2001) *Routes to Resolution* (London, HMSO).

—— (2002) *Full and Fulfilling Employment: Creating the Labour Market of the Future*, (London, HMSO).

—— (2006a) *High Performance Workplaces: The Role of Employee Involvement in a Modern Economy* (London, DTI).

—— (2006b) *Success at Work: Protecting Vulnerable Workers, Supporting Good Employers* (London, DTI).

Edwards, P (2007) *Justice in the Workplace: Why it is Important and Why a New Public Policy Initiative is Needed* (London, The Work Foundation).

Fredman, S (2004) 'Women at Work: The Broken Promise of Flexicurity' 33 *Industrial Law Journal* 299–319.

—— (2011) 'The Public Sector Equality Duty' 40 *Industrial Law Journal* 405–27.

Gibbons, M (2007) *Better Dispute Resolution. A Review of Employment Dispute Resolution in Great Britain* (London, DTI).

Hart, S (2010) 'Self-regulation, Corporate Social Responsibility, and the Business Case: Do they Work in Achieving Workplace Equality and Safety?' 92 *Journal of Business Ethics* 585–600.

Hepple, B and Morris, G (2002) 'The Employment Act 2002 and the Crisis of Individual Employment Rights' 31 *Industrial Law Journal* 251–69.

Hoque K and Noon M (2004) 'Equal Opportunity Policy and Practice in Britain' 18 *Work Employment and Society* 481–506.

James P and Walters D (2002) 'Worker Representation in Health and Safety: Options for Regulatory Reform' 33 *Journal of Industrial Relations* 141–56.

James, P, Johnstone, R, Quinlan, M and Walters, D (2007) 'Regulating Supply Chains to Improve Health and Safety' 36 *Industrial Law Journal* 163–87.

Kahn-Freund, O (1970) 33 'Trade Unions, the Law and Society' *Modern Law Review* 241–67.

Kersley, B, Alpin, C, Forth, J, Bryson, A, Bewley, H, Dix, G and Oxenbridge, S (2006) *Inside the Workplace* (London, Routledge).

Kilpatrick, C and Freedland, M (2004) 'The United Kingdom: How is EU Governance Transformative?' in S Sciarra, P Davies and M Freedland (eds), *Employment Policy and the Regulation of Part-time Work in the European Union: A Comparative Analysis* (Cambridge, Cambridge University Press).

Lambourne, E, Brown, S, Hawkins, J and Allen, D (2008) *Employment Law Administrative Burdens Survey* (London, BERR).

Marchington, M, Grimshaw, D, Rubery J and Wilmott H (2005) *Fragmenting Work: Blurring Organisational Boundaries and Disordering Hierarchies* (Oxford, Oxford University Press).

McColgan, A (2000) 'Family Friendly Frolics? The Maternity and Parental Leave Etc Regulations 1999' 29 *Industrial Law Journal* 125–44.

McKay, S (2001) 'Between Flexibility and Regulation: Rights, Equality and Protection at Work' 39 *British Journal of Industrial Relations* 285–303.

Meeran, G (2006) 'The Employment Tribunals' in L Dickens and A Neal (eds), *The Changing Institutional Face of British Employment Relations* (The Hague: Kluwer).

Metcalf, D (2008) 'Why has the British National Minimum Wage had Little or No Impact on Employment?' 50 *Journal of Industrial Relations* 489–512.

Mitchell, D (2009) *Citizens Advice Client Research Final Report*, Employment Relations Research Series 99 (London, BERR).

OECD (June 2006) *Boosting Jobs and Incomes: Policy Lessons from Reassessing the OECD Jobs Strategy* (Paris, OECD).

Patel, S (2011) *Research into Employers' Attitudes and Behavior Towards Compliance with UK National Minimum Wage Legislation*, Employment Relations Research Series No 121 (London, BIS).

People Management (2011) Join the Green Shift (London, People Management) 25 June 28.

Podro S et al (2008) *Employee Representatives: Challenges and Changes in the Workplace* (London, Acas).

Pollert A (2007) *The Unorganised Vulnerable Worker: The Case for Union Organising* (Liverpool, Institute of Employment Rights).

Pollert, A and Charlwood, A (2009) 'The Vulnerable Worker in Britain and Problems at Work' 23 *Work Employment and Society* 343–62.

Reed, H (2010) *Flexible with the Truth? Exploring the Relationship Between Labour Market Flexibility and Labour Market Performance* (London, TUC).

Robinson, P (2010) 'Do Voluntary Labour Initiatives Make a Difference for the Conditions of Workers in Global Supply Chains?' 52 *Journal of Industrial Relations* 561.

Sanders, A (2009) 'Part One of the Employment Act 2008: Better Dispute Resolution?' 38 *Industrial Law Journal*.

Simpson B (1999) 'Implementing the National Minimum Wage: The 1999 Regulations' 28 *Industrial Law Journal* 245–53.

Streeck, W (1997) 'Beneficial Constraints' in J Hollingsworth and R Boyer (eds), *Contemporary Capitalism* (Cambridge, CUP).

Tailby S, Pollert A, Warren S, Danford, A and Wilton, N (2011) Under-funded and Overwhelmed: The Voluntary Sector as Worker Representation in Britain's Individualised Industrial Relations System' 42 *Industrial Relations Journal* 273–92.

TUC (2008) *Hidden Work, Hidden Lives*, Report of the TUC Commission on Vulnerable Employment (London, TUC).

Weil, D (2009) 'Rethinking the Regulation of Vulnerable Work in the USA: A Sector Based Approach' 51 *Journal of Industrial Relations* 411–30.

Weil, D and Mallo, C (2007) 'Regulating Labour Standards via Supply Chains: Combining Public/Private Interventions to Improve Workplace Compliance' 45 *British Journal of Industrial Relations* 791–814.

McCrudden, C (2007) Equality Legislation and Reflexive Regulation' 36 *Industrial Law Journal* 255.

Weekes, B, Mellish M, Dickens, L and Lloyd, J (1975) *Industrial Relations and the Limits of Law* (Oxford, Blackwell).

Williams S, Abbott, B and Heery, E (2011) 'Non-union Worker Representation Through Civil Society Organisations: Evidence from the United Kingdom' 42 *Industrial Relations Journal* 69–85.